YOUTH WORKING WITH GIRLS
AND WOMEN IN COMMUNITY SETTINGS

Youth Working with Girls and Women in Community Settings

A Feminist Perspective

JANET BATSLEER
Manchester Metropolitan University, UK

ASHGATE

Published by
Ashgate Publishing Limited
Wey Court East
Union Road
Farnham
Surrey GU9 7PT
England

Ashgate Publishing Company
110 Cherry Street
Suite 3-1
Burlington, VT 05401-3818
USA

www.ashgate.com

British Library Cataloguing in Publication Data
Batsleer, Janet.
Youth working with girls and women in community settings: a feminist perspective.
– 2nd ed. 1. Social work with teenagers. 2. Social work with women. 3. Teenage girls–
Services for. 4. Feminism.
I. Title
362.7'083–dc23

Library of Congress Cataloging-in-Publication Data
Batsleer, Janet.
Youth Working With Girls and Women in Community Settings : A Feminist
Perspective / By Janet Batsleer.
    pages cm
Includes bibliographical references and index.
ISBN 978-1-4094-2579-3 (hardback : alk. paper) — ISBN 978-1-4094-2580-9 (ebook)
(print) 1. Young women—Services for—Great Britain. 2. Girls—Services for—Great
Britain. 3. Non-formal education—Great Britain. I. Title.
HV1425.B38 2012
362.83'530941—dc23

2012029644

ISBN 978-1-4094-2579-3 (Pbk)
ISBN 978-1-4094-2580-9 (Ebk-pdf)
ISBN 978-1-4724-0004-8 (Ebk-ePub)

Mixed Sources
Product group from well-managed
forests and other controlled sources
www.fsc.org Cert no. SA-COC-1565
© 1996 Forest Stewardship Council

Printed and bound in Great Britain by
MPG Books Ltd, Bodmin, Cornwall.

Contents

Acknowledgements

This book exists because there has been a movement within youth and community work practice, referred to as 'the girls' work movement'. It is an attempt to record some of the work that has gone on. More immediately, this book exists because of the encouragement of particular colleagues and the sense that 'something should be written down'. Specific help in the form of supply of documents and references, discussions about particular ideas, reading of early drafts, encouragement to press on and support in domestic and family life came from: Gregory Batsleer, Julian Batsleer, Margaret Beetham, Erica Burman, Sue Campbell, Sylvia Caveney, Kate Clements, Sue Cockerell, Jill Dennis, Sakinna Dickenson, Maureen Green, Steph Green, Lorraine Hansford, Moira Hill, Netta Hughes, Kath Hunter, Rehana Hussein, Julia Keenan, Kate Kirk, Ken Leech, Mary Madden, Lydia Merryll, Debbie Mitchell, Louise Murray, Liz Neat, Cath Nicholls, Carol Packham, Bhaggi Patel, Nikki Patterson, Poddi Peerman, Janet Preece, Mark Smith, Parvinder Sohal, Alima Sonne, Yasmin Sonne, Michelle Walmsley, Viv Whittaker, Vanessa Worrell, Margaret White and Tracy Yankowski.

I would like to thank all the projects whose reports and publications I have drawn from in compiling this book. Where I have drawn on project reports, on group discussions, or on the work of youth and community work students, this is acknowledged in the text. Thanks especially to the Feminist Webs network, acknowledged throughout this book, for encouragement to get on with a second edition: especially, Amelia Lee, Alison Ronan, Sally Carr, Jean Spence, Kimberley Osivwemu, Ali Hanbury, Niamh Moore, Viv Whittaker and Maggie Cole. Feminist Webs participants were interested in the Pearl Jephcott Questionnaire: thanks to all the youth workers who asked young women to complete the revised questionnaire based on Jephcott's original study. Although it is not analysed in depth in this book, a copy of the questionnaire – which was completed by 75 young women – is attached as an appendix.

Thanks to colleagues in the wider Youth and Community networks too: Finn Cullen, Steph Green, Karen McCarthy, Carol Packham, Diane Watt, Susan Morgan and Jean Spence for interest and inspiration.

Thanks especially to people who have contributed the new case studies throughout this second edition: Alison Healicon, Diane Watt, Kimberley Osivwemu, Ali Hanbury, Amelia Lee and Steph Green.

I am grateful to the Education and Social Research Institute (ESRI) at Manchester Metropolitan University (MMU) for their support, releasing me from some teaching commitments to enable this work to be completed. As the research for this new edition has been ongoing, papers which have been presented include:

J. Batsleer and A. Lee (2010) 'Youth Work as a Feminist Method: Encouraging Feminist Webs', CRESC (Centre for Research on Socio-Cultural Change), University of Manchester, 'Feminism and Its Methods: An Inter-Disciplinary Colloquium', July 2010
J. Batsleer (2010) 'The History of Youth Work with Girls in the UK. Targets from Below'; First European Conference on the History of Youth Work and Youth Policy, Ghent, July 2010
J. Batsleer and I. Barron (2010), 'Social Pedagogy and Social Education. Can they embrace diversity and difference?', Minding the Gap? International Conference on Work with Young People, University of Strathclyde, September 2010;
J. Batsleer (2010)'From Feminism to Queer and Back Again', 'Thinking Seriously about youth work with girls and young women', March 2010'Youth and Policy Colloquium', , Leeds
J. Batsleer ((2011) 'What Sort of Eyebrow Bar Should I have', BERA National Conference London
J. Batsleer (2011) 'Taking Offence? Making Exception? The Politics of Gender in Work with Young Women in Urban Multiculture', Nordic Youth Research Symposium, Turku, Finland and UCLAN Children and Young People's Participation Seminar.

And thanks to Fay Entwistle and Julie Wood for support in preparing the manuscript.

Introduction
'Threat'

Somehow, youth work and informal education that focuses attention on girls has always been associated with threat. It seems to be a threat to the boys, who have been getting more than their fair share of attention. It seems to be a threat to long-held assumptions about who and what youth work and informal education are for, and to the 'we've always done it this way' school of practice. And it is initially threatening to women, as well as energising, to realise that 'the way things are' is not as inevitable as the weather, but can change.

Yet this practice, which seems so threatening, is itself always under threat. First it was under threat from the boys: banging on the door and demanding to be let in to the girls' night. Then the persuasions of supportive professionals were also potentially threatening: 'There is such a need for progressive and supportive work with boys as well as girls, on sexual health and teenage pregnancy for example.' Of course this is true. But because the larger share of budgets still goes to boys, anti-sexist work needs to recognise and respect the power of agenda-setting in autonomous work with girls.

Models of anti-discriminatory and anti-oppressive practice have contributed to the professional formation of informal educators in youth work for more than thirty years. Recognising the impact of patterns of discrimination and exclusion on the lives of young people and communities is essential to any good practice in informal education. There has been significant discussion of group work based in young peoples' awareness of specific identities which mean something to them, which matter. Culturally sensitive and culturally specific work has been discussed, as has gender-specific and gender-sensitive work. Autonomous work with girls as it is discussed is a significant stream flowing into the wider river of anti-oppressive practice (Thompson 2006, Ledwith 2011, Batsleer 2008, Young 2006, Banks 2010).

When the first edition of this book appeared in 1996, the threats to such autonomous anti-sexist work with girls – closures, cutbacks, the numbers game, measurable outcomes –were crude and much more powerful than the threat from any boys who were still banging on the door. In 2012, these pressures are still present, intensified as they were by the policy frameworks of accredited outcomes and 'Every Child Matters', with youth work sessions expected to meet particular policy targets and now expected to demonstrate social impact. In 1986, the National Association of Youth Clubs (NAYC) closed down its Girls Work Unit which had provided a national focus for the work in the early 1980s, and there was a backlash against positive and progressive autonomous work with girls. The resistance to the unit's closure was strong and swift and clearly surprised the NAYC. The organisation reviewed its strategy and continued to support some focus on work with girls, but by the late 1990s, most feminist girls' work had disappeared, fulfilling the fears which Kerry Young, one of the first workers at the Girls Work Unit, had expressed:

> As the years have passed it has become increasingly easy to organise activities days and concentrate our emphasis on establishing groups for girls. To a certain extent that aspect of our work has gained some acceptability – credibility even. But the purpose of the work, like the purpose of so many youth and community work methods, has become blurred at the edges. If the general gist of contemporary literature on the subject (little that there is) is anything to go by, it may even be that the purpose of working with girls and young women has become obscured at its very centre. The purpose of the work was never so narrow as simply providing space and opportunity for young women on their own. Specific work with young women, whilst important in its own right, was also (and remains) the central plank by which the challenge to sexism in youth and community work was and still is to be forged. (Young 1992: 17)

It seems that the threat posed to the status quo by anti-sexist work with girls and young women is always becoming blurred, whilst the threat to anti-sexist work means that it is continually on the edge of disappearance. The first edition of this book was written as a testimony because we must leave evidence or too much work is lost. This is still the case, but in 2012, there is a recovery of the inspirations of feminisms and it seems worth re-presenting this book in that context. Each chapter has been revised by adding new material from the current context, some chapters have been reorganised as has the order of chapters and a new final chapter has been added, so that the book can still provide something of a map of practice mainly but not exclusively in the United Kingdom. Whenever possible, the 1996 material has been retained in its original form, with 2012 material incorporated, to highlight the specific history of closure and decline which underpinned the original text and to show continuities with the present. The intensity of the impact of globalisation in the context in which this book has been revised, especially the impact of war and migration as well as that of the current global and political financial crises, has been far wider and deeper than I would have imagined even in the very difficult years of the 1980s – this too is reflected in this new edition.

Stories About Practice as a Source of Knowledge

The extension of this study is based on a survey of practice and on practitioner research projects undertaken as a tutor in youth and community studies in the 15 years since the first edition. It has been particularly inspired by my participation in the Feminist Webs project (Batsleer 2010a) and especially by the work on the Feminist Webs oral histories and archive housed in the youth and community department at Manchester Metropolitan University (MMU). Working as a tutor and researcher in the youth and community work team gives me a particular access to stories about practice, stories which offer valuable perspectives on the feminist theoretical frameworks of the first edition. It also has given me access, beyond the library, to project reports, conferences and meetings, and to internet sources and extended email conversations. Since 2008, the systematic critical reflection, including the two periods of research interviewing and participant observation on which this revised book is based, has been inspired by the work of Feminist Webs (<www.feministwebs.com>, Lee and Withers 2012). I am very grateful to a number of colleagues, who are acknowledged throughout the revised edition, who have contributed vignettes and case studies to illuminate the practice discussed here.

This book attempts to offer a context for the stories I have heard, to trace the connections between them and between the stories of youth and community work practice and other aspects of contemporary communities and society, and to make connections with the current concerns of 'girlhood studies' in the research community. Because of my involvement in educating and assessing them, I developed a particular concern for and interest in the support and well-being of practitioners, especially women practitioners, but also men positioned as 'other' and who support anti-sexist work. The phrase 'conscious use of self in relation to others', as a prerequisite of practice in informal settings, in many ways encapsulates the concerns of this book, as informal education draws so strongly on personal relationship as the basis for practice. Self-understanding and the ability to draw on that resource in being with others has long been a central professional task and for women this can be a highly subversive activity. Patterns of mutual support, including reflection and analysis, are essential to women if we are to continue to build up our strength. I hope this book will contribute something to this process. Its major focus therefore is on questions facing practitioners in practice.

Feminist Practice

This book advocates a feminist practice and also recognises a need to unsettle the term 'feminism' so as to embrace the struggles for emancipation and justice of all women and not simply to make a claim for equality with men of the same caste or class (hooks 1984). Feminism is understood as the theoretical and political perspective which aims to end women's oppression on grounds of their sex, and which makes common cause with other perspectives which resist domination. The feminist practice embraced here is therefore necessarily pluralist and diverse. It does not analyse a single cause of women's oppression on grounds of sex nor imagine a single ending to it. Much attention has been given in this context to questions of commonalities and differences between women and men, and between men and men and women and women, and to the intersectionality of subject positions which empower and constrain. This debate is closely linked to the political debate about the appropriateness of demands for equal rights while at the same time recognising and valuing women's 'sexual difference'. Attention to questions of commonality and difference arises from the recognition that finding oneself interpolated by the category 'woman' does not necessarily mean finding oneself a member of a group which shares the same social experience, let alone the same biology (Riley 1988). Subjects positioned by the category 'woman' are enormously different and some of the differences between women are also marks of powerful divisions and injustices: poverty and comfort or even wealth, or patterns of racism based on nationality, language, or skin colour are obvious examples. They are not merely differences but highly significant differences. It is to these significant differences that a feminism with a strong commitment to social justice is drawn.

Feminist Practice and the Politics of Difference

For some writers and activists, the whole question of difference and division between women has become so problematic that they no longer see autonomous work with women as an appropriate focus for activism and organisation. Against this perspective I argue for a recognition of the continuing strength of the category 'woman' as a vehicle of positioning and subordination. To collect and organise under the sign 'woman' is to organise against subordination and it is a necessary place from which to resist. The recognition of difference becomes a resource for resisting and challenging oppression which depends in part on a construction of 'woman' as uniform and the same and defined by a uniform experience of biology. The political theorist I.M. Young drew on the philosophy of Jean Paul Sartre to argue that it is possible to conceptualise women as sharing membership of a series which exists passively in relation to enforced heterosexuality, and in relation to a sexual division of labour, in which those who care for bodies and babies are defined in distinction from those who do not. This is strongly related to the case made by Judith Butler in *Gender Trouble* (1989) that it is the heterosexual matrix which gives rise to gender and not the reverse. Being positioned as woman implies neither shared experience, shared identity, nor shared interpretations, but women can consciously collect as a group in relation to that positionality. It is that active self-naming and grouping which enables feminist activism as a collective praxis to occur. Such feminist praxis at its best, in its turn, challenges the notion that all women are the same and values difference as a resource in the movement for emancipation (Young 1994).

This understanding of the positionality of 'woman' also allows us to understand some key social elements in the transition from girlhood to womanhood. From the point of view of feminist practice in informal education, growing up as a woman is a social process which changes from generation to generation and yet has some consistent boundaries. The 'marks of womanhood' are in part defined through their difference from, and subordination or superiority to, the 'marks of manhood', and there is a persistent discourse of normative heterosexuality and of the role of carer for bodies and babies. Feminist practice works from a recognition of these structurings as they are lived in the habitus of young women and also explores the ways this is lived through difference in the process of becoming an adult woman. For it is in these real, historical differences that the friction and creativity of change is to be found. And it is the friction and creativity of change which is constantly both challenging and reworking the positioning of women as subordinate.

When 'difference' is addressed, it is possible also to reveal areas of privilege and the ways difference can be mobilised to reinforce privilege. Significant difference is not just a sign of ready-packaged diversity. I have tried in what follows to give an account of the practice of community-based education with girls and young women which recognises diversity and sees it as a strength. It is also important to see how difference is 'power-charged'. The problem of the agenda of women's movements being dominated by the agendas of already privileged women can then be more easily addressed.

The question of the role of the woman worker inevitably touches on questions of inequality and injustice among women and differential access to power and resources. The project of coalition building is an essential strategy advocated in this book. One of the critical problems for coalition building, including with male allies, is the question of 'on whose terms' coalitions can be built. An analysis of power relations is an essential part of coalition building.

A major deficit in this text is the absence of the voices of young women who have participated in girls' work projects. It has not been possible to address this in a second edition. However, the priority has been to give support to youth and community workers in critically investigating and developing practice and it is this which remains at the heart of the book. An earlier writer on youth work with girls and women, Pearl Jephcott, with whose work I hope this book has a strong connection, started a project of research into the lives and conditions of girls which it would be good to see organisations adopting again today. Although the project of including a new version of that survey in this book has not come to fruition, I have included the questions by way of encouragement as a reminder of the close links between youth work and research in the interests of social justice.

Chapter Outline

The early chapters of this book – on the history of work with girls and the principles of practice – attempt to offer a broad picture of current approaches. They use case studies to show the diversity among women who carry out youth work in terms of race, class and cultural histories, lesbians, bisexuals, heterosexual women and trans people. I hope the stories this book tells do reflect that range. Later chapters focus on themes that arise consistently in relation to the practice of social and political education: sexuality, health and poverty, violence, disability, culture and community. The book concludes with chapters on the role of the youth work professional in community settings, some reflections on the changes between 1996 and 2011, and the urgency of youth work's contribution to a wider challenge to neo-liberalism.

1 Girls in the Modern World: Moments of Danger and Delight

The 1880s: The Girls' Clubs

Maude Stanley's volume *Clubs for Working Girls*, published in 1890, contains a mixture of handy hints and ideological resonance which characterises much writing about youth work. She wrote for ladies who were interested in the rapid spread of girls' clubs – 'this most modern of schemes':

> ... it is from the repeated requests of ladies who wish to form new ones, who consult us as to how they should begin, what rules they should have, how often they should get together the girls, that these pages are written, in order that they may assist others in the work of which we have such pleasing experiences. (Stanley 1890: 14)

However lady-like her approach, Maude Stanley – founder of the Soho Club and recorder of the work of the Girls' Club Union – clearly knew her business. Anyone who has tried in the face of lack of support and understanding to establish provision for girls in a youth club or other youth project will recognise her account of disruption and near anarchy. One hundred years later, we can still hear the boys banging at the windows and barging through the doors:

> We remember one sad night when two bigger girls who were sitting happily at work round a little table with a bright lamp, while a story was read to them, suddenly quarrelled about a thimble and in a passion one girl threw the table over; others, mad with excitement, began to act in the wildest, utterly indescribable fashion. The unfortunate teacher seized the dangerous lamp, which went out in her hands and came downstairs to get help. Meanwhile the girls threw up the window, and hanging out of it, with loud shouts and rude laughter presently had a crowd underneath, with whom they exchanged chaff and abuse. Downstairs the crowded kitchen was too noisy in its play for any upstairs sounds to be audible.

They, however, were cautioned to be quiet while the ladies went upstairs with a lamp to quell the disturbance and close the window. Coming down with the subdued and sulking girls, found hiding in corners and tolerably ashamed of themselves, as soon as the light came the horrified workers found the lower room in still worse confusion. Boys were banging at the shutters and door, the girls inside shouting and singing, and even fighting, slates, books and sewing being used as missiles; and one or two of the girls were reading the books at the desk, and finding out who had paid the club money and who not, and other interesting details, One of the ladies went to speak to the lads outside and one threw his cap in and getting his foot in the doorway prevented the door being closed. Remonstrances were of no use. They wished to come in and play with 'the lasses'. At last the cap was thrown out, and the door shut and locked for fear any girl might open it. An attempt was then made to get peace restored, but the boys had taken up the cellar grate outside, had dropped into the dark cellar, groped their way up the stairs and three grinning lads emerged through the cellar door into the kitchen amid shrieks of terror from the girls. The ladies greeted them with silence, and locking the door through which they came, put that key too in safety. The boys struck across the kitchen to the outer door and found themselves trapped. They didn't like it. 'Now' said the lady, 'I suppose we must give you in charge for house breaking. You know what the house has to say about burglars?' (She didn't, but the effect of these was just as impressive) (Ibid.: 196).

The ladies who began with a feeling of sympathy for the girls and who had themselves a set of high moral values they were concerned to share, found themselves threatening to call the police. In this way, care, concern and control have run hand-in-hand along the path of charity for more than a century.

Maude Stanley well recognised some of the qualities necessary in workers who would run along that path and for whom her book was written. She advised ladies to start slowly and to give some consideration as to whether the club should be organised on a neighbourhood basis, whether it should be limited by the girls' occupations, and whether it should be linked to a particular church. She made many useful organisational points early on – concerning age groups, bookkeeping, the establishing of a girls' committee – and her book contains what must be one of the earliest discussions of the role of volunteers and paid workers. She stressed the importance of recognising that the role of the philanthropic organisation must have priority over the need of the lady helpers, especially over the desire of ladies to be of assistance.

She saw the role of the club as primarily concerned with raising girls' standard of education. The curriculum reflected that provided by the school boards and aimed to provide girls with the means to fulfil their female role, within the context of their station in life. Cooking, needlework, pattern cutting, laundry and Bible classes formed the staple subjects: singing, dancing and drill supplemented the curriculum.

The First Women Youth Workers

> The ladies themselves 'must have a dignity in themselves which will command respect' and must be able to encourage a love of learning.
>
> Our work with many girls is to help them find out their own powers and to raise them more in their own estimation, for if a girl is stupid the fact of being thought so will put out even the small spark of intelligence that remains in her. (Stanley 1890: 72)

At the same time, the club might find it necessary to employ a superintendent: a full-time worker who would inevitably become closer to the girls than the ladies of the committee. The question of the social class of the superintendent was considered carefully by Maude Stanley, but, in the spirit of cross-class influence which permeated the philanthropic initiatives of the time, she hesitated to opt firmly for the employment of a lady:

> We have had the experience of a lady as a superintendent and also one of the same class of the girls and we do not recommend either one or the other as absolutely the best; the essential is to find a woman with great friendliness, love for the girls, warm sympathy, order and liveliness, who will never be tired or who rather will never let her feelings, mental or physical, interfere with the work of the club. (Stanley 1890: 31)

This job description for a saint is usually written in more detail nowadays and with less direct emphasis on personality. Yet Maude Stanley's account contained one of the central elements of a contemporary definition of professionalism: an ability to prioritise the work and the project rather than the worker's own needs, when they are in conflict. Unfortunately, her account continued in a vein which is still all too recognisable, especially when the status of part-time workers who comprise the majority of the workforce is discussed:

> The salary required for a superintendent will be some consideration when funds are low, but as it will only occupy the evenings of a working woman, a very large pay should not be required. Should the superintendent be a lady, her salary need not be much more, as it would not be wise to engage one who would have to depend on this salary for her maintenance. (Ibid.: 32)

Maude Stanley clearly intended the girls' clubs to be run with scarcely a voice or a salary being raised.

Keeping Girls Off the Streets

Maude Stanley also relished a challenge to her authority. In a chapter dedicated to the discussion of differences in social position among the work girls, she is not afraid to name them:

> But there are other classes of work girls, factory hands, who after the day's work are always in the street, who are rude, vulgar and boisterous. In one part of London, where a girls' club has been established they have been seen on a Saturday night fighting with one another bared to their waists, and yet these, by the gentle and kindly influence of a good matron in a girls' club, have been, may we not say, tamed and civilised. Many of our readers may never have seen the class of girl I now refer to – girls who will roll about the pavement three or four together, their hair cut straight over their foreheads, shawls over their heads, insulting every decent woman they meet; but even these, if they can be brought to the club, may become quiet and well-behaved. (Ibid.: 193)

Keeping girls off the streets was clearly as much on the agenda of the girls' clubs as it was of the lads' clubs in the same era and the distractions of drinking, dancing and other 'commercial' opportunities were real. Cleaning up the slums, similar to present-day regeneration, also meant cleaning out the population of the slums, and yet Maude Stanley spoke warmly of her relationship with the 'wild girls', rather as Baden Powell would later declare that 'the best sort of boy is the hooligan' (Pearson 1983). Writing of Newport Market and Princes Row in Soho, Stanley comments:

> These abodes, formerly the possessions of princes, had become so low in their surroundings, that we are thankful they are now swept away with the improvements of Charing Cross Road and Shaftesbury Avenue.
>
> The wild girls who used to call themselves the forty thieves and lived above these courts, and the lads who assumed the like designation, where are they gone to? We see them no longer about Soho. (Stanley 1890: 263)

The 1980s: The Girls' Work Movement

Perhaps, a lifetime later, it was the grandchildren of these wild girls who returned to Soho and to many other places celebrating wildness and power in the name of the women's liberation movement – not off the streets but on the streets instead. Maude Stanley wanted to tame the wild girls and send them off to domestic service, despite her nostalgia for them. In 1982, girls were writing for themselves in a collection called *Girls are Powerful*, edited by Susan Hemmings at *SpareRib,* the women's liberation magazine. This collection of lively, aggressive essays found its way on to the shelves of many young women's projects in the 1980s, where women workers were attempting to understand young women's perspectives on the world and to work out a new language for talking about discrimination and oppression. This involved a new vocabulary, and the word 'sexism' in particular became shorthand for a whole burgeoning understanding of how women are oppressed.

There are certainly persistent themes from the earlier attention to girls in the 1880s: particularly lack of opportunities for education and employment of a satisfying kind, and the experience of low pay. *Girls are Powerful* contains pieces on hairdressing, babysitting and Saturday shop work. But on the whole, the spirit of the enterprise and the way in which girls are a focus of attention has been recuperated in a transformed and reinvigorated capitalism.

First, young women spoke and speak for themselves. No one is going to speak on their behalf or define their best interests for them. Young women who produced the magazine *Shocking Pink* wrote:

> So no matter how much older feminists think it's important to put their energy into young women' s projects, girls nights in youth clubs and so on, it won't work if they see their role as educators. That's a patronising basis, neither equal nor conducive to trust.

> What we are saying is that we are already feminists. There are at the moment many hundreds of young women, politically aware and active, defining their sexuality, organising women's groups in schools and colleges, forming bands, starting magazines. Your ageist assumptions deny us our ability to think for ourselves, to create and make our own decisions. In your minds, you place our feminism on another level, below that of yours. We've all got it hard. We must stop turning it into some kind of competition and recognise each other's struggles. (Hemming 1982: 155)

Secondly, it was clear that young women's ambitions for change would extend far beyond the conventional definitions of politics into questions of personal life: looks and friendship, the age of consent, and lesbianism were, and remain, as relevant as themes for imagining a better future as educational and employment opportunities.

Thirdly, although many of the pieces did address and express a sense of threat and powerlessness experienced by young women (despite the courageous title), the source of danger was now understood on the whole to be in the workings of an unjust system. The appropriate response was to be found in collective organising. For Maude Stanley in the 1890s, the dangers facing girls were in the form of dancing, prostitution and drink. Her responses lay in a concern for morality and spirituality, religion and purity. Wider feminist responses in the same period lay, for example, in the agitation to raise the age of consent.

By the 1980s, the age-of-consent rules were being described by girls writing in *Girls are Powerful* as part of the problem. In a reversal of expectations, Asian girls, who are described as 'Growing Angry, Growing Strong', rejected the exaggerated lady-like passivity to which British culture seems to assign them. Racist and sexist expectations are the problem and the dangers. Organising collectively and speaking on our own behalves are the antidotes.

Early in the 1980s, it seemed as if the agenda for youth work with girls and young women might have shifted away from the philanthropic focus to girls as people with potential. The sense of excitement and movement made collective organising as women exhilarating and exhausting. Accounts of practice in a particular setting could always be framed by reference to a wider movement. For example, even as late as 1989, Dominelli and McLeod could claim that feminist campaigns and networks formed the basis of feminist social work, and feminist community work could only retain an identity if it was not totally incorporated within a professional community work network (Dominelli and McLeod 1989: 46).

In *Feminism for Girls: An Adventure Story*, Trisha McCabe communicated this sense of movement by talking about the differences and arguments among feminists, in a way which current accounts of the movement's history seem to erase:

> With the WLM (Women's Liberation Movement) there are lots of different politics and women put their energy and time into the areas that they see as the most important or relevant to them. We have big disagreements, not to mention rows. Women aren't nice to each other all the time! Our ideas can be so different that it can make it difficult, or impossible, to always work together. And feminists outside the WLM may have different ideas again. But that doesn't mean that we shouldn't listen to each other or that we aren't all fighting for the same thing. The however-many-thousands-of-women that are involved in the WLM in this country (and there are millions more, in every country of the world) obviously don't agree on how to end women's oppression or exactly what kind of society we want to build. The WLM is a movement, not a political party or a social set, precisely because it can encompass so many different political positions. The movement has broad aims – not a political programme – and what we have in common is that we all want women's liberation, we all want changes and we all want choices. (McCabe and McRobbie 1981: 14)

Girls are Powerful and *Feminism for Girls: An Adventure Story* are books which bridged the gap between a sense of a wider women's liberation movement and the practice of youth and community work which became known as 'the girls' work movement'. Some of the history of this movement, particularly its connection with the Girls Work Unit at the National Association of Youth Clubs (NAYC), is recorded in detail in the book written by the NAYC workers who were subsequently made redundant by the Association: *Coming in from the Margins: Youth Work with Girls and Young Women* (Carpenter and Young 1986). What follows is only a brief and very partial snapshot. But it is undoubtedly the spirit of the girls' work movement which informs the rest of this book.

Organisations of Women Youth Workers

In the mid-1970s, projects had begun to develop in London and Manchester. By the late 1970s, there was pressure on the NAYC to establish separate events for girls and women. These continued until the mid-1980s, along with the publication of the *Working with Girls* newsletter (Spence, 2010). The events and publications of the Girls Work Unit became a major resource for the work. The unit was closed very suddenly in 1986; the actions of the NAYC managers who made the decision to close the unit brought about a nationwide campaign of women workers and their allies in the trade unions to restore the unit, or at least to restore the organisation's support for girls' work. A 'pirate edition' of the *Working with Girls* newsletter, with the cover illustration 'The Grass Roots are Bloomin' Wonderful', appeared on the desk of every committee member who attended the executive meeting in which the closure decision had been made. Women workers' groups, trade union branches and young women's groups picketed the hotel. Resolutions from regional organisations threatened to disaffiliate and break up the NAYC. All this collective organising was evidence that the movement did not belong to the NAYC, nor even to the Girls Work Unit.

Two other forms of organising had emerged: the Women's Caucus within the Community and the Youth Workers Union, in which women had gained the right to organise autonomously within the trade union structure and were using their organising very effectively to promote the interests of women and girls with a particular focus on promoting the interests of part-time youth workers; and secondly, the National Organisation for Work with Girls and Young Women (NOWGYW) which was in existence from 1981 to 1994. The original working group for the NOWGYW circulated proposals for a constitution with the following aims in 1980:

Some of the aims which we aim to develop are:

- An information and resources unit
- A network of women youth and community workers
- Support for workers who are starting to work with girls in an alternative way
- The initiation of a training programme both for workers and young women
- The acquisition of campsites and residential premises for use by young women's groups
- The setting up of a training college specifically for women youth and community workers.

While many of these aims are very long term, action has been taken on some already. We hope that more clubs, projects and women youth workers' groups will join as soon as possible, so that they will be involved in determining the nature of the organisation from the start. No hard and fast decisions have been made, except to actually get the organisation moving.

The National Organisation for Work with Girls and Young Women could radically change the thinking on girls in the Youth Service. From being seen primarily as a problem, they could be recognised as a positive force with a great deal of energy and imagination, which, at present, is wasted in most clubs and projects. (NOWGYW: 4)

Throughout the 1980s, this democratic and autonomous organisation developed strong and active regional organisations. Annual meetings were well attended. The NOWGYW established a small base in Manchester and was able to appoint paid workers. As Michelle Walmsley and Liz Osborne have noted:

At the time it was seen as innovatory to have headquarters outside London or Leicester but the National Organisation was never afraid to respond to its members' radical and progressive ideas. Indeed the central debates which took place in the National Organisation were always focused on issues originally seen as marginal by mainstream services but which are now identified as central. The whole notion of 'empowerment' came from the direct practice of women succeeding in raising young women's esteem, self-confidence and skills so they were really taking control of their own lives. Today's curriculum has been shaped by these women's ideas, so that services' delivery plans now routinely include equal opportunities and monitoring processes to try to ensure that work is directed to previously excluded groups (currently young carers, young lesbians, disabled young women, bisexual young women, mixed race young families etc.). (Osborne and Walmsley 1995: 3)

The 'Sisters Are Doing It for Themselves' young women's conference was organised by members in 1986 and launched the young women's council, enabling young women's participation in the executive level of the organisation.

Sadly, as a result of a sustained attack on the funding of girls' work during the early 1990s, the decision to wind up the NOWGYW was taken at its AGM in Manchester in July 1994. In an essay which documents the history of the NOWGYW, Liz Osborne and Michelle Walmsley pointed out that the inequalities, which the organisation was established in part to address, have persisted:

Work with boys and young men has failed to keep pace with the gains and sheer weight of the work achieved by girls and young women's workers in past years. Ironically, whilst the 'B' team provides some sort of national resource, at least in training and materials, new girls' work resources rarely appear. Indeed the bright and challenging NAYC 'Girls Can Do Anything' poster set is making a reappearance in some centres – flares and pigtails have gone out of fashion and in again yet nothing comparable is available!

Unlike these images, the means whereby women workers and young women empowered themselves and each other have never gone out of fashion. We continue delivering a 'core curriculum' of work with girls and young women (identifying power and inequalities in our lives; challenging all discrimination and oppression at every level; esteem/confidence building; developing political awareness; anti-sexism; learning to support each other; individual growth through group challenges) with unchanging methods (assertiveness skills; groupwork; new experiences in a safe setting; peer education; communication skills; inter-agency co-operation etc.) but in more difficult circumstances.

Women workers are used to having to be more active, more accountable than male colleagues. We are often at considerable personal and professional risk through being outspoken, and increasingly women in management positions are made similarly vulnerable.

We hope that a different national body will one day be called for by women workers, building on the history of work with girls and young women once more. (Ibid.: 9)

Forward to the (18?)90s

Self-activity or Protection? Risk and Challenge/Risk and Danger

It is clear that the optimistic energy and activism of the girls' work movement – with its stress on self-activity, risk and challenge – has not yet been sufficiently strong to transform the long-standing agenda of risk and danger with which girls' work has been continually embroiled. Indeed, Maude Stanley would certainly recognise the language spoken in many girls' and young women's projects today. The continuities with the philanthropic agenda of the late nineteenth century seem very strong. Maude Stanley ended her book with a discussion of the danger of overpopulation and the link between overpopulation and poverty:

> We are always aiming at improving the education of the masses, we make it possible for the lowest to pass through the primary to the secondary education, we teach the adults by means of lectures within the reach of all. We enable all parishes at their own will to levy a rate in order to establish free libraries, we look after the health of our population and we establish by means of poor rates excellent hospitals for fevers, smallpox and diphtheria, where the working man gets as perfect treatment and nursing as could be given in any land.

> Countless other schemes are afloat and a vast army of unpaid workers are gallantly doing their utmost to improve our overgrown population; and yet we are never even abreast of the flood, that seems to be always surging around us, of destitution and poverty. And will not all unite in saying that the chief cause of this perplexing difficulty is that of over-population? And is not this evil mostly the result of early marriages? (Stanley 1890: 234)

Many projects concerned with work with young women in the 1990s were framed by the 'Health of the Nation' agenda of reducing teenage pregnancies. Maude Stanley's concerns with the dangers of dancing and drinking found their contemporary echoes in drugs education projects, and the distractions of popular culture still seem to challenge a serious educational focus of girls' work. Stanley's sense that girls on the streets are at continual risk of sexual exploitation finds some echoes in the place of the safeguarding agenda in work with girls and young women today, especially in the renewed attention to girls and gangs.

This consistent agenda of seeing girls as 'at risk', in need of protection and appropriate training in becoming a woman, is concerned with retaining and shoring up existing class relations and existing relationships between the sexes. It is in itself a recognisable focus for feminist political activity. The fact that work with girls and young women can shift so readily from an agenda concerned with challenging existing forms of power relationships to an agenda which is essentially rooted in them whilst promoting practice of charity is a major theme of this book.

The Difference Between Dominant Assumptions About 'Separate Spheres' and Autonomous Feminist Organising as Women

In analysing this shift from challenging the status quo to sustaining it, albeit with care for the girls, it is useful to pay attention to the links between arguments about separate spheres and arguments about autonomous organising. The difference made by the principles and aims which underpin practice, rather than by the methods alone, is made manifest here. It is after all perfectly possible and consistent to undertake separate work with girls and women which is not concerned with challenging women's subordination. 'Separate spheres' work is work which enables girls to undertake activities 'appropriate to their station in life' and not get into too much trouble. Autonomous anti-sexist work, by contrast, is based on the breaking-out of the position of women defined and categorised by their sex as persons of secondary importance. It therefore provides a potential base from which to recognise and challenge women's subordination.

However, in practical terms, it is quite possible and even likely, that a young women's group engaging in a health-and-fitness body workshop is not easily distinguished from a girls' club where make-up and beauty sessions are the most popular request and most frequent activity. It is the focus, direction and movement of the work which makes the difference: that it moves away from established patriarchally defined hierarchies, that it moves from the local to the global, that it seeks dialogue and transformation. All these contribute to the power of autonomous work. As well as having different aims and purposes, the role of the worker in autonomous anti-sexist work is seen as different. Alongside the practice of charity comes the development of the patronising attitude of the ladies towards the girls. In autonomous work with girls, the worker is positioned in solidarity with the girls and young women she is working with. While not denying difference of role, status and histories, it is essential that commonalities are not denied either and that both difference and commonality are worked with in the interests of challenging women's subordination. In anti-sexist work, it can be acknowledged that women workers have something to gain, as well as something to give, in the work they do.

Taking Risks and Acknowledging Difference: Sources of Creativity and Strength

This book seeks to celebrate some of the 1970s rediscoveries about autonomy, self-activity and collective action. It also locates current practice in relation to those ideologies of risk and danger which date back over a century and which still frame dominant social thinking about girls and young women. In moving from oppressive constructions of sameness to an attention to difference, not as a threat to unity but as a promise of greater strength, it was the work of Black women which pointed the way. At the very beginning of the work of the Girls Work Unit at the NAYC, the research undertaken by Laxmi Jamdagni and commissioned by the Department of Education and Science was a focus for this shift. It offered an early challenge to women workers to address the links between the identification of 'difference' and 'risk' and the exercise of power.

Having chosen to focus attention on Asian girls, Laxmi Jamdagni wrote:

> My aim in the groups was to provide the girls with the opportunity to talk about their experience of being Asian girls in Britain. Whilst they often need to talk through with me some of the problems they faced as girls in relation for example to their families, the specific focus of my research was to challenge the stereotyped notions of Asian girls being 'at risk' per se – a view popularly held by white professional workers including those who designed the project. (Jamdagni 1980: 3)

Like Jamdagni, I wish to question those ideologies of risk, danger and protection. I would like to re-associate the idea of 'risk' with excitement, rebellion, wildness, pleasure and potential. Like Maude Stanley, but with a quite opposite purpose, I shall ask: 'Where are the wild girls now?'

By the end of the first decade of the twenty-first century, the issue of how to respond to difference – especially as constructed through global power, politics, resurgent nationalisms and xenophobia – is inescapable in the context of youth work.

In public policy terms, two models of responsiveness vie with one another. First, there is multiculturalism which both promotes a commodified view of 'difference' and 'otherness' and seems somehow to fix and make static what for feminists and anti-racists remains a question, a moving horizon (Hall 2000). This corporate version of multiculturalism is perhaps best understood as an approach which calls for a 'live and let live' toleration. Secondly, there is assimilation/expulsion. When in Rome, do as the Romans do. Or leave. This is best exemplified by the burkha ban in continental Europe (currently France and Belgium). The contrast between these two policy stances is often seen as the contrast between French and British approaches to Islam, post 9/11 and the attack on the World Trade Centre in New York and both need to be understood in the context of 'new racisms, old pathologies.' (Shain 2003)

In urban centres across the UK and Europe, there are significant communities who have well-established traditions concerning the distinct and separate place of women and men, a commitment to single-sex education. This is sometimes associated with views that women should not work outside the home after marriage. There are also communities with traditions of head, face and sometimes whole body covering for women. In Manchester, for example, these may include Somali, Bangladeshi, Pakistani, Sudanese, Iraqi, Afghan as well as Orthodox Jewish communities. Of course not all women and men in these communities follow such traditions, but frequently the designation of separate spaces for men and women is firmly based on a strongly gendered set of expectations in which men's role is in the public domain and women's in the domestic and private domain. In Islam as practised in these communities, these separate spheres are mirrored in patterns of worship when Friday prayers are said by men at the mosque and by women in the domestic space of the home.

In Europe, the banning of the burkha in public space was agreed first by the government of France. In Belgium in 2011 the burkha ban was the only legislation on which its divided Parliament was able to agree. Public space in law includes educational space, potentially creating an extreme example of the clash for some girls and women between expectations in the family and expectations in the secularised Christian state. In the UK, the capacity to establish single-sex faith-based schools mitigates this tension for some girls as family and school expectations can be more aligned. However, the existence of such schools is thought by many to reinforce the segregation of communities. Faith schools seem to connect to segregation of communities. Schooling strategies are criticised when they reinforce segregation. There is a direct link between the critique of such schooling strategies and policy moves 'against multiculturalism' (Back et al. 2002, Shukra 2010).

These move 'against multiculturalism' involve a misrecognition of multiculturalism as a strategy, which has in fact always promoted association (Thomas 2006, 2011). In practice, such policy is leading to an increased reluctance to fund separate community associations and projects for Black and minority communities and for women. A number of long-established organisations – most notably Southall Black Sisters – have had threats to funding in consequence of these policy directions.

There is a sense in which women's bodies and women's dress have become the symbolic site in which the fears of the 'other' (depicted as militant Islam) are being played out.

At the same time as women's dress is a politicised site of attack on Islam, the 'slutwalkers' across Canada, the US and the UK have been protesting the assumptions of a Canadian police officer who said that women who want to stay safe on the streets 'should avoid dressing like sluts'. One of the organisers of the slutwalks in the UK said: 'Comments like these only serve to shame victims into silence.' They are reclaiming the old feminist slogan: 'Whatever we wear, wherever we go, yes means yes and no means no.' The campaign group Object is mounting a major campaign against what they term the 'pornification' of high street shopping. These new feminist campaigns have strong links to the student movement. The existence of women's groups as lesbian space has also developed strongly in major cities with lesbian youth groups as part of lesbian, gay, trans and bisexual community and youth projects (Batsleer 2012).

In youth and community work, single-sex organisations and practice still include the Girl Guides and Boy Scouts as major organisations. The main girls' work projects which had significant support from local authorities when others were closed were projects working with Asian (now usually designated as 'Muslim' girls) who met separately for cultural reasons. The ambivalence of the space occupied by Muslim girls work has been well captured by Gill Cressey in 'The Ultimate Separatist Cage? Youth Work with Muslim Girls' (2007). For some young women, the reclaiming of Islamic as against western dress codes and the exploration of ideas of the respect for women which they feel is offered by 'true Islam' is very important. Such young women seek to distinguish between 'true Islam', and what they argue are cultural interpretations of religion which limit women's place and potential. The space behind the scarf and the veil may sometimes become a space from which to challenge the assumptions about femininity. On the other hand, it may be seen to be as offering as limited a view of female sexuality in its own way as Page Three of the *Sun* does in its. In the UK, the Muslim Youth Work Foundation has been creating a space for these issues to be explored (Khan 2006a).

So, in urban contexts, there is always more than one possible meaning to be assigned to women-only spaces and that meaning cannot be assigned in advance. It is also clear that the assumption that mixed coeducational space is 'normal' and single-sex space as 'deviant' is an assumption that is being strongly challenged from a number of very different directions.

There is a great deal of scope for the development of work with girls and young women across communities, which explores these issues and this question of difference, and its meanings will be investigated throughout the chapters which follow. The point is that feminist approaches do not foreclose or assume the meanings associated with difference, whether the difference is sexual difference, national difference, cultural or linguistic difference, or difference of faith. Difference remains as a question to be investigated and as a sign of a new and constantly shifting horizon.

2 Autonomy and Relationship

The Tensions Between Autonomy and Community

Practice occurring in projects and groups from which boys and men are excluded may be informed by the principles of separate and autonomous provision. This is often referred to as `separate work' or 'gender-specific work'. It is youth work with girls and women, by girls and women, controlled by girls and women. The term 'separate work' can easily be taken to mean no more than work in which only girls participate. However, from the point of view of practice which advocates feminism, the term has a stronger meaning. It suggests the independence of girls and women from boys and men, and a commitment to enable girls and women to set and control the agenda. 'Separate work' might better be termed 'autonomous work', as the act of separation and exclusion of men from groups needs to be understood as an action in the direction of empowerment, not 'on our own' so much as 'with one another'. It is not 'separatist', as it remains in dialogue with wider networks of provision for both boys and girls.

Of course the autonomy of girls' work is profoundly circumscribed by organisational hierarchies and the control of funding. Nevertheless, it is now widely recognised that the dynamic of work from which boys and men are excluded is very different and potentially very creative. It may well be appropriate for particular girls and boys to work together, but if such mixed work is undertaken on the basis of the experience of autonomous girls' groups, girls will join the negotiations in mixed groups from a position of greater strength.

Acceptance of the need for 'separate space' unites women whose analyses of the position of women and the nature of women's subordination differ. For some women, the commitment to separate space is tactical and temporary. For others, it is strategic and very long term. And for others again, it is visionary and prefigurative of an alternative form of community.

21

All these positions share a recognition that separate space can provide a basis from which male dominance can be understood, negotiated and resisted. New possibilities can emerge when women meet in the absence of men and are temporarily released from the need to act as 'relative creatures'.

Some characteristic explanations given by workers who choose to work separately with women and girls include the following:

- It offers girls the opportunity to meet without pressure from boys and men.
- It offers girls the opportunity to build up and value female friendship and mutual support.
- It enables the creation of a safe environment in which self-confidence can develop and new skills can be tested.
- It enables the creation of an environment in which silences can be broken and difficult, challenging questions explored.

In addition, the following community-based rationales are offered:

- It offers girls the opportunity to do work that is appropriate to women's role in the community.
- It provides the opportunity to do work that is seen as appropriate by religious and community organisations.
- It facilitates the welfare of the whole community.

Within and between these statements, there are a number of potentially conflicting positions. For example, a growth of self-confidence and individual ambition in a young woman may endanger her role as someone who works to facilitate the welfare of the whole community. The exploration of difficult and challenging questions may mean that the work ceases to be 'appropriate' in the eyes of the organisations, be they religious or not, who are sponsoring the work. Autonomous work always raises the question of 'in whose interests?'. There is a tension between promoting young women's rights as individuals and promoting young women's interests as members of communities. Separate, autonomous work can explore what is possible for young women as individuals and what is at stake for them in their membership of communities.

In some projects, the exclusion of men has been a formal policy position. In others, the exclusion of men derives from a commitment to working within existing friendship and community networks and giving priority to work around young women's own identified concerns. Women's projects in working-class communities, including projects which have focused on work with Asian women and projects which have worked with women of African and African-Caribbean descent, have been strong when they have recognised and drawn on the strength and resourcefulness of women as community-makers. In such contexts, women's groups occur 'naturally' as sources of community, support and constraint (Hill Collins 1991, Jarrett Macaulay 1996). In some neighbourhoods, work with girls and young women can build on the achievements of the earlier generation, particularly among Black women who focused on building up voluntary organisations and self-help networks, in the face of the racism of the 'host' community. Working with young women, in this perspective, involves more than a resistance to male dominance. Release from subordination for women in poor communities has never been only a matter of tackling 'the sexual Toryism of men'. It becomes rooted in a practice of resistance to oppression which includes male dominance, but in which men may sometimes be allies (Wilson 2006). And it affirms women's already well-developed strengths and capacities for survival. Autonomous work needs to be understood as work which challenges all patterns of dominance, including sexism, but not confined to it.

The principles underlying separate and autonomous work with women need to be explored and discussed each time a project is established and each time links between projects are proposed and alliances suggested. In this way, some of the tensions of the practice can be explored and the work strengthened. It is possible to anticipate some of the tensions which may need to be confronted. Such practice of exploration may now be referred to as 'gender-specific' work in recognition that such explorations are of value to both girls and boys (Batsleer 2008).

Autonomy and Young Women's Rights: The Tension Between 'Autonomy and Relationship'

The tension between the commitment to girls' groups as offering autonomous space and the need to recognise and debate the place of women within communities of women and men is present in the question of the particular aims of informal education with girls and young women.

Underlying much feminist practice in which girls are offered opportunities for development is a commitment to young women's development as persons in their own right, of equal worth and dignity to men and boys, and with the potential to create their own perspectives in social and political education.

At the same time, young women can be viewed as essentially co-operators and community-builders: the cornerstone from which everything else develops. From community-based perspectives, the liberal, individualist perspective inherent in the commitment to 'rights' is regarded as inadequate to promote the well-being of young women, which must be a collective enterprise (Frazer and Lacey 1994). On the one hand, to become adult means to become an autonomous person, with rights. In the language of developmental psychology, autonomy is seen as a developmental goal for girls as well as for boys. On the other hand, to become an adult means being prepared to take up adult duties and responsibilities. And for women, whose subordinate status means that definitions of adulthood are always open to question, both points of view about what it means to be an adult will be questioned in the process of challenging women's subordination.

Many women working in informal education have identified the 'small group' and 'working through relationships' as methods both for good educational practice and as an alternative forum where such questions – and in particular the tension between rights and community – can be addressed (Cruddas and Haddock 2003). Small-group work can enable both the recognition of the reality and importance of relationship and the differing life-stories of the individuals who form the groups. It enables the identification of common ground and multivocality about what it means to be a woman and, in relation to empowerment, the exploration both 'what is within our grasp' and 'what is outside our power'. The focus for working with and through relationships on which small-group work depends means that these questions can be addressed both by individuals and collectively.

If relationships become a focus for small-group work, as is often the case, then the group work can focus on a number of potential relationships:

- between girls,
- between young women and older women, particularly sisters, mothers and grandmothers, and cousins and aunts,
- with fathers and brothers,
- with young men, including boyfriends and children's fathers,
- with professional workers such as health visitors, teachers, social workers and GPs who have an impact on their lives and who are 'gatekeepers' of enormous power,
- between neighbourhoods,
- with political representatives and
- between communities in different nations.

It is these relationships which form most of the curriculum for informal education with girls and young women.

Most young women's projects effectively combine in practice an orientation towards the 'development of individuals-in-community' – and an orientation towards social change. It is important to be able to identify the primary orientation of any project, for projects to be able to shift from one orientation to another, and for projects to be able to make links with one another on the basis of discussions of differences and similarities in interpretation of the term 'empowerment'. The following examples illustrate, I think, the ways in which two projects with different initial orientations both addressed aspects of women's subordination and resistance. The Hag Fold Project seemed to have a strong orientation to the achievements of particular young women, while the Youth Support Project's orientation seemed to focus on community, engaging with the organisational or 'command' aspects of power. Both made connections, but in different ways, between the lives of the particular young women and society-wide power relations.

The Hag Fold Young Women's Centre

In the context of Wigan Youth Service's commitment to young people's rights, the workers at Hag Fold Young Women's Centre, Poddy Peerman and Julia Keenan, expressed their aims in the following ways:

Within the constraints of the budget, Hag Fold Young Women's Centre aims to:

1. provide an environment that challenges oppression within society;
2. ensure that the physical environment of the project is conducive to all women;
3. increase young women's confidence and stimulate personal development;
4. encourage young women to learn to value themselves and other young women;
5. increase young women's knowledge of their rights and the political climate in which they live;
6. increase young women's expectations of their rights and goals;
7. help young women understand what blocks them from having control;
8. enable young women to make informed choices;
9. support young women making changes in their lives.

The workers then went on to express these aims in terms of what they hoped the outcomes for young women who participated in the project might be. They hoped the women would:

1. take up training opportunities inside and outside the project (e.g., enrolling for courses at the local college; learning to use the word-processor at the centre);

2. take up Youth Service opportunities (e.g., taking driving lessons through the borough-wide driving scheme; going on senior members' training courses; joining the Young People's HIV Education Project);
3. take up new opportunities of all types (e.g., one young woman went into car mechanics; several women tried 'fantasy' activities like windsurfing and abseiling);
4. feel valuable and be prepared to consider their own needs (e.g., learning to leave their child in the crèche for two hours so as to have space; thinking about what they want from a relationship);
5. gain knowledge and skills for self-development and to aid employment prospects (e.g., overcoming agoraphobia and being able to come out of the house and mix with others; developing tolerance for the opinions of others; e.g., a young woman herself became a youth worker; women developing marketable skills like sewing, typing, welding, childcare);
6. experience the benefits (and difficulties) of collective working and team work (e.g., organising fundraising activities together; campaigning; group discussions and support);
7. challenge put-downs of women; themselves and others;
8. become analytical/more aware about their child-rearing;
9. learn about discrimination and prejudice and the position of oppressed groups;
10. direct their anger in appropriate ways in order to effect change (e.g., a young woman challenging her partner about their behaviour and setting an ultimatum that demands change; complaining to a local councillor about their dissatisfaction with a local service; campaigning to save the project);
11. be involved in making decisions about the life of the project (e.g., via the structure of centre meetings). (Peerman and Keenan 1993)

The Youth Support Project

The Youth Support Project was a Manchester-based voluntary organisation which has worked mainly but not exclusively with young women. Reflecting on the prospects for improving young women's health by improving their diets (the link between ill health and poverty being as clear then as now), the project workers turned their attention to the fact that local stores were stocking poor-quality produce and selling products which were past their expiry date. They called on their local MP to lobby national food organisations, the National Consumer Council and the Health Inspectorate, as well as the agricultural minister, and used the national media to good effect, including the BBC *Watchdog* programme.

In the same year, the project was involved in Women's Action for Benefits, a campaign linked to a nationwide campaign against social security cuts. The group organised a conference to examine the current position of women within the benefits system, to share information and discuss campaign strategies for the future. The Youth Support Project ran a well-attended workshop on maternity benefits. Overall, the conference attracted 120 women. Jo Richardson MP and speakers from the Child Poverty Action Group were well received.

As the project workers noted in their report: 'As a high percentage of Project users are women claiming benefits this campaign is particularly relevant to them' (Youth Support Project 1986).

Characteristics of Feminist Practice

After 1986, there was something of a decline in campaigning, and the attempt to turn 'private troubles into public issues' or the desire to turn 'cases into issues, issues into movements' has taken different forms. The long period of Conservative rule in Britain led to a loss of confidence in what were well-established forms of collective advocacy and collective action. This – along with the stress on identifying 'outcomes' so necessary for the funding of projects in the 1990s – may account for such continuing differences in orientation.

A commitment to empowerment has unified the practice of community-based informal education with girls and young women. It is possible to offer, at this stage, a statement of some characteristics which seem to inform feminist-inspired informal education practice with girls and young women. This summary should be read as open to change, critique and modification on the basis of continuing debate.

These are some characteristics of feminist practice in informal education with girls and young women:

- There is a commitment to autonomy – the desire to see girls and young women have the opportunity to develop as subjects of their own lives, rather than merely as the objects of professional intervention. There is a recognition of the shared and distinct experiences of adult women workers and of young women in relation to the goal of autonomy, in particular in exploring, from different perspectives and ages, the meaning of 'adult status' for women.
- There is a commitment to openness – this does not exclude the possibility of working with closed groups, or working with women who have been referred to a project. It does, however, mean that young women are to be free to participate or not. It also means that there is

positive encouragement for new and different groups of women to participate. There is development and change within the project.

- The work of the project entails active participation – doing and being – by girls and young women. They are not merely consumers, but also creators. Characteristically, the work of informal educators starts from the strengths and concerns of participants, rather than from an already fixed curriculum

- There is negotiation of the project's programme and agenda of work. Workers or funders are not able alone to define the agenda, goals and purposes of a programme. Young women are critically involved in the development of the project (though not necessarily 'burdened' with management in the name of empowerment). There is a continuous dialogue about the work of the project that 'starts where young women are at, but does not end there'.

- The approach to the work is informal, flexible and not geared to assessment. It is evaluated in relation to its process as much as its end results. Its subject matter is developed from key themes in the lives of young women. Its method draws on oracy, literacy, arts education, outdoor education and community action, and they link to the school-based curriculum of social and personal education, as well as to women's studies in adult education. It is not subject to assessment at age 7, 11, 16 or older, but the achievements of young women within the frameworks it offers can be recognised and recorded.

- The work uses the methods of social group work and collective action to build on individual young women's strengths and to turn 'private troubles into public issues'. The focus of group work is enjoyment, association, education and community development, as distinct from therapeutic group work. However, it also recognises the need to provide support, both material and emotional, to individuals.

- There is commitment to making connections with other women's projects and with other projects which share these principles in some degree and are engaged with empowerment/anti-oppressive practice. There is a recognition that women workers, as well as young women who are participants in the work, have much to gain from such initiatives.

A Deepening Understanding of the Problems of 'Autonomy'

Since the first edition of this book, the increasing focus on individualised and personalised agendas in youth work has made the focus on 'autonomy' seem even more problematic than it did in 1996. Nevertheless, the tensions still remain, as, for many women all over the world, access to claims based in a human rights/women's rights agenda provide the basis from which they can and do challenge oppression. This is especially the case in relation to women's access to such basic resources as health care, contraception and abortion, and education. Others emphasise the importance of rights-based regulations in supporting practice, such as the Public Service Equality Duty.

April 2011 saw the gender, race and disability duties in public services replaced by a new Public Service Equality Duty which covered age, disability, gender, gender reassignment, pregnancy and maternity, race, religion or belief and sexual orientation. It applies in England, Scotland and in Wales. The general equality duty is set out in section 149 of the Equality Act (2010). In summary, those subject to the general equality duty must have due regard to the need to:

- eliminate unlawful discrimination, harassment and victimisation,
- advance equality of opportunity between different groups and
- foster good relations between different groups.

The duty to have due regard to the need to eliminate discrimination also covered marriage and civil partnership. The Equality Act (2010) gives ministers the power to impose specific duties through regulations. The specific duties are legal requirements designed to help those public bodies covered by the specific duties meet the general duty.

However, the depth of the neo-liberal reshaping of the global economy makes it more important in 2012 to emphasise the distance between community-based and individualist approaches to work with women and women's empowerment.

The ways in which individualist approaches can shape practice is clear in relation to what came to be known as the 'equalities strands' and the reconstruction of ideas of 'empowerment' to become coterminous with consumer/client/pupil choice in a series of marketised public services. The human rights framework in this context becomes a framework rooted in law, litigation, compliance and regulation; empowerment becomes a matter of the capacity to enforce such laws. There is a danger that compliance with the 'gender duty' becomes the basis of feminist politics and the space for a cultural politics which seeks collective undoings and transformations of our understandings of gender is squeezed (Butler 2004). Such an approach positions young people as consumers rather than creators, as checkers, monitors and regulators, in a reversal of roles which does little to challenge the system.

The shift to a neo-liberal managerial approach to issues of power is made clear in the following case study which highlights the way statements concerning youth work, power and inequality in England have shifted since the first edition of this book was published. It serves to illuminate the ways in which discourses which emerged in a periods of activism and struggle have been first transposed into policy statements and then turned upside down so that creative activists become consumers and recipients of policy once again.

Case Study: The Development and Debate about National Occupational Standards and Regulatory Frameworks for Youth Work

The first quotation below, from the National Youth Agency (1990), shows how a commitment to 'redress all forms of inequality' was eventually written into policy about youth work. Following a period of powerful contestation in the 1980s among youth and community workers about the purpose and direction of the profession, the following statement was agreed. It powerfully reflects the engagement of youth workers in social justice struggles during the preceding decade:

> National Youth Agency Statement of Purpose 1990
> The purpose of youth work is to redress all forms of inequality and to ensure equality of opportunity for all young people to fulfil their potential as empowered individuals and members of groups and communities and to support young people during the transition to adulthood ... Youth work offers young people opportunities which are ... designed to promote equality of opportunity – through the challenging of oppressions such as racism and sexism and all those which spring from differences of culture, race, language, sexual identity, gender, disability, age, religion and class; and – through the celebration of diversity and strengths which arise from those differences.

The second example, taken from the National Occupational Standards (2008), shows how that commitment had been minimised as a sub-set (2.3.1) of a much wider set of statements. The development

---

of 'competence'-based approaches to work-based learning and employment standards was also highly contested, as it seemed to downplay the need for a broad education as a knowledge base for professional formation. However, with the development of National Vocational Qualifications (NVQs) across a range of employment contexts, the competence framework was established as the basis for assessing competence in youth work. What had been a social movement seemed to some to have been reduced to a 'Tick-box list' of requirements, and reference to challenging oppression has been removed from the 'Statement of Purpose':

National Occupational Standards for Youth Work 2008

2.3.1 Promote equality of opportunity and diversity in your area of responsibility (MSC B11)

2.3.2 Develop a culture and systems that promote equality and value diversity

2.3.3 Challenge oppressive behaviour in young people

2.4.1 Fulfil the legal, regulatory and ethical requirements relevant to youth work

Final version approved February 2008 The key purpose of youth work is to …'Enable young people to develop holistically, working with them to facilitate their personal, social and educational development, to enable them to develop their voice, influence, and place in society and to reach their full potential'

This statement refers to the holistic development of young people, recognising that personal, social and educational development can also include, for example, physical, political and spiritual development.

Finally, the combination of a resurgence emphasis on young people's rights to have a say in matters which affect them and a need to develop regulatory frameworks for outsourced, local authority commissioned services has led to an emphasis on engaging with young people in their role as consumers of services. A major thread of current policy therefore positions young people as auditors in an audit culture.

The Young Inspectors Programme 2012

This programme is the product of a successful 2 year training pilot called Youth4U – Young Inspectors and supports the government's 'Big Society Agenda'. Youth4U – Young Inspectors encouraged young people to help over 33 local communities across England assess their services. The results of the pilot showed both the participating organisations and the young people involved had hugely benefited from the exercise. The pilot project resulted in over 1400 young inspectors contributing to society by actively engaging with their peers to address issues they had identified in their community's local services. This responsibility had a huge impact on the young people involved, who gained confidence and channelled this into beneficial action and invaluable work experience. Experience that otherwise, with the majority of volunteers from marginalised backgrounds, they would not have had the opportunity to gain.

The feminist practice which is advocated in this book seeks to return the discussion of empowerment away from such monetised and consumerist approaches and to re-engage with questions of whether there is an alternative vision of empowerment to those encapsulated in current policy.

3 Empowerment?

Work with girls and young women is still widely regarded with scepticism and mistrust, and where good practice exists it is due almost entirely to women workers who are challenging the system and offering to young women a curriculum of relevant social education in an environment where they feel confident and secure. (DES, WO and NACYS 1989: 6)

Kate Clements, the Youth and Community Worker responsible for the development of the Girls Work Unit in Lancashire, tells an important story. She was appointed to her full-time post just as the Girls Work Unit at the National Association of Youth Clubs was being closed down. One of her first 'official appointments' in her new post was to attend the demonstration which had been called in Leicester to coincide with the meeting where a decision about the Girls Work Unit was to be taken. The banners that were flying and the crowd of women and men who gathered seemed, both then and now, to mark a turning-point. For the Girls Work Unit at NAYC, it was a full stop. For the Girls Work Unit in Lancashire, the banners were heralding a beginning.

There were six girls' groups in Lancashire in 1986. By 1996, there were 66. Work with girls persists despite its often reported demise. New generations of workers become involved and ask the same basic questions: 'Why should we work with girls and what sort of work should we do?' The basic concepts which underpin the work need to be stated and discussed again and again.

The aim of this chapter is to present and discuss some key concepts and the thinking behind them, so that the conceptual framework which underpins community-based education with girls and young women can continue to be developed and to change. The original approach to empowerment which was presented in the first edition of this volume is broadly retained here; this is then followed by a new section which explores the impact of the New Labour period on the debate about empowerment in youth work.

The Debate About Empowerment

A commitment to empowerment is often claimed to unify the practice of community-based informal education work with girls and young women. However, the term seems elastic and capable of such a wide range of reference as to be of doubtful usefulness. Rather than abandon the term and the struggle to define its meaning, this chapter offers a specific perspective on the debate about empowerment which derives from a feminist analysis. In doing this, I intend to shift the debate away from a fruitless polarisation between individual and structural accounts of power and root the discussion of empowerment in an analysis of the links between the personal and the political.

In the 1990s, many writers on 'empowerment' drew a sharp distinction between approaches which seem to be based on an individualistic model of self-help and the consumer movement, and those which are based on a collective model of resistance to structures of oppression. This distinction is drawn particularly sharply by David Ward and Audrey Mullender:

> Broadly, empowerment is associated at one end of a continuum with the New Right's welfare consumerism and at the other end with the user movement which demands a voice in controlling standards themselves. One is 'the essential expression of individualism'; the other rests on a collective voicing of universal need. (Ward and Mullender 1992: 21)

They argue that it is only on the basis of a clear analysis of the structural nature of oppression that community work practice can promote empowerment. This commitment to a structural analysis of power relations is clearly a necessary antidote to the 'power to the people' rhetoric of free-market Conservative and Liberal social policy, in which the power of the citizen is her purchasing power, that is, her ability to choose to buy or not to buy certain services.

These two versions of empowerment do represent two different political orientations. However, from the point of view of a feminist analysis of power relations, the distinction between the individual and the structural rests on a mistaken account of the personal and its separation from the political. The much-discussed tension between structure and agency and the relationship between the personal, the social and systemic and the public as it has been theorised and debated in critical theory is very significant here and contemporary feminist social and political theory has much to offer this discussion. The individual/structural dichotomy prevents an analysis of the social and a recognition that all power, even when it is exercised by individuals, derives from the social order. Even the physical force of the natural world experienced in hurricanes, floods and earthquakes, even the apparent domain of spiritual power (the realm of angels and archangels!) can be analysed most convincingly as power exercised through the social domain. Hannah Arendt's formulation reinforced this emphasis on the social as the source of power, emphasising the distinction between power and force and leading to a recognition of the significance of drawing the social back into the public realm and the realm of politics. This distinction also forms the basis of Gramsci's discussion of hegemony which has been so important for community work practice. Because of the significance of the struggle for ideas, for imagination and culture in Gramsci's analysis, it has offered a framework within which radical educators, including feminist educators, have been able to imagine their work contributing to a counter-hegemonic alliance. Here. empowerment is not about individuals as consumers but supports a fundamental challenge to existing social relations and contributes to a vision of new ways of ordering society.

Power

The most general definitions of power build on the account given by Max Weber: 'to achieve one's will, even against the resistance of others'.

In its widest sense, the power a person has indicates their ability to produce intended effects upon the world around them, to realise their purposes within it, whatever their purposes happen to be. Power in this general sense depends upon certain preconditions: the presence of personal capacities or powers, such as health, strength, knowledge and skill; the possession of material resources; and the space or scope, in the sense of freedom from control, obstruction or subservience to the purposes of others (Beetham 1991).

Power is Socially Organised

Other theorists have emphasised that the definition of power needs to be social from the very start. Hannah Arendt argued that 'Power corresponds to the human ability not just to act but to act in concert. Power is never the property of an individual; it belongs to a group and remains in existence only so long as the group keeps together' (Arendt 1986: 64).

On this basis, when individuals hold and exercise power, they are able to do so only because it is socially sanctioned. Power is invested in individuals by groups, and can be removed from them. This is currently visible in global politics in the events of the Arab Spring, as socially sanctioned power crumbles and is reconstructed. So the expression 'power to the people' is profoundly misleading. Power belongs to the people and derives from the people. This reality can even appear to give legitimacy to the power of markets as an apparent expression of popular power as consumer power. Power is only ever lent to rulers, and it can be reclaimed. Rulers can be overthrown. Power relations can be reconstructed.

Power is Channelled Through Socially Sanctioned Relations of Domination and Subordination

Power is unequally accessed and flows through channels and relationships which are structured in patterns of dominance and subordination. These are systematic and continuous relations whereby one group defines and limits the power of another group, legitimately, and through their hegemonic direction of the purposes of society. The problem for the subordinate group is that the dominant group has the power to define what are legitimate forms of domination. A number of means to power can provide the basis for these social relations. To be dominant means to be able to direct these means to power and exclude others from them. Power relations operate through processes of possession, direction and exclusion.

What are the Means to Power?

Many social theorists have identified the following as significant aspects of power. First, there is the possession of, or exclusion from, material resource: on the one hand, the means of life – such as food, water, clothing and all other material goods; on the other hand, the means of death, the capacity to control and use physical force destructively. Secondly, there is the control of socially necessary activities and the possession of skills associated with their performance: this includes the whole area of the division of labour and the reproduction of life and new generations, as well as caring for the sick and the dying. Third, power is invested in positions of command and in the ability to generate the rules of social life and of legality. Fourth, power is invested in the work of naming and defining the aims and purposes of society: it is educative, cultural and moral.

Those aspects of power exist in all societies, and it is through the social relations of exclusion and possession that domination is secured.

Power and Discourse: The Productive Capacities of Power

Following Foucault, the discursive aspect of all these forms of power is well recognised. They are productive as well as repressive; they bring into being particular types of subjectivity as well as laying down principles of exclusion. Power is creative as well as regulatory and always involves and brings into being the possibilities of resistance.

Because of its attention to subjectivities and because of the ways in which accounts of discursive formations enable resistance to domination to be described and analysed, Foucauldian perspectives and those following the work of Butler remain very important. Views of gender as a social construction have long been important for feminist politics and this perspective has been developed by Butler and others to make visible the politics of intersex (Butler 2004). Despite the arguments of some that Butler's analyses destabilise the basis of feminist politics by proposing the deconstruction of the category 'woman' which founds such politics (Benhabib 1995), the enquiry Butler instigated into 'the heterosexual matrix' has been fruitful for unsettling assumptions about what belongs to 'women' and therefore for a feminist politics which embraces the possibility of an end to gender controls.

Feminist Accounts of Power

All feminist accounts of power which share in the project of analysing domination and subordination pay particular attention to gender as a conduit for power relations. Sometimes this involves analysing the power relations between women and men, sometimes between masculinity and femininity, and sometimes it involves deconstructing the practices of gender themselves.

Such analyses of power and resistance attempt to uncover the ways in which power flows and to create alternative conduits for the flow of power, through which practices which subordinate women are undermined and changed. Feminisms are therefore involved with questions of economics, of wealth and poverty. Feminisms also address the gendering of coercion, the control of means of physical force and violence, especially militarisation. They question how the power of the body is channelled through sexualities. A variety of feminist analyses address the issue of the sexual division of labour, particularly the work of reproduction and mothering, and care for the sick or frail.

Feminist analysis considers the 'relations of ruling': the gendering of access to positions of control and command, related to the practice of government, but also to the command and control of major social and economic institutions and the practices of governance.

Finally it is concerned with challenging cultural hegemony, with the sources of cultural and educative power.

Working with girls and young women in community settings can best be understood as empowering when it engages with one or more of these aspects of power. It can be understood as challenging hegemonic power as discussed in community development strategies. Drawing on the thinking of Gramsci, the role of the community development worker or activist has been discussed in terms of the role of organic intellectual, who works with working-class communities to educate and form the 'good sense' which can challenge received ideas and the fragmented inherited 'common sense' of popular culture (Ledwith 2011). In developing the challenge to prevailing ideologies, especially those which support male dominance, the campaigning strategies of community development work seek to turn 'cases into issues, and issues into movements', generalising beyond the local neighbourhood to the national and international.

Empowering practice addresses the problems of poverty and understands the nature of women's access to wealth. It creates places of relative safety, where women can build up strategies for resisting or escaping violence. It explores the responsibilities of motherhood or the realities of 'community care' for other dependants. It enables young women to explore sexualities. It makes connections with society-wide and global democratic movements; it challenges the law as a critical point of control and direction of violence and seeks to influence legislation to the benefit of women. This connection-making, from the local to the national and international, is central to any claims on the part of youth and community work to be contributing to processes of change. So, projects responding to violence are also likely to affiliate to Women's Aid and support those campaigns and to be ready to support women across cultures who are challenging traditional practices which involve control of women and their sexuality.

Empowering practice is always about participating in and naming the issues for public debate, rather than accepting the terms of the dominant discourse. There is good reason for a commitment to separate and autonomous women's groups. Women are still relatively unused to accessing the power to act and name on their own behalves. In such settings, new agendas can be rehearsed and emerge. Michael Fielding and Peter Moss (2011) have termed this 'democratic experimentalism' and it is essential that such experimentalism can occur at both local and national levels. Democratic audits which have undertaken gender audits have identified a preponderance of women active at the local community level; this is reversed in processes of formal democratic representation, both in local councils and in Parliament where men are in the majority (Berry and Oyteza 2007, Batsleer, Hanbury and Lee 2010).

Power relations between men and women were historically structured through the public/private divide and this persists both spatially, where women are confined to the domestic and prevented from entering the public domains of employment or politics, and culturally by the designation of many of women's concerns, such as control of fertility, childbearing, contraception and abortion as not political matters, but matters of 'private' or 'personal' morality. Feminisms have both challenged these forms of the public/private divide and sought to unsettle them by working 'from both sides' in a recognition that 'the personal is political' and seeking to make a beginning by pioneering new ways of being in the world, even in hostile conditions. Empowerment is both personal and structural.

Empowerment is Personal

Even within present conditions, it is possible to support young people in a personal process of making choices, taking what responsibility they can, acknowledging potential and recognising the barriers to the fulfilment of their potential. In the case of work with girls and young women, this involves developing a curriculum which is concerned with developing choice within personal relationships, especially perhaps sexual relationships, discussion of the meanings of motherhood and daughterhood, and practical support in relation to contraception/abortion and/or the positive commitment to children. Questions about employment and economic independence can be explored, and personal and group strategies for understanding and tackling poverty can be developed.

It involves a recognition of the existence of violence and the possibility of abuse in various forms in the lives of young women. It means raising questions about dependency and independence, the strengths that can be gained from relationships with others and the constraints that the same networks of relationships, the same 'community' can impose. The person-centred approach to empowerment constantly confronts the question of confidence building, self-confidence and motivation. Lack of power leads to lack of confidence and thereby to inertia.

A primary aim, expressed over and over again in professional reports, is the building up of self-confidence. Self-confidence is built up in a number of ways, but they each involve careful attention to the particular young women who are participating in a project, their particular interests and strengths, as well as their particular difficulties. Being on the receiving end of positive personal attention can in itself boost confidence enormously. Workers have often used methods drawn from assertiveness training to enable young women to have more confidence in defining small steps which can be taken to improve their situation, to rehearse different strategies for handling relationships and to help young women think about their own needs as well as their children's or the needs of other dependants. A good deal of the practice is about encouraging self-reflection by young women, encouraging a sense of lifescripts and autobiographies, seeing young women as potentially 'authors of their own lives' and also encouraging awareness of how lifestories interconnect.

Offering new opportunities and challenges is also a common method of building up self-confidence: as young women try new activities, they grow in confidence to tackle new ways of living that are within their grasp. Such new activities can include survival activities such as cooking on a low budget, or joining a credit union to help in the management of debt, or learning basic health measures (such as fertility awareness, early pregnancy testing, or the practice of 'safer sex'). New activities can also be opportunities for personal enjoyment and development: taking part in sporting or drama or arts activities is a common resource in youth work. This can extend to opportunities to attend formal education programmes and to take part in political campaigning and advocacy. The development of the 'Participation Worker' role in the New Labour years enabled widespread advocacy opportunities to be made available, which were significantly more likely to be taken up by young women than young men.

Programme planning derives from a combination of the skills and areas of interest of workers and a careful attention to the personal stories of girls and young women who make up the groups the projects work with. The aim is to build up pride and self-confidence among girls and young women who have been denied the opportunities to develop this confidence and this can be done in any setting.

Empowerment is Structural

A structural emphasis often addresses the organisational and 'command' aspects of power. Its origins are in democratic traditions of community work practice, which focus on making power structures accountable to the people they are supposed to assist. Movements such as London Citizens, Citizens UK and ChangeMakers draw on Alinsky-based community organising tactics to bring power holders to account (see Alinsky, 1971). It is the process of making public hitherto 'private troubles' and turning them, as C. Wright Mills (1959,2000) suggested, into public issues. Currently, the feminist campaign Object is taking direct action against the 'pornification of the high street', the Million Women Rise movement is challenging violence against women, while Slutwalks have challenged the dubious assumptions of the judiciary who continue to distinguish between slags and good girls in rape trials. Empowerment is the process of struggle for definition of those public issues, often against the agenda-setting processes and definitions of the currently powerful.

Examples of empowerment in practice can be relatively small scale. A project might invite a speaker from a feminist project such as Women's Aid; it might encourage young women to analyse advertisements and take part in a public debate about representations of women. It might create opportunities for young women to take part in work traditionally or currently designated as being for men, such as carpentry or computer science.

On a slightly wider scale, young women's projects have been involved in establishing resource centres and libraries which give young women access to the debates about their position in society, and projects have run literacy programmes, publishing projects and websites which enable young women to voice their own perspectives on contemporary politics. Larger initiatives, embracing national and international campaigns, have remained a persistent feature of practice in some projects, such as campaigns about the Child Support Agency, or those in support of young women affected by immigration and asylum rules, or against funding cutbacks, or for women's access to education internationally. Young women's projects have organised to make public bodies such as health authorities, schools and youth training schemes more girl-friendly. Links have been made with user movements, particularly in the field of mental health, which challenge the role of 'experts' in defining the nature of, and solutions to, mental health problems.

In such campaigning activity, youth work-based local young women's groups have become part of wider women's networks and campaigns at a national and international level.

Empowerment is Social/Cultural

From an explicitly feminist perspective, Sandra Butler and Claire Wintram (1991) distinguish between feminist group work and political and community action. They see dangers in focusing empowerment on political and community action: that women are asked yet again to prioritise the needs of others before their own selves. In *Feminist Groupwork*, they explore some of the processes of collective action which draw on a prioritising of women's selves in feminist group work:

> Individual power, stemming from a positive attitude towards Self, precipitates collectivity. Collective action which involves sublimation of the Self becomes a training in conformity in the name of a sense of belonging. The last thing a women's group wants to do is to provide yet another source of social pressure for women, in which the words may be different but the song remains the same. (Butler and Wintram 1991: 152)

These writers are very aware of the problematic nature of personal and social change which can be precipitated by feminist group work, including the potential for an increase in women's sense of frustration and helplessness as our consciousness of our own rights grows: 'The implications of personal and social change while occupying a position of economic and social dependence are great' (ibid.: 158).

At the same time, Butler and Wintram argue that a shift in focus is possible, once women begin to prioritise themselves and other women:

> The motivation for social change is that women are fighting for other women, and this proves to be a major turning point for group members who habitually act on behalf of families and children. Women in poverty have no legitimate socially granted power to determine their own fate economically, socially or politically. Yet through membership of the group, women can bring about anything that is within their grasp by placing each other centre stage. (Ibid.: 159)

It is within this tension between 'what is within our grasp' and 'what remains outside our power' that much of the most creative work with girls and young women occurs. The distinction between women's lack of legitimate, socially granted power to act as women on our own behalf and the empowering possibilities of small women's groups in 'bringing about what is within our grasp' is very helpful. It helps to assess the claims made on behalf of small projects and particular moments in small-group work: small groups of women who are in positions of dependency facing big power structures do remain dependent and structurally oppressed. However, it also enables a challenge to purely functional accounts of power systems: the creativity of small groups is already a place where change and challenge to women's subordination occurs. We do not have to wait until 'after the revolution' or for the election of the next reforming government.

Feminist insight into the links between the personal and political offers a way beyond the polarity of 'individual' and 'collective' approaches to empowerment. No one who has shared the energy of young women at the end of a residential weekend focusing on confidence building or assertiveness, perhaps using some very traditional youth-work approaches to outdoor education, will doubt that young women's sense of achievement and self-worth is empowering. The group may never meet again as a group, and yet young women are taking a belief in themselves and their own potential with them which will conflict with the far too low expectations they encounter.

One frequently used 'workbook' for feminist work was entitled *Greater Expectations* (Szirom and Dyson 1986). The work of raising expectations already participates in a movement of resistance. However, such work alone is easily marginalised and repackaged as a form of individualism: 'You can do it if you really want.' It can then pathologise those who fail to take initiatives, or who fail to take up the opportunities offered. Confidence-building work needs to link to public debate and dialogue with those organisations and practices which destroy young women's confidence and limit or lower their expectations. It is the practice of small-group work which can provide that link and ensure that feminist practice does not disappear into individualism.

Links between women who work in informal education and allies within major social institutions are very important. For example, a project was established to explore the levels of use of Depo Provera (an injectable long-duration contraceptive with serious side-effects) among young women in a particularly poor neighbourhood; the project began by focusing on the problems which young women presented to the medical profession and the qualities in the young women which led to them being seen as unreliable contraceptive users and therefore likely to be prescribed Depo Provera. However, it soon became apparent that it was perhaps more useful to explore the attitudes of doctors and other medical professionals in the area. Empowerment for young women in relation to contraceptive choice is only partly a matter of young women's own self-confidence. It also depends critically on a public debate which informs the decision making of medical professionals.

The Personal is Political

Analyses of power that locate the sources of power only in the economy ('the market') or in formal legal and democratic processes ('the State') neglect significant aspects of domination and regulation. Bodies and identities are sites of power play – whether through the control of fertility, through sexual violence, through women's relationship with food, or the manipulation of body image, including perceptions of skin tone by the beauty industry.

Power relations operate not only through the market and the economy, but also run right through us, in the social construction of the self. Sometimes it can seem that what is most personal is most intensely thereby the focus of domination and regulation, especially for women who have been for long periods of history seen as belonging to the private, domestic, personal sphere. Feminist analyses of the working of power relationships challenge such separations of the public and private realms on which liberal political theory depends.

The major social institutions such as schools, hospitals, clinics, churches, mosques, temples and synagogues, the press and media all themselves challenge the division between the personal and public. They are sources of power in their own right and do not simply reflect power relationships produced elsewhere, for example, in the factory and the courtroom. They are productive in their own specific domains of domination, subordination and resistance. This means that the work of empowerment that engages with young women's relationship to schools, to employment training schemes, or to the health-care system, cannot be viewed as secondary to a real struggle occurring elsewhere. Young women's access to social and cultural power is as important as access to economic and political power. These forms of power are not connected in a hierarchy from base to superstructure, but are mutually dependent in a material, historical matrix. Change in any aspect of this matrix will affect the whole.

These understandings of the exercise of power also rely on a recognition of the power of language in social relations. The power to name and define is understood as a significant aspect of power relations, and the commitment to processes of 'finding a voice' among subordinate groups are a direct recognition of this power in language.

All this means, in effect, that matters previously regarded as 'personal' or 'private' can now be acknowledged as social and potentially in the public domain, and open to public discussion and debate. It also allows us to recognise that the apparent 'lack of self-confidence' of many young women may be a result of social processes which render young women either invisible or visible only as problems to be regulated, and that therefore, any attempts to build self-confidence is, at least potentially, an act of resistance within existing power relationships.

Feminist Analysis and Analysing the 'Matrix of Domination'

The work of the African-American feminist Patricia Hill Collins is helpful in arguing the variety of levels at which resistance to and experience of oppression happen. (Similar ideas have been developed by Neil Thompson in the very widely discussed PCS (personal, cultural, structural) model of anti-oppressive practice ((Thompson, 2006). Hill Collins developed the idea of a 'matrix of domination' to explore the complexities of oppression and domination. She suggested that approaches which prioritise one aspect of domination 'fail to recognise that a matrix of domination contains few pure victims or oppressors' (Hill Collins 1991: 229).

A broader focus stresses the interlocking nature of oppressions that are structured on multiple levels, from the individual to the social structural, and which are part of the larger matrix of domination. Adhering to this inclusive model provides the conceptual space needed for each individual to see that she or he is both a member of multiple dominant groups and a member of multiple subordinate groups (ibid.: 230).

In this perspective, collective and personal empowerment are intrinsically linked. Personal fulfilment as a goal is insufficient. The feminist movement is not primarily a movement for self-fulfilment, but a movement for justice. It may indeed involve some short-term sacrifices by some women (including those who have chosen to put defending girls' work before their career promotion and sometimes even their employment). Working out how the connections between the personal, social and political can be channelled is a difficult task, especially as women have so often been that place of connection for others. Nevertheless, the processes which increase women's sense of their own value overflow into movements which protest the injustice of treatment which other women receive. This is embodied in the existence of national and international feminist campaigns, organisations, publications and now websites, such as Feminist Webs, Feminista and DIY Feminism.

Groups which enable friendships to develop can also enable wider connections to be made within a community or neighbourhood, and alliances to be formed between women who occupy different positions and roles. The question of alliance is essential to community-based practice. It is through alliance that community-based work with women and girls is part of the wider stream of movements for justice. As a movement for justice, feminism embraces and seeks out as much self-fulfilment and joy as it can.

It is good to remember the excitement and pleasure which can be generated by young women enjoying dancing together without inhibition;

the girl abseiling down a rockface to the delight of her friends and to her own delight; willingness to trust from the girl who feels safe to speak about her experience of abuse; 'falling in love' in the young lesbian group; the end of suicide threats; the celebrations at the Eid disco; young women confronting policy makers and politicians about the lack of resources for children and young people on the estate; 'saying no' to drugs and dealing as the only option for their children; refusal of sex without condoms; young women becoming engineers or car mechanics; and accompanying it all, the laughter that means we can imagine and understand that the world might change for the better.

Equalities and Empowerment: From Collective Practice to Neo-liberal Individualism and the Return?

In 1997, the New Labour government was elected, led by Prime Minister Tony Blair, and hopes were high for a renewal of commitment to work with young people, including young women.

The initiatives introduced by New Labour such as those arising from the work of the Social Exclusion Unit led to a new focus on targeting provision to those most in need and creating links into the mainstream for those at risk of exclusion. Sharon Gewirz (2002) has characterised the 'modernising' policy settlement of New Labour as 'neo-liberalism, authoritarianism and humanism'; this policy settlement impacted in particular ways on youth work, including youth work with girls.

A series of key policies reshaped youth services. These were contradictory, embodying both an intensification of surveillance and increased use of youth custody, and a positive recognition of young people as citizens in the making (Milbourne 2009, Davies 2008).

Negative policies included the approach to young people embodied by policy agendas such as those promoting Anti-Social Behaviour Orders (ASBOs), 'youth nuisance' strategies and the development of the use of dispersal orders, all of which prevented young people gathering in public places. Targeted work focused strongly on young people at risk of social exclusion led to a new predominance of case work-based approaches in the wake of public concern at the failure of child safeguarding strategies.

Positive encouragement for youth participation built on the adoption of United Nations Convention on the Rights of the Child (UNCRC) in 1989 led eventually to the appointment of the Children's Commissioner and strongly influenced the development of the 'Every Child Matters' agenda (DfES 2003). Following the work of the Policy Action Teams (PATs) and the Social Exclusion Unit, the Connexions Service was established, along with a new role of Personal Advisers.

The specific policy papers 'Transforming Youth Work' and 'Resourcing Excellent Youth Services' (DFES 2001, 2002) formed the framework for policy in England with 'reach', 'participation', and 'recorded and accredited outcomes' being the preferred measures of success. As a result of these changes, universal and open-access aspirations for youth work were mediated through the performance management of targets for newly integrated children's and young people's services, so that social education did indeed become a vehicle for delivery of social policy, with 'youth work methods' widely sought after for their effectiveness in meeting social policy agendas in relation to such targets as 'youth nuisance' and 'teenage pregnancy'.

The Russell Commission (2004) on volunteering led,by to 2006, to the establishment of the charity V-Inspired and 'Youth Matters!' (DfE 2005), led to the development of the Youth Opportunities Fund and Youth Capital Fund. This was followed by the Children's Plan (DCSF 2007) and it was during this later period that the most significant power shifts towards young people as co-creators of services rather than merely as targets of them seems to have occurred.

The shift in emphasis to targeted work was accompanied by a superficially gender-neutral language in policy (with reference, for example, to parents rather than mothers, to young people rather than young men and young women), which had the effect of rendering much recent history of positive feminist work with young women invisible.

Nevertheless, some feminist work with girls did continue through this period, as the following case study by Steph Green, who was director of services for young women with the YWCA England & Wales throughout much of this period, shows. It illuminates the ways in which some of the pressures of this period were negotiated by feminist practitioners seeking to keep alive youth-work principles of 'starting where young women are, with their issues and concerns', in a period where feminist agendas were largely side-lined and policy was couched in gender-neutral language.

Campaigning under New Labour contributed by Steph Green

Under New Labour and the Teenage Pregnancy Strategy, things changed dramatically. From then on, in policy terms, the only important thing about young women was their status as mothers. The policy aimed to reduce the numbers of young mothers and the numbers of their children, and to get the mothers into education, employment, or training. In the forward to *Teenage Pregnacy(SEU,1999)* Prime Minister Blair described the British rate of teenage pregnancy as 'shameful' and leading to 'shattered lives and blighted futures'. This is not at all how young mothers described their own experiences (Arai 2009, Duncan et al. 2010) but it embedded a 'monochrome, negative stereotype' (ibid.: 20) in policy, which translated into a wider public discourse of demonising young mothers, blaming them for all manner of social 'ills'.

The effect of this on the young mothers themselves was devastating. They and their children were stigmatised. They felt the hostility in every aspect of life, from pregnancy onwards. One young woman interviewed about her experience of becoming a young mother said: 'I'd have just liked one person to turn round and say congratulations like they do to all people who are older' In 2003 and 2004, I worked with young women with children and their (women) youth and community workers on a national 'Respect Young Mums' campaign. The campaign, led by YWCA England & Wales, was primarily intended to reposition the public perception of the charity, but there was also a genuine commitment to ensure that the campaign gave the young women a voice in the whole process. The youth and community workers and the young women worked with professionals specialising in media, policy, campaigns and fundraising.

The Respect Young Mums campaign challenged the 'common-sense' perspectives that oppressed these young women as young mothers. These were Black and White working-class young women, mainly heterosexual and aged 14–25 years.

During the campaign preparation, the young women had support from youth and community workers to examine their experiences of becoming and being young mothers. Many of the workers saw that the campaign had the potential to be about young women's right to control their own sexuality and fertility. This would challenge the policy and public view that these women couldn't and shouldn't be trusted to make decisions about whether and when to have children (because of their age and often their poverty and poor education).

During the early stages, groups of young women from different parts of the country met at several national residential conferences to share experiences and prepare for the campaign. These very different young women found that they had a lot in common once the conversations between them developed. The young women informed the focus and direction of the campaign and took part in most stages of the decision making. Many of the workers working with the young women in their local projects and during the national residentials, worked explicitly with a model I had introduced, to help generate critical questions about how power and oppression operated. It was important to help workers and young women to move beyond the 'common-sense' ways of understanding young mothers' experiences and actively examine the lived experiences of the young women together. This model focused on three levels – internal, interpersonal and institutional. The language of this model was compromised, we couched it in terms of discrimination not oppression, because the organisation felt that the term 'oppression' was too strong. Still, it sparked useful critical questions which helped the young women explore how power and oppression operated in their everyday lives.

Through these processes, the young women indicated that they felt it was most important to tackle the negative attitudes they experienced daily, rather than any specific element of government policy. For example, they felt that lack of money was a problem but that it was less debilitating than the constant erosion of their self-esteem which resulted from the hostility they experienced from professionals and their own communities.

Throughout the preparation and campaign activities, the young women grew in confidence and began to see their experiences in political, not just personal, terms. Many of the young women spoke directly to national and local media during the campaign. They and their youth and community workers designed and led local campaign events, supported by media and campaign staff.

Working on a media-based campaign, and distilling the young women's experiences into one shared set of campaign messages, often submerged their differences rather than exploring them fully. For example, Black young women and workers were involved in the campaign, but we didn't draw out specifically Black perspectives for the campaign. Nor did we specifically draw out the perspectives of young women who were not British, though some were involved. The campaign work was politicising, positive and empowering for the young women in many ways, but it potentially challenged some forms of oppression while colluding with others.

The power and perspective of the professionals involved in the campaign and the politics of the organisation as a whole played a very significant part in both facilitating the campaign and framing its boundaries. For example, it would have been interesting to examine the term 'young mums' with the young women before it was decided as the term to be used in the campaign. 'Young mums' was the term widely used in the organisation to describe work with young women with children, or pregnant young women. The option to consider other language was quickly closed down. 'Young mums' was deemed preferable because it would make the campaign messages more palatable to the media and public. It was interesting to note that the youth and community workers wanted to stick with this language because of concerns about funder's perceptions.

The young women themselves (around 200 of them) enjoyed the campaign work. They grew in confidence, knowledge and skills as a result of both local and national activities. They were able to make sense of some of the power relations in their own lives and feel stronger to reject the negative public messages. It was hugely important to them that the organisation had decided to stand alongside them, value them and work from their experiences.

The power of recognition and of language that demeans, and the potential empowerment involved in challenging stigma cannot be underestimated as an important aspect of work with girls and young women.

The Beauty Myth

A significant form in which the radical discourse of women's empowerment has been individualised, undermined and co-opted has been through its incorporation by the beauty industry; yet this has been much less discussed in the context of youth work. Personal body improvement is presented as empowering, while at the same time being a marketing ploy. The minute attention to the (female) body which accompanies growing up, and the scrutiny of young women's bodies, has been identified as a major source of anxiety for young women and also as a lucrative international market. The Cosmetic Company of the UK markets its services under the slogan 'Your body, your choice', while the international beauty companies L'Oreal and Maybelline offer women the opportunity 'to improve their well-being and self-esteem' 'making a difference because every-one has the right to beauty', and claiming to be 'focused on helping women feel more beautiful and enhancing their individuality through education and empowerment' (Banyard 2010). Even the Dove campaign which delighted many women by challenging the 'size 0' mentality still emphasises beauty and beauty products and increased Dove's sales. The body image campaign 'Endangered Species Women' seeks to challenge the invisible and corporate pedagogy which is instructing all of us in our appropriate gender roles, in pursuit not of well-being but of profit.

The strongly gendered forms of these body markings and the debates which surround them mean that the significance of gendered space as a subject for collaborative enquiry has not yet had its day. In the context of the beauty industry, the commodification, alienation and emotional labour involved in the presentation of self in everyday life is the source of limitation and constraint for young women and empowerment for the businesses who market the products. The impact of such everyday pressures on young women, and the persistent question of young women's agency in negotiating such pressures alongside the constraints on them and the complicity of their agency in practices not of their own choosing, has been widely discussed (Gill and Scharff 2011, Levy 2005). In the context of such appropriations of the term 'empowerment', a return to and re-examination of the democratic impulses which have underpinned modern European feminist politics is salutary. This is especially the case at a moment in which the democratic impulses associated with the 'Arab Spring' and with a renewed student movement and direct action in the 99%/Occupy protests are strong. Fielding and Moss (2011) emphasise democratic experimentation as a key aspect of radical education and I believe this points out a significant direction for the revitalisation of a more open, less constrained youth work.

Feminist Youth Work and Democratic Practice

Fielding and Moss (2011) have articulated a vision of an alternative which challenges, in their words, the tyranny of 'no alternatives'. In their definition, democratic values and practice need to shape educational spaces. Democracy is conceived as a way of being that shapes relationality. A democratic, as distinct from a hierarchical, way of being is grounded in equality, so in the context of work with children and young people, the wish on the part of adults to listen to 'the hundred voices of children' shapes practice. Collective deliberation, and concern for the common good, define public space; education along with welfare is a public good. Associationalist traditions provide ideas of fellowship: a deliberative and creative form of personal encounter and the values of social and political justice, solidarity and plurality underlie these encounters. From the socialist-feminist writer Sheila Rowbotham and from the Marxist Erik Olin Wright, Fielding and Moss take the ideas of prefigurative practice and real utopias. It is with this dissident tradition that any renewed discussion of feminist practice in youth work belongs. Fielding and Moss have suggested a number of characteristics of a practice which embodies this radical democratic tradition. These include:

- a proclaimed democratic vitality;
- insistent affirmation of possibility;
- the centrality of dialogue and co-creation of knowledge as a pedagogic practice;
- the importance of intergenerational working;
- positional restlessness and the ability to experiment with democratic forms and relations of authority, including an exploration of the role of school meetings in this process, and
- a sense of connection with the regional, national and global.

All of these principles are recognisably among the principles of critical youth work and informal education in the UK. Such a statement, however, leaves unvoiced the question of the place of women's groups as part of democratic experimentation.

Feminist Youth Work and a New Wave of Activism

Renewed engagement in the UK with feminist agendas as part of the new wave of activism can be dated to the 2005 Feminist Webs initiative 'Done Hair and Nails: Now What?'. In offering an alternative practice to the 'target-driven' focuses on teenage pregnancy, personal safety and anti-obesity healthy-eating practices, or the 'pampering' offered as part of outreach to girls via hair and beauty sessions, the conscious starting-point of Feminist Webs is democratic and against the tyrannies of 'no imagination possible'.

Since 2005, the Feminist Webs network has been revitalising such democratic practice through informal education in the North-west of England and beyond. Explicit in its purposes to reconnect with feminist histories of girls' work and to make girls and young women count, Feminist Webs organises through a loose network which is not 'owned' by any one institution, but in which there are key figures who have worked across institutional boundaries to support the work. The method of oral history in relation to feminist-inspired youth work with girls and young women has created cross-generational dialogue; the initial provocation, 'Done Hair and Nails? Now What?', spoke across centuries of feminist restlessness with the problematic association of women and beauty. The presence of women from all over the world in youth work in the North-west of England has enabled international connections to be made, and the existence of feminist-inspired institutions – especially archives and Women's Studies networks in universities – has enabled national connections and learning. An arts-based project on body image called 'postfeminisms' included a postcard campaign which cheekily challenged the status of feminism as 'post' and invited young women to express their anger at the ways their bodies are represented in popular culture.

Youth-work methods of democratic collaborative enquiry have enabled women's spaces to become spaces of democratic experimentalism. Feminist educators can draw on counter-histories and narratives which go back as far as Mary Wollstonecraft, who wrote *A Vindication of the Rights of Women* (1792) in order to count women and make women count in the democratic, egalitarian movement. Wollstonecraft saw reason, virtue (especially courage) and knowledge (rooted in experience) as the foundations of women's education that equipped them to fight tyranny. Furthermore, Wollstonecraft analysed a system which encouraged women's attachment to prettification as the compensation for social and political subordination. This, Wollstonecraft argued, was the first practice which would need to be challenged if girls were to grow into full citizenship.

Such anti-oppressive approaches to youth work practice have recently been well-captured in the 'lens-model' proposed by Susan Morgan and Ken Harland (2009). Seeing the establishment of separate spaces for men and women as spaces for enquiry rather than as spaces primarily for action offers a way through the production of difference as diversity, another commodity for consumption, and returns youth work to its affinity with DIY movements and democratic experimentation.

4　Informal Education and Feminist Pedagogies

The elements of informal learning in youth and community work are widely taken to include experiential learning (Ord 2011B); challenging 'common sense' and problem-posing/problem-solving (Batsleer 2008, Packham 2008); participation and group work/association (Jeffs and Smith 2005, Coburn 2011); advocacy and accompaniment (Green and Christian 1998); engaged pedagogy and community development (Smith 1988, hooks 1994, Ledwith 2011), and making voices heard and resisting corporate pedagogies (Batsleer 2008, Steinberg 2011). This chapter illuminates briefly each of these approaches from a variety of feminist perspectives.

Informal Education in Youth Work Involves Experiential Learning

The theorisation of learning from experience has its roots in the writings of the American pragmatists, and in particular in the work of John Dewey (Ord 2012)(Ord 2011a). 'Experiential learning' also refers to a process of social learning not contained in the formal subject-discipline based elements of the National Curriculum for schools in England and Wales. In youth and community work, 'experiential learning' usually refers to 'learning by doing' rather than 'learning by instruction'. Sometimes, it means the opportunity to take part in new activities and experiences, to 'broaden the horizons'. Sometimes, the project of experiential learning can offer support for 'going to the roots': reflection on both the difficult and the positive experiences of life within a particular group/community. Knowledge and understanding are believed to be the results of such learning processes, rather than to arise as a result of instruction or direct induction into received ideas. It is an educational tradition capable of inspiring passionate adherence. It is useful, following Dewey, to point out the two distinctly different modes

55

in which 'experience' can be understood as an aspect of learning, that is, *actively* and *passively*. We learn through experience when we are like 'little scientists', actively enquiring into the world; we also learn through experience, as people who take in and 'endure' whatever life offers us in the way of environments and experiences. And yet the concept of 'experience' on which it is based is one of the most slippery in the whole of philosophy, and because of the difficulties associated with it, the term 'experience' has often been rejected altogether. Nevertheless, the sense that traditional subject-based formal instruction erases the experience and knowledge of subordinated groups remains, despite numerous philosophical critiques of the concept of 'experience'.

The claims of 'experience' as a touchstone against which social and political strategies for emancipation can be tested remain vital. There can surely be no political emancipation of women without an engagement with the day-to-day realities and experiences of many different groups of women (hooks 1994). And, although experience cannot speak itself without language, language must be scrutinised for its ability to communicate and express, or to disguise, the things that matter in relation to the lived realities of particular groups of women. In universities (traditionally the home of abstract knowledge) feminist teachers have reflected in depth on the place of 'experience' in the development of women's studies. Donna Haraway (1991) argued that experience still continues to be central to women's studies. She emphasised, however, that it is reflection on experience, the process of making sense of experience, which constitutes the explosive terrain of political change, rather than 'experience' alone. Haraway writes:

> Women do not find 'experience' ready to hand any more than they/we find 'nature' or 'the body' preformed always innocent and waiting outside the violations of language and culture. Just as nature is one of culture's most startling and non-innocent products, so is experience one of the least innocent, least self-evident aspects of historical, embodied movement. Through the politically explosive terrain of linked experience, feminists make connection and enter into movement. Complexity, heterogeneity, specific positioning and power-charged difference are not the same thing as liberal pluralism. Experience is a semiosis, an embodying of meanings ... The politics of difference that feminists need to articulate must be rooted in a politics of experience that searches for specificity, heterogeneity, and connection through struggle, not through psychologistic, liberal appeals to each her own endless difference. Feminism is collective; and difference is political, that is, about power, accountability and hope. Experience, like difference, is about contradictory and necessary connection. (Haraway 1991: 109)

Case Study: Adventure and Experience

Getaway Girls was set up in Leeds in 1987 and emerged directly from women's engagement in the world of outdoor education. It now offers a classic example of the strengths of experiential learning in its offer to address young women's lives in terms of health and well-being, cultural identity and diversity and voice and influence.

The project offers an 'inclusive and innovative approach which places young women at the control centre of their own experience and learning. Programmes incorporate the outdoors, the arts, multimedia, IT, discussion and residential which help young women explore their dreams, aspirations and potential.'(http://getawaygirls.co.uk).

One young woman said of her experience at Getaway Girls. 'I have learned:

- To make new friends
- To get on with people
- To communicate
- To be more open
- To be more assertive and less passive
- To calm down and not go off my head
- To not be scared
- To work as part of a team
- To give new experiences a try
- To be honest.'

This statement clearly articulates some of the powerful gains to individuals which emerge from experiential learning.

A hopeful account of the place of learning from experience as a place of learning from struggle and connection can be of enormous benefit to youth and community workers, and it points to the role of the educator in assisting young women in making sense of existing and new experiences. When young women make sense of their experiences and make connections between aspects of their lives and the lives of other women which they had previously held separate, they are acting as feminist theorists as much as anyone involved in academic work as a trade.

Case Study: The Mothers and Daughters Project, Cheetham Hill Community Centre 1985

A group of young women attending the club were having difficulties with their parents, who didn't want them to be out at night. One of the workers was a mother of daughters herself and felt that she could understand the parents' anxieties. Some of the mothers were members of a community group which met at the community centre during the day.

The worker decided to set up a 'mothers and daughters' project, to enable each group to express their own perspective. The young women experienced their mothers as lacking in trust. The mothers were fearful that their daughters would 'get into trouble'. The fear of trouble was sexual, but not only sexual.

The method the workers chose as a starting-point for the work was, first, to undertake in-depth interviews with both mothers and daughters, and then to develop a life-history project. In this storytelling project, the girls became both chroniclers and the storytellers of their mothers' lives. Beautiful, bound biographies were produced, with photographs and narratives.

The worker's aim of establishing trust once more was certainly achieved, and across the truly explosive terrain of mother–daughter differences, some new understandings of women's condition of life in a North Manchester community were generated.

Informal Education in Youth Work Involves the Critique of 'Common Sense', Problem-posing and Problem-solving

Youth and community work practice needs to avoid the taken-for-granted 'common sense' which pathologises young women and removes a sense of agency (Batsleer 2008). For example, community and youth work practice has often focused on the assessment of needs. This potentially places young women in a position of passivity, waiting to have their needs met by others. While the address to needs enables women to make some legitimate call on resources, the language of rights should also be used, as this encapsulates women's participation as citizens in defining and seeking solutions for social problems. A good example of this process of working on the definition of problems and needs is in the common process of working with young women with small children. Quite often the attention of young women focuses initially on the problem of what to do with the children and on the needs of the children for play facilities. A youth and community worker's involvement in establishing a mother-and-toddler group may also assist the process of young women exploring their own needs, as mothers, for time away from the children. It may even eventually lead to a questioning of what is expected of mothers in our society, and to discussion of the rights of women *vis-à-vis* the rights of men. The following case studies illuminate some of the ways youth workers have engaged with 'common sense' through critique of popular culture.

Case Study: Visual Images

Photography, collage and digital imaging have been used in a number of projects as a basis for reflection on experience and struggle over meanings. Feminist work in cultural studies has created an understanding of the power of visual images in shaping women's experience, self-understanding and subordination/survival. Informal education projects working with young women are able to explore the impact of visual images, often through young women becoming creators of their own images. The following focuses of work have been extremely popular.

Critical reflection on magazines, especially on advertising – Here workers use collage work, ideas about 'positive' and 'negative' images, focus on representations of 'body parts' in relation to discussions of ideas about beauty and female sexuality. The website of the 'Dove Campaign for Real Beauty' contains fascinating examples of the 'airbrushing' techniques used in fashion and advertising photography.

Photography and video workshops – Young women produce their own alternative posters, photo-stories and DVDs. As well as giving greater access to understanding the reality of visual representation as 'productions' as well as 'images', projects of this kind have given young women a forum in which to discuss relationships, romance and their own dreams and fantasies. Using photo-collage to develop young women's fantasies has been a successful method. Here, young women use photographs of themselves and then amend or combine them in order to produce dream images and alternative scenes. The photo-love/alternative endings storyline remains popular. Common alternative endings to the 'girl gets together with boy' storyline are girls successfully resisting rape, and girls dumping their boyfriends in order to stick with their best friends.

Visual images are powerful for the exploration of anti-racist and international perspectives, since both visual images and their absence are important in the construction of 'whiteness' and of Black women's identities in Britain and globally. There is still an absence of representation of European Black women, with North American imagery being the dominant source of representations. Women from the Southern Hemisphere are still often depicted as impoverished, backward, victims, or as grateful recipients of aid. Or else they are represented as entirely 'other' and as the repositories of a smouldering sensuality available for the dominant North to consume.

Development education projects have used images from the South to challenge such dominant representations. The practice in one development education project was to fund photographers to work with poor communities over a period of time in both Somalia and Pakistan to produce more appropriate images. Rehana Hussain, a youth and community worker working with women from Asian communities in Sheffield, recognised the power of such images for her own practice in building and retaining community links. However, she also points out that the reception of such images, even among communities now settled here but with strong connections with the South, needed attention and work. The worker has a vital role to play in assisting in the interpretation of such images and the creation of meanings which challenge the codes of 'otherness'.

The movement away from being pathologised as a source of problems is an educational movement and a liberating one. It involves being able to recognise the fact that limitations are being placed on us as well as our own possibly self-destructive response to this limitations. However, when so many official discourses problematise young women, it is good to be able to turn the tables and to point to official discourses and practices as the source of the problem.

Case Study: The Activate Group

The Activate Group is a mixed group of black and white young women. Initially, due to the difficulties they were having at school, we enabled them to explore these difficulties and ideas for action. This involved them coming up with proposals for changes (concerning racism, sexism and respect from teachers) they would like to see in school, for example, choosing teachers they felt would listen, and arranging a series of meetings with them on their territory to discuss these proposals. Some positive outcomes arose due to the teachers listening to them and taking on board some of their suggestions and involving some of the young women in their implementation.

This brief account of the work of a Leeds-based group gives a clear indication of the critical role of problem-posing and problem-solving as a method. It involves a clear shift away from seeing girls as a problem or as growing into women whose role it is to deal with other people's problems. The motto of the Leeds young women's workers is 'Think opportunity, not problem.' Young women themselves defined the starting-points and terms for the work. To begin with, workers identify, from discussion with young women, key areas that are influencing their lives. Through group discussion, they began to identify the voices and perspectives that influence young women's thinking about the chosen topic. There are a number of useful methods here: discussion of newspaper reports, current episodes in soap operas, magazine features – especially problem pages, drama exercises and focusing on popular music – all provide resources. The second stage is a process of positive identification of starting-points by young women and the workers themselves.

'Youth' has long been seen as a problem, and the terms from which 'the problem of youth' is constructed – such as unemployment, crime and deviance, the transition to adult status – are focused for young women through attention to sexuality. Youth and community work practice can clearly contribute to the pathologising of young women (Batsleer and Davies 2010). Consciousness-raising about these powerful definitions of young women's experience is an important starting-point. It can seem as if to be young means constantly to be measuring yourself against a standard of 'normality' and finding yourself lacking. Conversations about what is 'normal' and who decides, if continued over time and offered in a context of positive opportunities, can help young women shake off some of the effects of negative ascriptions as 'deviant' or 'a problem'. Through youth and community work processes, the 'problem' can be relocated away from young women and in a wider appreciation of systemic problems.

Informal Education in Youth Work Involves
Learning Through Participation and Group Work

Feminist practice attempts to develop ways of working which move away from hierarchy and towards democratic organisation. It also attempts to move away from individual pathologising and blaming, towards a participation in community groups and networks, a sense of citizenship and the right to influence the direction of society.

There is a growing literature on group work, as a key method in community action and in feminist education (Mullender and Cohen 2003, Lather 1991). bell hooks, the Black feminist educator and cultural critic, writes:

> Small groups remain an important place for education for critical consciousness for a number of reasons. An especially important aspect of the small group setting is the emphasis on communicating feminist thinking, feminist theory in a manner that can easily be understood. In small groups, individuals do not need to be equally literate or literate at all because the information is primarily shared through conversation, through dialogue which is necessarily a liberatory expression. (Literacy should be a goal for feminists even as we ensure it is not a requirement for participation in feminist education.) Reforming small groups would subvert the appropriation of feminist thinking by a select group of academic women and men, usually white, from privileged class backgrounds. (hooks 1989: 24)

Understanding of the place of small groups as a vehicle for education has developed in tension with therapeutic accounts of group work. The educational focus of group work demands that connections be made between the work of the group and life outside the group. Therapeutic accounts more often draw on group processes themselves as a source of healing.

Group work can be undertaken informally. It can also be undertaken within an explicit and agreed framework, with links to the curriculum of formal education. The worker characteristically develops programmes of work, study, community action and social events in discussion and negotiation with young women whom she has come to know, often using already existing friendship networks as a basis for building up a project.

It is at this early stage that many choices are made about the focus and membership of groups, and it is also here that exclusions occur. Sometimes, it is only later that these patterns of exclusion are noticed and addressed. For example, a worker working in a 'racially mixed' neighbourhood notices recruits from only one group in the neighbourhood: the one to which she is most closely connected herself. Hulme Girls' Project in Manchester, which was established in the same building as the oldest Lads' Club in the area, addressed this issue and began a programme of positive work with Black girls. Here, the worker describes building up and working with a group of 14 young Black mothers.

Case Study: Hulme Girls' Project

Since the very encouraging beginning, we have built up our experience and a more ambitious plan of activity. This was based on what we felt was now possible with this group and on what the young women have said was needed, this includes:

1. Courses on woodwork, basic electrics, computers.
2. Discussion using educational work packs on women and health issues and other relevant topics.
3. Support work with young women before they leave our local school, using informal contacts and home visits, also special sessions.
4. Preparation and build-up for the Educational Exchange Visit to Jamaica, including:
5. Educational courses on Jamaica – January to March. These included history, culture, Black women in history, women's issues, historical buildings and places in Jamaica.

We feel that the work has developed in a way that really holds together and involves the group members as it is highly relevant to them and their lives.

The aim of such a programme is clearly to develop the understandings of the group. The worker's ability to respond to the issues and potentials introduced by group members is critical. It is the worker's interest in the agendas of young women which is often the catalyst which allows

---

young women to move from being consumers to creators, from being in a role of dependency to one of active participation.

The other aspect of such community-based group work which cannot be stressed too strongly is the necessity of continual outreach work and of workers getting to know individuals well, in their own right, before and during the time they are members of a group. It is on the basis of such knowledge of individuals and the building-up of relationships of trust that workers can feel free sometimes to jettison programmes and arranged agendas in favour of responding to issues in the here-and-now:

Last night one of the young women brought her new baby into the club with her. We jettisoned the planned talk on drugs which I had carefully prepared and we talked for hours in the girls' room about having babies or not and relationships. The fact that Jane was there with her baby and was talking seriously made the young women listen to her and join in in a way they would never have listened to me.

This comment came from a student on placement, working with a girls' group in a youth club. It beautifully encapsulates what is involved, both in the effort to plan learning through small-group work, and even more importantly, in the ability to let those plans go. Working with small groups in community settings is the central focus and defining feature of informal education practice. Group work forms the crucible from which other ways of working emerge.

The important place of projects focusing on visual images and on the romance narratives of popular culture has already been mentioned. The relationship between informal education on questions of sexuality and the work undertaken by the teen magazines, television soaps, YouTube, music channels and social networking sites is of great significance.

Reflecting on Informal Sex Education in a Girls' Group

The 'problem page' has an honoured and useful place in discussions of the perils of emergent heterosexuality. The genre is easily imitated and has instigated many useful discussions of relationships about topics such as 'why sex is scary' and what to think about before you have sex for the first time, sexual abuse by a grandfather, not wanting to have sex when your boyfriend does, having a crush on someone, feeling ashamed of your body and 'falling out of love' with someone. Reading aloud tackles the problem of different levels of literacy among young women, and it also allows the worker to gauge young women's reactions and make a 'safe' choice of topic. Most youth and community workers are highly skilled at working with and responding to the here-and-now in terms of the passing trends of youth culture, but need resources of conversation and dialogue which enable them to move with young women into the exciting and sometimes troubled territory of emerging sexuality.

If the worker can work with a small group to build on already existing trust and friendship, she will, from this small beginning, readily build up an atmosphere in which a positive sex education programme can develop. It is, of course, very important that the worker herself is well informed on the issues she is tackling, and is supported by knowledge of and access to local family planning services, the attitude to abortion in her local GP network and information about local young lesbian groups. Such resources are now widely available through the specialist services of organisations such as Brook (www.brook.org)

Informal Education in Youth Work Involves Advocacy and Accompaniment

Advocacy work need not be limited to work with individuals, and the process of collective self-advocacy has strong links with concepts of community development. Work with groups which may begin as self-help or mutual aid, often has implications for women beyond the ambit of those small groups, and feminist practice must encourage the making of connections, especially with the people and agencies which have the power to create positive change.

Case Study: Health and Self-help

The Y-Wait Group in the North Manchester Health Authority offered an important model of young women's participation in a self-help project which had a significant impact on the power structures of the health authority.

The group began as an initiative of young women in a community centre in a North Manchester estate, who felt that the services their GPs offered were not appropriate to young women of the area. They established their own group with the support of a community health worker, employed their own nurse and began to develop projects which could reach out to young women in the area, for whom the current services seemed out of reach and inappropriate. There was a strong emphasis on sexual health in the project, and the group became seen as a pioneer of 'peer education' within the health authority, facilitating a determined rethinking of the health authority's own approach and publicity.

Case Study: Sound Women – Community Radio

Phil Smith, a youth and community worker at Knowsley Community Radio, was forced to reflect on his advantage as a man when he discovered that he was in an exclusively male group receiving Sony Radio Awards in 2009. He was not alone in noticing this, as a campaigning group, Sound Women, was established immediately afterward to campaign for better representation of women at every level in the sound radio industry. In alliance with Platform 51 (formerly YWCA) and with Sound Women, Knowsley Community Radio celebrated International Women's Day by turning the radio entirely over to women, in both presenter and backroom roles, including both local girls and young women campaigners from Sound.

The youth and community worker has been memorably described as 'useful friend'. The usefulness lies, above all, in access to information.

Information is Power

Working with girls requires the worker to become a walking resource centre, equipped with up-to-date knowledge on money, housing, health and maternity rights. A number of projects have concentrated initially on building up an information resource and have focused a good deal of attention on understanding young women's rights, both to resources and to participation in processes that affect their lives. Information packs and websites are constructed with the assistance and participation of young women in the project. They characteristically include information about benefits and health services for women, information about other resources for young people and women's groups in the borough and surrounding area, information about Women's Aid and Rape Crisis, information about Lesbian Link and groups for young lesbian/bisexual women. They may also include information about concessionary travel and other cheap or free services, including leisure facilities. They may include information relating to homelessness, including matters such as where to find free cleaning and laundry facilities. They will direct workers and young women to other specialist advice projects, such as Citizens' Advice Bureaux and law centres. Some projects have specific information and experience in relation to industrial tribunals, particularly where there is a claim of race or sex discrimination, or other human rights issues.

However, the availability of such information is only part of the story. Hence, the importance of the term 'friend' in the expression 'useful friend'. It is the friendliness, accessibility, reliability and dependability of the relationship a worker has with young women which can make information accessible. But the term 'friend' may disguise at least as much as it reveals. The relationship between a woman worker and the young women she works with is certainly based on mutuality. However, it is not based on equality in the way of friendship.

It is important to recognise some of the difficulties involved in offering friendship on a professional basis, and there are a number of important questions about professional boundaries and ethics here (Young 2006, Sercombe. Lesbian workers, in particular, have been instrumental in developing codes of ethics which can assist in recognising when you are becoming over-involved, while also recognising the dangers of apparently detached professionalism. Receiving payment to undertake the work of informal education, or even undertaking such work in a voluntary capacity, does place serious limits and responsibilities on workers, which women, on the whole, have been quick to recognise. Codes of ethics have been developed which include statements about:

- non-violence and non-discrimination;

- health and safety of women workers;
- the importance of co-working;
- use of project funds to buy items for young people, particularly payment for alcohol and cigarettes;
- the non-permissibility of sexual relationships;
- the importance of reliability in relationships with young women;
- the importance of reliability in timekeeping;
- how crisis situations will be dealt with;
- availability of workers' home telephone numbers, and
- confidentiality and the limits of confidentiality.

The benefits of such a clear statement lie in allowing the boundaries of the work to be made explicit, shared and discussed. It means that young women know that while a worker may become very involved with their lives and be a very important source of support and advocacy in the context of power systems which they are forced to deal with, the relationship is a professional one, in which the young woman has certain rights and the worker has some very clear responsibilities. The relationship does not impose on the young women personal obligations to provide support to the worker, and although the worker always learns a great deal from her work, the relationship does not have the purpose of enabling the worker to explore her own difficulties.

Informal Education in Youth Work Involves Engaged Pedagogy and Community Development

bell hooks introduced the notion of engaged pedagogy as a development of Paolo Freire's ideas of liberatory pedagogy in order to emphasise two things (hooks 1994). First, educational processes are implicated in the everyday realities of learner's lives and that a refusal of this by educators cannot lead in the direction of freedom. Secondly, she emphasised engagement in order to emphasise the capacity of education to make a difference through action and to bring about change. The following account of participation in the informal learning of a community carnival conveys both these aspects of engaged pedagogy.

Learning through Carnival (contributed by Kimberley Osivwemu)

Manchester's Caribbean Carnival hosted the 'Raging Roosters', a carnival held annually in Alexander Park and on the streets of Manchester. The roosters mirrored the marauding movement presented by cockerel in Barbados. The annual carnival is rooted firmly in the slave traditions of the Caribbean, whereby each one teaches one to sew, dance, share masks and parade the carnival.

Grandmothers encourage and inspire granddaughters and pickendem telling tales of past carnivals, stand offs and competitions. Weekly workshops in community venues culminate in the crescendo of public street parade. Stamping the streets of Manchester for half a day a year gives a sense of culturally loaded freedom not otherwise enjoyed. Watching back through masked eyes in part human form at humdrum existence of bus travel, shopping and car travel. Seeing amazed incredulous gaze at the audacity of such stamping facilitates a view of self outside of self thus far envisioned. Being something audacious and incredible for a few hours is great reward for the planning and preparation. The oneness of spectacle and the elevation of sense of self as something greater than ordinary is empowering. Playing with the humdrum rules of personal presentation and imaginary self draws out creativity and enables play. Playing with blackness as public spectacle and gazing back bounces back the looks and glares that might otherwise malign. The hidden code my people are roosters strong independent separate and a group invisible ties that bind through the collective conscience. We are oneness when we hail each other: 'Jump and wave! Jump and wave! Jump jump jump jump and wave!' Indelible rhythms planted in your stamp. Stamp at the police. Stamp at the ivory towers. Raging around without hindrance and without regard to social decorum and signs. Waft the codes away with your wing. The streets are ours today sista stamp your stuff my sistren. Make your mark on the city wend your way and leave your prints. Clear tracks of presence and messages of routes marked out as right to roam on the Queen's highway. Come down my sistah make your mark. Lead your picken through the streets, make your presence known. Let them see the streets and city through different eyes. Take up the road as your own, own the space and make your mark. Not now the time for the motor with little regard for foot and walk, not now the time for haste. Wend your way, follow the rhythm, dance the beat! Tek time, tek time. It is yours for the taking. Black presence met with police hostility, stop and search. Stop and Search is met with joviality, jump and wave, jump and wave. A distortion of a national norm. Dance with the police, dance with the police. Not now the cosh and the shackles but the smile and the soca down. Disrupt the national norm, occupy a different space!

The critical role of group work and association in promoting learning means that the worker has a responsibility both to support individuals who participate in their programmes and towards community groups whose interests are wider and more generalised than those of the particular small groups she is involved with. In responding to the first responsibility, she may find herself concerned with the themes of personal development. In responding to the second, wider responsibility, she will find herself concerned with themes of community development (hooks 2004).

There are a number of difficulties associated with the term 'development' (whether 'child development' or 'economic development'), which it is important to highlight at this point (Burman 2008a, 2008b; Mies and Shiva 1993). Like the term 'community', the term 'development' is capable of imparting a warm glow while bearing a number of different meanings.

Youth workers need to recognise the normative connotations of the term in the context of both personal and economic development. There are highly elaborated accounts of stages of growth (often rooted in biology) to which all individuals and societies are expected to conform. These models of 'normal development' which claim universal validity are masculinist and rooted in western capitalist power, relying on a concept of progress which appears to see the experience of North American societies and of successful young men in such societies as the goal of development.

It is therefore essential that women workers are aware of the normative pressures contained in the term 'development', which may, for example, be used by other professionals, such as educational psychologists, or by funding bodies concerned with urban regeneration. They can then frame their own projects and ways of working to permit young women (and themselves) some say in what constitutes progress and development for them, some control over the agenda of 'development projects'. Current critical discussion focuses on 'sustainability'.

In community development work, this often involves extensive and carefully thought-through consultation processes and the creation of non-bureaucratic democratic forums. In the context of unequal and unjust social relations, this is likely to lead to conflict over priorities with funding and resourcing bodies, and women need to have strategies for engaging in or avoiding such conflict. In any case, women are most likely to be engaged at local neighbourhood level in such democratic processes with representation in local and national government still being dominated by men (Berry and Oyteza 2007).

In relation to community development, there is an apparently permanent economic conflict between a self-help agenda which believes the costs of welfare can be reduced by community development and the clear demands of most community-based groups for more resources; in particular, for more sustained opportunities for employment accompanied by affirmative socio-cultural education and animation. These conflicts are also worked through internationally in neighbourhoods where there is still a practice of supporting those (extended) family members who remain in countries of origin, even after several generations of presence in the UK.

Case Study: Abasindi (contributed by Diane Watt)

The establishment of Abasindi during the early 1980s was but one expression of women in the African diaspora's support for Black women of South Africa in their struggle against apartheid. This support – as in the South African origins of both the organisation's name and the names of children such as Sibongile, Malaika, Thembikile, Nkosi and Dziko – is a testimony to Abasindi's commitment to an activist form of mothering, which '[h]ighlights the community workers' gendered conceptualisation of activism on behalf of their communities, often defined beyond the confines of their families, households and neighbourhoods. Activist mothering includes self-conscious struggles against racism, sexism and poverty' (Naples 1998: 114). Given its links to Pan-Africanism, the organisation was also inspired by the work of Amy Jacques Garvey, who refuted the false dichotomy between motherhood and political activism. At the 1945 Pan-African Congress which was held at Chorlton Town Hall in Manchester, Amy Garvey chaired the session on Britain's racial problems.

My contribution to the development of Abasindi was very much influenced by the late Kath Locke, who made a clear distinction between one who is a 'Black professional' as opposed to being a 'Professional Black'. In terms of the latter, she was referring to those whom she saw as having no political commitment to the development of the Black community. Instead, the concern lay with the privileging of whiteness specifically for their own self-aggrandisement. From Paula May Jones and Shirley Ann Inniss, I learnt that it is possible for one to be a Black professional and a community activist with a good sense of humour. It is against this background that I became involved in the development of the cultural programme thus giving me the opportunity to embrace and celebrate myself as a Black woman of African heritage.

Prior to my involvement with Abasindi, I was merely one of many female spectators to performances based on traditional West African dance forms and drumming patterns. Within the group, this was indeed Abena's area of specialism and she can be counted amongst those people whom the Arts Council concluded were 'influenced by a consciousness of ancestral heritage and the immediate experience of life in contemporary Britain, these artists have developed a powerful voice which if heard and acknowledged, will have a profound and enriching influence upon the artistic life of our multi-cultural society.'

Although Abena worked tirelessly to encourage the other women such as myself to move from a position of spectators to that of performers, initially I resisted in that I could not see the relationship between community activism and grass skirts, which I associated with stereotypical images of Africa. However, my visit to Barbados to the Caribbean Festival of Arts (CARIFESTA) was a significant turning-point in that the relationship between performer, spectators and audience were all interlinked. On our return to the UK, and through discussion with other members of the organisation, the group agreed to establish the Abasindi drummers on arrival back. In commenting on the emergence of the African diaspora, the group wrote 'embracing the diversity of African women, we travel the Ancestral Journey. We remember and celebrate in ways handed down over generations; drumming, dancing, singing. The Journey takes us finally back across the ocean to the Caribbean where drumming and dancing continue to be part of the lives of Africans providing both resistance and celebration.'

Young Women's Centres Have Acted as a Focus for Personal Development and Community Development

Wigan Youth Service developed a number of young women's centres, and these offered a focus both for personal development and community development. Worsley Mesnes Young Women's Centre pioneered an approach to work with young women based on young women's rights, which linked advocacy, personal development and community development. The following extracts from one Wigan Youth Service project report illustrate some of the methods which the workers used:

> Following a supervision session, it was decided to do some work on the rights and entitlements of young women particularly looking at young women's rights in terms of:
> 1. The individual
> 2. The project
> 3. The local community
> 4. Wider social and political issues.
> The workers then chose a number of themes to address. Under the heading 'The Right to Live Free From Abuse: Physical, Sexual, Emotional', they considered the following matters:
>
> 1. The individual
>> Information – refuges, rape crisis, solicitors.
>> Space for one-to-one work.
>> Self-esteem and confidence.
>> Don't judge young women who stay in violent relationships.
>> Support and training for workers.
>> Links with other agencies.
>
> 2. The project
>> Make sure information is available, put in the toilet (private) and kitchen (public).
>> We create an environment that refuses to accept that abuse is OK.
>> Create physical space for one-to-one work.
>> Keep all project members informed and updated.
>> Make the ethos of the project groups safe for young women to talk about violence.

3. The community

> Housing Department – policy on rehousing women poor, but good relationships with local housing officer ensure it happens.
>
> Work with young men; issues for estate worker team.
>
> Ensure new workers from other departments understand our perspective on this issue.
>
> Links with other women on estate through meetings, etc. means project is an educational force on this issue.

4. Wider social and political issues

> Wigan Youth Service Homelessness Group – liaison with Housing and CHAR to seek changes in policy on young women's housing.
>
> No Rape Crisis in Wigan or support groups.
>
> Contribute to development of guidelines on sexual abuse and to training programmes for professionals.
>
> Campaigning against violence against women.
>
> Refuge in Wigan not linked to Women's Aid.
>
> Issue of rape in marriage.
>
> Treatment of women in rape trials.
>
> Make links nationally with bodies doing work on these issues.

Having made their current thinking in each of these areas explicit, the workers then identified an action plan of work which they could tackle.

Informal Education in Youth Work Involves Making Voices Heard and Resisting Corporate Pedagogies

The aspects of informal education discussed so far – experiential learning, learning through problem-posing and problem-solving, learning through group work and participation, learning through advocacy and accompaniment, learning through engaged pedagogy and community development – can all be understood as moments in a process of education for liberation. The writer who most crystallised these processes for educators of recent generations is Paolo Freire, according to whom, all these processes are to be rooted in an explicit commitment to literacy. Not to a merely functional literacy either, but to a literacy whose purpose is to enable those who are denied expression and participation in the current social order, especially through corporate pedagogies, to act in ways which transform their own condition.

Although Freire's (1972) work on the nature of consciousness and authenticity and the relation between consciousness, education and liberation has been developed and modified, its central themes remain of the utmost importance. It is, after all, still the oppression/liberation axis which remains the focus of attention in feminist work with girls and young women. The complexity and heterogeneity of the experience of oppression and the project of liberation is now widely recognised. The poet June Jordan expressed this brilliantly in her essay 'Report from the Bahamas': 'When we get the monsters off our backs, we may all want to run in very different directions' (Jordan 1989: 144).

In this essay, June Jordan is exploring the basis for alliances against a shared oppression which recognise a diversity of visions of liberation:

> I am reaching for the words to describe the difference between a common identity that has been imposed and the individual identity any one of us will choose, once she gains that chance ... I am saying that the ultimate connection cannot be the enemy. The ultimate connection must be the need that we find between us. It is not only who you are, in other words, but what we can do for each other, that will determine the connection. (Ibid.)

Such a recognition of the need for alliance to be constructed across diversities, rather than recognised, once we are in the process of release from a state of alienation, modifies some central aspects of Freire's account. In creating opportunities for young women to 'name their own monsters' and to speak about their visions of the future, youth and community workers quickly discover that young women all want to run in different directions. The movement of feminist work is away from an imposed common identity as 'women' to a place where we choose our own connectedness of mutual support – and solidarity is not an automatic effect of consciousness-raising. Education programmes must actively and consciously promote this. Freire's emphasis on voice, language and literacy, and his claim that 'silence' remains the single great theme of emancipatory education will be recognised by feminist educators very clearly.

The movement from silence to speech is of central importance to many aspects of the role of the woman worker. In all the case studies which have been used in this chapter, it is this moment of finding and giving voice which is critical. It may be daughters giving voice to their understandings of their mothers; it may be a young women's group giving voice to a sense of the importance of their history as Black women, or young women writing a photo-love story with a different kind of ending and giving voice to hopes differing from the hopes of heterosexual romance. It may be young women asserting their rights not to be discriminated against. It may be young women asserting their needs for health care to be offered in appropriate and non-patronising ways. It may be young women collectively voicing the need for resources: whether of housing, or play facilities, or free education. All these processes are underpinned by literacy as a basic necessity, and all participate clearly in that movement from silence to speech, from object to subject, which Freire identified as the basic movement of education for liberation. Feminist engagement with Freirean traditions of critical pedagogy has taken a forked road; some writers and thinkers such as Shirley Steinberg and bell hooks remain critical friends of Freirean approaches with their emphasis on critique and breaking silence in the interests of emancipation, whilst others have dared to question the very basis of 'critical pedagogy' and have in response been attacked by its contemporary proponents (Ellsworth 1992, Lather 1991, Spivak 1989). These 'post-critical' thinkers open up challenging and productive questions about critical pedagogies as political strategies beyond a kind of heroism in the classroom; about the situatedness of teachers and about the possibilities of multiple meanings. In contrast, feminist work which remains located in critical pedagogy continues to take the unmasking of ideology, the critique of corporate pedagogies as its central focus.

Case Study: Feminist Webs – Using the Arts to Challenge Myths/ Corporate Pedagogies (Contributed by Amelia Lee)

Body image and body image pressure are issues central to the identity of many young women.

Body image pressures are numerous, and come from magazines, from one's peer group, one's community, from TV, the porn industry, the Internet and wider society in general.

Most of these pressures come from a pervasive capitalist structure which in essence peddles the notion that it is not ok for women to be happy with their bodies, and that in order to achieve happiness they must regularly consume expensive products and clothing. Happiness for women, it seems, comes in a can, a mascara tube, a boob tube, or an Armani veil, and most certainly can be bought.

These pressures include:

- expectations to wear 'feminine' clothing;

- wearing clothes that conform to one's culture (for example, wearing a hijab/burkha when in public, or wearing a short skirt and low-cut top on a night out);
- navigating both being sexually available to boys (reinforcing women's role as 'objects' for men and heteronormativity), as well as reinforcing innocence for fear of being labelled sexually 'easy' or being reprimanded by family members;
- being slim, more than slim (size 0), and preferably not eating;
- having clear skin, no body hair, beautiful and groomed head hair (achieved through expensive GHDs);
- walking and moving 'gracefully';
- artificial faces (achieved by buying expensive make-up and facial products);
- orange skin achieved through tanning machines or 'fake tan';
- considering plastic surgery (boob jobs, liposuction, lip enhancement);
- sub-cultural expectations (for example, looking strong and tattoos for young lesbians; wearing dark clothing and self-harming for Goths and Emos), and
- dressing to impress other girls, not for sexual purposes, but for competitive purposes (for example, definitely not having the same dress as anyone else on prom night).

The 'Post-Feminist' and 'Bin the Beauty Box' projects devised by Feminist Webs sought to explore these issues and help young women decide for themselves how they felt about their bodies.

First, we did a number of sessions with young women looking at air brushing, body image, pressures we face, how much money we spend on ourselves, the risks of skin cancer through tanning, and so on.

Then we did some arts workshops with women artists. In one workshop, the young women used magazines to create images that they thought showed real beauty, or the contrast between pressurised beauty and positive body image. We photographed these images and used stop-frame photography to make an animation called 'More than a face'.

In another workshop, the young women talked about how make-up, Barbie dolls, frills and pink made them feel. They then created a textile banner in the shape of a question mark called 'my body', which had painted, shaven-headed Barbies on it, and comments about what the young women liked or didn't like about their bodies.

For the Post-Feminist workshop and project, we asked young women to create and send us postcards. On the postcard, they could draw or write what it means to be a young woman today, what feminism means to them (if anything), and what positive body image means to them. We got 153 postcards and we made them into a postcard book – post-feminist because it was in the post, and NOT because we think we are beyond feminism!

5 Sexuality

Friends
You hold my hand
Smile and talk
We're friends aren't we
Would you walk off
Or hold me close
I want to hold you
  Kiss you
You let go of my hand
  Hug me
And turn to leave
I call your name
  You turn
  I smile
Maybe I'll tell you tomorrow.
     (Shona, Manchester Young Lesbian Group)

Talking about sex and sexuality is inescapable in talking about and with girls and young women. The poem above expresses clearly some of the uncertainties involved in the expression of sexuality for young women, the fears of rejection and the links between love and friendship, between affection and sex, which are so important in one common experience of female sexuality. The poem could plausibly have been written about a possible boyfriend. In fact, it was written by a member of Manchester Young Lesbian Group and is about another girl.

Sex and sexuality are widely understood to be defining preoccupations of adolescence. Women pass from girlhood to womanhood in ways which are understood as essentially to do with female sexuality. Some feminist theorists have suggested that sexuality is the main mechanism of female subordination: 'Sexuality is to feminism what work is to Marxism; that which is most one's own, yet most taken away' (MacKinnon 1982: 1). It is not necessary to share this view to understand that this is important ground for informal education with girls and young women.

Yet the question of what is understood by sexuality and its link to sexual practice remains oddly obscure. Women workers are used to having their sexuality questioned. It is sometimes assumed that we must all be queer, simply because we choose to do separate and autonomous work with girls. For many people, sexuality seems to be linked to a taken-for-granted sense of self-identity and gender; being a woman, being a man seems to relatively straightforwardly define gender. In order to grow up heterosexual, one must identify as a woman or as a man. A woman who does not identify as heterosexual throws the dominant understandings of gender – what it means to be a proper woman or a proper man – into confusion. To gain a positive lesbian or bisexual identity, young women are forced to question such understandings of gender, and in particular to question the norms of femininity they are offered. When young women undertake such questioning, they share common ground with a feminist project which identifies and tries to change the restrictive patterns associated with conventional, dominant models of femininity. One of the most long-established assumptions about femininity is that it is a 'passive' role, compared to the 'active' role associated with masculinity. These assumptions have been associated with a sexual double standard in which young men who are sexually active are seen as 'sewing their wild oats', whilst young women who are sexually active are deemed 'at risk'. Second-wave feminism challenged these assumptions, but there remains a significant debate about how to respond to overt expressions of sexual availability by teenage girls. Such phenomena as girls posting overtly sexual images of themselves on social networking sites (Ringrose 2011) have led to a complex debate about the sexualisation of girls and young women.

Our understanding of our sexuality is clearly linked to our sexual desires and our actual or anticipated choices about sexual practice. Sexuality encompasses far more than sexual practice and should not be reduced to it. At the same time, it is impossible to speak and write about sexuality without speaking and writing about sex. Education about sexuality and education about sex are separate and connected areas of work. This chapter aims to offer a series of approaches and methods to work on both sexuality and sexual practice, from both heterosexual and lesbian perspectives.

What is Sexuality? Current Frameworks

First, it is useful to consider some of the available frameworks for understanding sexuality, which can be shared with young women in the context of informal education. Discussion of sex and sexuality which was developed by feminists in the 1980s and 1990s remains a useful resource – despite the many legal changes, there remains a concern with 'pinkification' and the powerful gendering of sex which many feminists seek to critique and challenge.

Sexology and Developmental Psychology

Probably the most widely available account of human sexuality is still the one which derived from sexology. The successful achievement of heterosexual identity at adolescence has been seen as a key development task. For a woman, this also supposedly involves a recognition that her satisfactory, normal, heterosexual development is bound up with the possibility of becoming a mother. The precarious path to the achievement of this prized, normative identity is littered with difficulties and distractions, including the fact that even according to the sexologists, 'exclusive heterosexuality' is only one end of a continuum of possible orientations. For example, Kinsey, whose surveys of sexual behaviour have offered a continually influential framework to link sexuality with sexual practice, used a 0–6 scale to rate individual's sexual orientation:

0 exclusively heterosexual,
1 predominantly heterosexual, only incidental homosexuality,
2 predominantly heterosexual, but more
than incidentally homosexual,
3 equally heterosexual and homosexual,
4 predominantly homosexual, but more
than incidentally heterosexual,
5 predominantly homosexual, but only incidentally heterosexual,
6 exclusively homosexual. (Kinsey 1948)

The variety of human experience of our sexualities has been mapped by the sexologists into a continuum with 'same' at one end and 'different' at the other. This continuum does not appear to be gendered. Along the way to 'normal' heterosexual relations, many of us are understood, even by sexologists, to enter into the 'passing phase' of same-sex friendships and homoerotic relationships. However, such dominant available models have regarded such same-sex relationships, at best, as a mark of immaturity and, at worst, as sickness or perversion. It is here that the feminist critiques begin. For, if it is so 'normal' and 'natural' to pass through the phase of same-sex attractions, why does 'growing up normal' need so much encouragement, attention, repetition? From this point of view, accounts of adolescent development which assume that heterosexuality is normal fail to account either for growing up gay or growing up straight.

There are now writers who retain a psychosexual model of development but who are more positive about gay identity. They argue that the 'development task' of achieving a strong identity at adolescence needs to be understood separately from the presumption that this identity must be heterosexual. Achieving a strong identity is argued to be a developmental task to be accomplished as an adolescent. It is possible to achieve such a sense of identity as a homosexual. It is possible to be normal and well-adjusted and gay.

However, for feminists, developmental psychology models as such have long appeared problematic. They are highly normative, and the account they give of 'developmental tasks', whether for heterosexuals or homosexuals, is strongly masculinised. Motherhood appears as the pinnacle of female sexuality. The normative accounts of 'gay and lesbian identity development', which are presented later in this chapter, should be treated with a similar caution, although many practitioners continue to find them useful in the context of a need to challenge stigma and oppression.

Psychoanalysis

Despite the fact that the traditions of psychoanalysis have offered a profoundly denigratory account of femininity (seeing it as a limited form of adulthood), a significant strand of feminist thinking engages more productively and critically with psychodynamic accounts of female desire than with developmental psychology. This is because psychodynamic accounts offer the possibility of attending to meanings of desires, and do not simply concentrate on behaviours. In drawing attention to meanings, such accounts hold open the possibilities of change of interpretation.

> The psycho-analytic concept of sexuality ... can never be equated with genitality nor is it the simple expression of a biological drive. It is always psycho-sexuality, a system of conscious and unconscious human fantasies involving a range of excitations and activities that produce pleasure beyond the satisfaction of any physiological need. It arises from various sources, seeks satisfaction in many different ways and makes use of many diverse objects for its aim of achieving pleasure. (Mitchell and Rose 1982: 2)

Our sexuality is always, in this perspective, about our pleasures and desires and the meanings we give to them, rather than primarily about our behaviours, although psychoanalytic accounts do acknowledge the ways in which these desires shape our behaviours. Feminist accounts attempt to change dominant understandings.

Female Sexuality: The Erotic as Power

The phrase 'the erotic as power' is drawn from work of the African-American lesbian poet Audre Lorde. Her account of the female erotic was not limited to lesbian experience, although it found its focus there, and is one of the clearest expressions of the power of sexuality which is not alienated or made into a commodity for profit-making:

> For as we begin to recognise our deepest feelings, we begin to give up, of necessity, being satisfied with suffering and self-negation, and with the numbness that often seems like the only alternative in our society. Our acts against oppression become integral with self, motivated and empowered from within.
>
> In touch with the erotic, I become less willing to accept powerlessness or other supplied states of being which are not native to me, such as resignation, despair, self-effacement, depression, self-denial. (Lorde 1984: 58)

Such an approach to the erotic for women, including young women, means moving away from a central focus on the negotiations of heterosexuality towards a sense of autonomy in our own bodies and our own desires. From this perspective, the dominant constructions of femininity are, in fact, disembodiments: they remove smells, hair, fat, fluids, movement. Women's material (for example, hairy, discharging) bodies are taken socially to be unnatural: 'Women's empowerment in confronting men's dominance begins with the ability to reclaim their own experience and claim their own bodies as the site of their own desires. This changes the meaning of sexual encounters and female sexuality' (Holland et al. 1994: 34, 36).

In order to reclaim our own experience and to experience our own desire as autonomous, we need words and imaginations and names which will enable us to do so. We need to be able to imagine, speak about and experience our bodies in new ways:

> Kiss me. Two lips kiss two lips and openness is ours again. 'Our world'. Between us the movements from inside to outside, from outside to inside knows no limits. It is without end.
>
> 'How can I say it?. That we are women from the start. That we don't need to be produced by them, named by them, made sacred or profane by them'. That this has always already happened, 'without their labours'. (Irigaray 1980, quoted in Humm 1992: 207)

Such poetry could inform feminist sex education programmes.

As well as naming our desires in new ways, feminist insights can help us name our bodies and understand them more accurately. Feminist work has encouraged a developing understanding of our bodies and not simple uncritical reliance on the accounts of the medical profession. The *New Our Bodies, Ourselves* has had a place of honour in every women's centre and project (Phillips and Rakusen 1989). Because the images of women's bodies which dominate our culture bear a largely alienated relationship to actual women, there exists a tremendous need to learn to live in and accept our own bodies and to understand for ourselves our potential for erotic love, our cycles and our fertility. There is a great deal which girls' work can do in support of such processes, and in doing this, 'we do that which is female and self-affirming in the fact of a racist, patriarchal and anti-erotic society' of female sexuality and female desire (Lorde 1984: 59).

Sexuality as a Social Construction

In this approach, a great deal of attention is paid to the ways in which female sexuality is constructed through social practices which tend towards the production of a preferred, if not compulsory, heterosexuality for girls and women:

> Young women are under pressure to construct their material bodies into a particular model of femininity which is both inscribed on the surface of their bodies, through such skills as dress, make-up and dietary regimes, and disembodied in the sense of detachment from their sensuality and alienation from their material bodies. (Holland et al. 1994: 24)

This 'particular model of femininity' is a model of heterosexuality, but its forms are very particularly created and change for each generation of young women. Close attention to dress and appearance, including attention to body weight and shape have been preoccupations of femininity since the mass-circulation women's magazines of the nineteenth century made them so (Beetham 1996).

The 'teenage' market is a market for the commodities of femininity: clothes, hair accessories, diet products, exercise videos, make-up, make-overs. It is also a market for the changing icons of femininity and heterosexuality in popular culture, promoting celebrities, stars and heroes of pop music and the soaps, the narratives of romance and indeed, the moralities and techniques of sexual intercourse as sources of instruction in femininity and heterosexuality. Social networking sites circulate these images and narratives alongside readily accessible pornography as part of a virtual world. The social construction of sexuality occurs in part through the purchase and consumption of particular commodities, and this includes a consumption of their meanings.

Constructions of femininity have always had strong class connotations too (Skeggs 1997), with different products marketed to different demographics, depending on the purchasing power of their readers. They also produce a clear identification of femininity with 'fairness' in skin colour, constructing all Black women as deviant by definition. The sexuality of Black women has, then, largely been understood in relation to a socially constructed White 'norm'. It can also be argued that the pleasure and desire associated with sexuality by the psychoanalytic tradition is caught up with this process of buying and using commodities, making the work and cost of producing a successful heterosexual identity a contradictory and potentially highly- desirable and highly pleasurable process. Such thinking informs much psychosocial analysis of contemporary popular culture.

Interactions between boys and girls, men and women, in small groups and in organisations, such as schools and youth projects, can also be understood as integral not only to the formation of gender identity, but also to the formation of heterosexuality. A number of early classroom studies demonstrated the nature of sexist behaviour and sexual harassment in classrooms, including the use of sexually explicit and derogatory language to control girls and to maintain boys' dominance (Herbert 1992, Jones and Mahoney 1989). More recent studies have identified such assumptions being continued both in mixed and in same-sex peer-group culture, in the ways in which girls harass and pressurise other girls, with additional pressure arising through social networking sites (George 2007a, 2007b). Such work reflects on the question of activity and passivity in sexuality. Is female sexuality still constructed as passive in relation to the activity of the male? Do girls still have to wait to be asked and take what they are offered? Can we recognise women's own active participation in the constructions of our sexuality? And do such active participation as girls offering oral sex to boys via their Facebook page suggest anything better for girls than a continuing phallocentric definition of sexuality?

This theme of women's active participation in the construction of female heterosexuality as passive was an important one, and has been developed in studies of the 'performativity' of sex and sexuality in neo-liberal femininities. When young women learn that their sexuality is meant to be experienced as passive and responsive in relation to male activity, they learn to suppress their own experience of active sexual desire and to pretend. This learned passivity then leads to an alienated experience of sex and to an incapacity to talk about and negotiate sexual practice, including negotiations about contraception. The difficulty in talking about sex in the context of intimate relationships remains a central problem for both girls and also boys.

Research studies such as these formed a useful basis for project work with young women's groups. They helped to clarify some important starting-points and principles for sex education, for example. There are now a number of possible ways in which girls who grow up heterosexual can imagine themselves being sexually active and able to take initiatives and make choices about their relationships with boys. The connotation of 'slag' or 'prostitute' still surrounds the image of sexually active women, even when, like Madonna, they are initially seen as strong and independent. However, the transformation in women's lives brought about by access to reliable contraceptives and to abortion, as well as, more recently, by discussion of 'safer sex' in relation to AIDS, cannot be underestimated. Current academic discussion of girls' negotiation of sexual identities – 'sexy, flirty, or slutty' (Ringrose 2011) – emphasises the complexity of girls' agency in negotiating these discourses whilst remaining alert to persistent patterns of both masculine sexual control and of the product marketing which accompany them.The interaction between academic study and the work of informal education with girls has been very evident in the past in a number of areas, including the work of understanding sexuality. For example, the work of Sue Lees analysed the use of the terms 'slags' and 'drags' in the construction/control of female sexuality (Lees 1986); this theme of the sexual double standard was taken up and explored in many girls' groups. The poster from the 'Us Girls' poster series 'We hate you when you call us slags', appeared in youth projects around the country.

Some of the work on popular culture undertaken in the 1980s – particularly Ros Coward's *Female Desire* (1984) and Judith Williamson's *Consuming Passions* (1986) – offered a highly readable and accessible resource for understanding the construction of female sexuality, and for acknowledging the pleasures of heterosexuality. The authors of the WRAP papers (Holland et al, 1994) were concerned to support a more active femininity in which girls can and do name their own desires. There was a recognition that, to some extent, young women's sexual health and ability to prevent pregnancy through the effective use of contraception will depend on the encouragement they have to name and acknowledge their own sexual desires. Informal education can clearly offer this encouragement.

Feminist discussion of sexuality which developed from Adrienne Rich's powerful essay 'Compulsory Heterosexuality and Lesbian Existence' (1980) made a detailed exposure and critique of the forms of heterosexuality available to women, and the forms of resistance to it. Rich developed a definition of the term 'lesbian' which rescued the discussion of female sexuality from the sexologists. Like heterosexuality, lesbian sexuality is (according to Rich) also a social construction, produced as a moment of resistance to compulsory heterosexuality or a refusal of it. Rich offered a model of women-identified sexuality which reconnects love, desire and resistance. Rich was rightly criticised for making the term 'lesbian' so broad as to fail to recognise the particular, outlawed nature of female-female sexual desire and practice, and for romanticising relationships between women as free from domination. It is still nevertheless important to value Rich's identification of female sexuality and female bonding as a source of empowerment and resistance.

Sexuality as Performance

Finally, there is a feminist critique which rejects altogether the dualistic accounts of male and female genders and works against attempts to map sexuality onto gender (Butler 1989). This work gives voice to a desire to 'fuck with gender' and with all accepted binary patterns. Here is the tradition of the 'mannish lesbian' and of other dyke identities that are not predominantly bound up with normative definitions of masculinity/femininity.

Instead, thinking about queer sexuality engaged with histories of lesbian existence and relationships, with the epistemologies of the closet and with the particular ways in which lesbian, gay and bisexual identities have been formed, acted out, lived and performed in different places and cultures. In one influential account, sexuality is not defined as identity, but as what is performed and acted (ibid.). Much work here makes a connection between lesbian sex and other so-called 'perverse pleasures'. Various forms of consensual sex are celebrated, even when they involve sadomasochism, for example. There is delight in the production of erotica and transgressive images.

There is an alliance here between lesbians, gay men and other 'sexual dissidents' who want to be able to practice exciting sex without risking AIDS.

Sexuality as performance and as unconnected with identity is the place for 'bad girls', slags and dykes, who delight in having transgressive fun. It is also, like the gay liberation movement and women's liberation movement previously, the place for spectacle and street theatre; a place which allows lesbians to claim a social and political identity, without necessarily accepting a minority status and pleading for 'tolerance' from the majority. In claiming a social and political presence, it builds on the feminist history of connecting the politics of sexuality and the politics of civil liberties. Women who had survived illegal abortions and who took to the streets in support of abortion rights made sexuality a civil liberties issue, as 'Pride' was to do later. Now bus adverts and other public spaces become sites of contestation between a new sexual citizenship: 'People are gay. Get used to it' and right-wing fundamentalist Christian agendas. Young lesbian, gay, bisexual, and trans groups become active in these public spaces as an aspect of their informal education practice.

Although much of the agenda of 'queer politics' is male-dominated and does little to challenge women's subordination or promote the emancipation of women, it does nevertheless offer and create a stage on which questions of the varieties of lesbian identification can be explored (McIntosh 1993). Transgression as a politics can sometimes seem to belong to the privileged, but it does open up space for exploration of multiple identities in ways which unsettle the binaries of gender(Haritaworn 2011). In this respect, current 'queer' politics seem to be building on earlier lesbian and feminist commitments to 'a woman's right to define her own sexuality'.

Post-feminist Sensibilities and Neo-liberal Subjectivities

A number of cultural analysts and theorists inspired by the work of Angela McRobbie have made the case that what they describe as the hypersexualisation and pornification of femininities in contemporary popular culture is in part a response to the gains of feminism and at the same time a repudiation of the second-wave feminist critiques of sexual objectification (Gill and Scharff 2011). In this context, there has been a renewed discussion of the constraints and possibilities created in such hyper-feminised discourses for young women's sexual agency, as well as for the sexual regulation of girls and women. The contemporary popular cultural genres of the 'make-over', and the discourses of shame, humiliation and abjection about the imperfect body which accompany them, are very much part of a neo-liberal packaging of femininities which different girls negotiate in different ways, with or without the products which are essential to the production. On the one hand, the 'mainstreaming' of porn enables girls to learn an explicit sexual language about sexual practice, but it is not obviously one likely to enhance female (or male) sexual pleasure or well-being.

How do Women Workers Educate Girls About Sexuality?

Sex Education/Education About Relationships (Contributed by Ali Hanbury)

Sex education and education about relationships has long been central to youth work practice and staff working in informal education can offer much to continuing thinking undertaken in the context of Department for Education guidelines for sex education in schools.

Good practice here can involve work in a number of areas, often undertaken with groups that are well-established and able to trust one another, and using residential work or closed-group work as a method. Sex education programmes and health education programmes clearly offer a positive focus, as do the important themes of female friendship and hopes for the future. There are always difficulties associated with finding a language for sex. This is particularly so for women, whose genitals have long lacked a sayable name.

Sex education in schools is currently guided by the Office for Standards in Education, Children's Services and Skills (Ofsted) and it is advisable for projects to develop their own policy in relation to current guidance on sex education, especially regarding permission from parents when working with girls of school age. The 'moral framework' presented in 1994, when the first edition of this book was produced, was not very hospitable to homosexuality:

> The Secretary of State believes that schools' programmes of sex education should therefore aim to present facts in an objective, balanced and sensitive manner, set within a clear framework of values and an awareness of the law on sexual behaviour. Pupils should accordingly be encouraged to appreciate the value of stable family life, marriage and the responsibilities of parenthood. They should be helped to consider the importance of self-restraint, dignity, respect for themselves and others, acceptance of responsibility, sensitivity towards the needs and views of others, loyalty and fidelity. And they should be enabled to recognise the physical, emotional and moral implications and risks of certain types of behaviour and to accept that both sexes must behave responsibly in sexual matters. (DfE 1994: 6)

The government did, however, recognise the need for education to prevent the spread of AIDS and thus opened up a way forward for sexual health education.

In 1997, the Labour Party was elected to the UK Parliament. The following 13 years saw a raft of significant policy that centred on children and young people's rights and welfare. And, tellingly, in 2007, the Department for Education and Skills (DfES) was renamed the Department for Children, Schools and Families (DCSF). Central to these changes was attention to Sex and Relationships Education (SRE), which was to be delivered as part of an ever-widening Personal and Social Education (PSE). In informal and community education settings, youth and community workers continued to deliver SRE that was rights-based and needs-led, with single-gender work being of particular importance. This was set against a backdrop of the introduction of various equalities legislation such as the Civil Partnership Act (2004) allowing lesbian, gay and bisexual people to formally recognise their partnership, the Equalities Act (2010) which brought together existing equalities legislation under one Act, and a range of Women's Equality work including women and work, women and domestic abuse, women's representation, and women in politics (Government Equalities Office <www.geo.gov.uk>).

Ofsted had produced a variety of guidance and their inspection framework for both formal education and 'leisure time' services included reference to sexual health and teenage pregnancy; expressing concerns that SRE was irregular and inconsistently delivered in schools often by teachers without training or qualifications. Education, and not least, Sex and Relationships Education has an intrinsically gendering effect on children and young people (Jackson, Paechter and Renold 2010). From early years of 'playing house', involving girls using the easy-bake ovens and boys being firemen, to the secondary curriculum options for Key Stage Three onwards, with young women encouraged into vocational subjects of Home Economics and Child Development and young men being encouraged to take up Woodwork and Resistant Materials, the world of school has a significant impact upon the gendered stereotypes of young people.

This theme can also be seen in the informal and community education settings in, for example, youth clubs and in detached settings. Youth clubs with sports halls and pool tables which occupy large and central spaces respectively, and often dominated by males, are juxtaposed with the dance studios and 'chill out' zones that are in the peripheral space and largely occupied by young women (Batsleer, Hanbury and Lee, in Batsleer and Davies 2010).This, along with the celebration of all things pink, provides the strongly gendered and heteronormative context in which sex and relationships education takes place (Alldred 2007).

Sex and Relationships Education vs Abstinence Programmes

Whilst SRE remained an optional subject for schools, Labour introduced the 'Healthy Schools' programme, which was made up of a variety of health strands, including SRE. Schools would be supported by a Healthy Schools adviser and would be able to be assessed and, if successful, awarded with a Healthy Schools status. The delivery of these programmes was, and continues to be very much attacked by the conservative right wing of UK society, and is often labelled as the paedophilic pedalling of pornography, by the mainstream press. Peter Hitchins, in the *Daily Mail* (3 March 2010) can stand as an example when he described a scene of 'the casual massacre of unborn babies in abortion mills … the free handouts of morning-after pills … and the prescription of contraceptive devices to young girls behind the backs of their parents by smiling advice workers'.

Despite this, findings show that young people continue to receive sporadic, misinformed, inaccurate and often value-laden SRE from teachers unwilling and/or untrained to deliver the subject, and young people have repeatedly voiced that SRE was 'too little, too late and too biological' (<www.brook.org.uk>).

Against this backdrop, many single-issue campaigning groups have begun to emerge. They took a particular hold in the US and received significant federal funding under the Bush Administration However, they have been less well-funded and well-documented in the UK. Nevertheless, such groups as Romance Academy and Challenge Team UK do exist on the margins rather than the mainstream of UK society. Following the election of the Conservative-led Coalition Government in May 2010, Conservative MP Nadine Dorries proposed the Sex Education (Required Content) Bill, which called for sex and relationships education to be replaced by abstinence-only education for girls. During its second hearing in early 2012, this Bill was voted down in the House of Commons to resounding applause from opposition organisations such as the British Humanist Association, Abortion Rights, Liberal Conspiracy, Education for Choice, the National Secular Society, Parents and Carers for Sex and Relationships Education (P4SRE), Youth Fight for Jobs, Feminist Fightback, Queers Against the Cuts and many others.

Affirmative work with girls about sex is connected first with confidence building. Girls are entitled to and deserve every encouragement to enjoy sex, to experience sex safely and without risk of unwanted pregnancy, and to refuse to participate in sexual activities which are neither safe nor enjoyable. Many of the activities undertaken as part of the girls' work programmes contribute to this basic aim of building up confidence (Allen 2004).

Secondly, girls are encouraged to find an appropriate language in which to explore and talk about their bodies and desires. Street language for sex, and particularly for the female genital area, is often either vague and inaccurate, or carries powerful derogatory connotations. Medical, professional language often seems distanced and alienated: in the same ways that medical diagrams seem to distort our own particular bodies, making our bodies seem wrong (Ingham 2005). Sex education is based in a process of naming, in which this disembodied and alienated language is laughed about and shouted about, and young women's feelings about particular words and associations they give to their bodies can be expressed. Once this has been done, young women are encouraged to choose and use their own words, and to understand the pleasures and potentials associated with them. Reconnecting the language we use about our bodies with pleasure and joy rather than with put-downs is enormously empowering. The actual words which are used in the end scarcely matter. Words as different as 'flowers' and 'cunt' have been owned by young women as words for the female genital area. It is the process of exploring meaning which makes the words empowering rather than alienating.

Finally, sex education with girls and young women refuses to separate discussion about sex from discussion about relationships. Possessiveness, love, jealousy, monogamy, and control and desire are all themes worth exploring in the context of sex education with girls and young women. The provision of information about the law on abortion, and the ethical debate about abortion, is an important area of work. By law, anyone who wants contraception can get it, including access to the 'morning-after pill'. In 1985, a court case decided that young women under 16 had a continued right to get help and advice with contraception. However, access, for example, to the 'morning-after pill' may vary in rather the way that access to abortion services has varied from region to region, and it is essential that youth workers make themselves well informed about the local situation.

The Ten Year Teenage Pregnancy Strategy 2000–10 was introduced with a view to strategically ensure that teenage pregnancy in the UK would be reduced by 50 per cent. As a result of this, at operational level, young women were being encouraged to opt for Long-Acting Reversible Contraceptive (LARC) methods such as the contraceptive Implant, Depo Prevera injection, or the IUD/IUS (coil). Messages of convenience and a hassle-free way of ensuring that women were not going to get pregnant (regardless of whether they wanted to) served to exacerbate and collude with the already dominant discourses of teenage risk-taking, deviant sexual practices and hegemonic hetero-normativity.

It appears that long gone are the feminist outcries against medicalising women's bodies as sites for regulation and control. Contraception is now seen as a safe and convenient way of controlling the population, despite classed and 'raced' undertones to the meta-narrative of choice, opportunities and independence. We must now look very hard indeed to find examples of work with girls and young women which prompt feminist critiques of the government health agendas that aim to make women's bodies, lives and choices unproblematic.

Sex education is about words and talking, because in sex education, we can explore the connection between what we want and what we do. In all this, the mouth, the tongue and the voice are the most important and powerful of organs.

Peer education has become a widely accepted practice in sex education and it is now possible for young women to train as peer educators to offer sexual health sessions in most areas of the UK.

Learning About Racism and Sexuality

So far, this chapter has assumed that there are clear common issues about female sexuality across cultures and communities. However, popular culture offers clear distinctions between the sexuality of White European women and of Black women. Women of African descent and women from Asia are subjected to a different range of representations, and are often set up in contrast to one another and in opposition to the dominant norms of White European beauty. It is important that these accounts, either of the 'wildness' and 'savagery' or of the 'passive sensuality' associated, in a racist imagination, with dark-skinned women, can be named and resisted (hooks 1992).

The sense in the dominant culture that Black female sexualities are uncivilised and uncontrolled, and that the 'whiteness' of the 'English rose', in contrast, is civilising, pure and motherly, connects directly to such practices as the prescribing of potentially dangerous contraceptives such as Norplant and Depo Provera to young Black women, who, according to the ideology, cannot be trusted to control their own fertility. Informal education needs to be very aware of these practices and help young women gain confidence in becoming assertive with medical professionals about such issues.

The question of the link between female friendship and autonomous female sexuality and of lesbian identification is likely to occur differently in different cultural groups. Among communities where the separation of the sexes is seen as highly appropriate and in no way detrimental to patriarchal heterosexuality, including most Asian communities, separate work with women does not automatically connect with discussions of the choice about same-sex relationships.

There are also a variety of ways in which marriage and motherhood are linked. Sexual practice and motherhood outside marriage are viewed differently by different communities. And understandings of the transition from girlhood to motherhood – particularly associated with different understandings of marriage – make understandings of heterosexuality varied and also mean that same-sex friendship and women's space and community are understood and valued in a variety of ways. For instance, there is a strong assumption of the appropriateness of separate work among many communities, particularly those from South Asia and also from rural African communities. This means there is little barrier to separate work with girls and that same-sex friendships may flourish. However, there is, at the same time, a very powerful taboo against explicit discussion of sex and sexuality, even among communities, with much less disembodied, more sensual cultures and resources than those offered by dominant European cultures. In some Black communities, there is the assumption that lesbian identification is a `White problem', a form of corruption which derives from an acceptance of European values. Black lesbians face both the possibility of homophobia in their own communities and the certainty of racist hostility outside their own communities. This makes the whole process of 'coming out' for White lesbians unlike the process of 'coming out' in Black communities (Parmar 1989).

The methods which workers use to develop education about sex and sexuality with young Black women are, of course, the same or similar in many respects to those outlined earlier in this chapter. The resources of popular culture are still worked with, although it may be more difficult to identify resources from popular culture, given the extent of the invisibility of Black women in the dominant culture. Other independent cultural resources can be drawn on: the independent film-maker Pratibha Parmer was for a long time involved with the development of work with girls, and young women, and the growing sector of women's magazines aimed at Black women. Project workers will not, on the whole, find material 'ready to hand' in the way that material which deals with White women's sexuality can be found. With the exception of work in the area of music, the cultural resources for positive work with young Black women must be created. They cannot be taken down from the shelf in packages made earlier. In this context, it is important to recognise the strengths of minority cultures, including family networks and religious traditions, which may initially appear hostile to the development of young women's autonomous understanding of sexuality.

Islam, in particular, has been depicted as exceptionally hostile to women. Women workers who themselves share a Muslim background and can recognise the strengths the tradition can offer women can also contribute to the development of the tradition and community in ways which assist young women growing up in Britain. They can be critical within their own community, without sharing in the hostility of the dominant Christian culture. Dominant representations of non-European cultural attitudes to female sexuality often single out practices which seem 'strange' or 'barbaric'. The 'arranged marriage issue' and 'the issue of genital mutilation' are the most obvious, and the use of attitudes to homosexuality as a citizenship test in some European countries has been used to fuel Islamophobia.

Any alliance between White feminists and Black women around issues of women's autonomy and choice will be most effective when it is based on support to young women from Black communities developing their own agendas. These agendas may well be concerned with issues within their own communities and in the wider society, and young women will not accept automatically either the terms set by their parents or the terms set by a dominant racist culture.

This is the context in which the issue of 'trafficking' needs to be set. There are times when the development of a European sense of feminist agency seems to depend on the depiction of the 'other' (typically the Thai or Albanian prostitute) as utterly victimised and without agency. These complex issues need to be tackled in alliance with women's organisations from the countries involved and whenever possible in alliance with prostitute women themselves (Haritaworn 2011).

Learning About Sexuality Through Discussions of Popular Culture

Popular culture remains important as a source of evidence of the ways in which heterosexuality is constructed as a form of learned ignorance of our own female sexualities and bodies. In 1986, Melanie McFadyean, then the 'agony aunt' for the girls' magazine *Just Seventeen*, described her mailbag: she was at that time receiving some 1,000 letters a month from girls aged between 12 and 18 expressing fear and ignorance about their bodies on a range of topics including menstruation, sexuality, relationships, contraception and sexually transmitted diseases (McFadyean 1986). Now the rise of celebrity culture and the rituals of humiliation which accompany it, both promoting perfectibility and trashing failure through 'the spot of shame', provide the basis through which young women must negotiate the meanings of their changing bodies.

Soap operas offer a useful focus, although the outlandish storylines may make the attempt to connect with young women's daily lives much harder. Brook and other sexual health charities have had strong support from such programming. One of the methods workers have used for working with material from soap operas, alongside the sort of focused discussion groups mentioned in relation to problem pages, include the creation of storyboards and dramas based on the characters involved. Through such activities, the focused conversation with a purpose, which is one of the main skills of youth and community work, can occur and be developed further. Popular music, rooted in its rhythms and lyrics in the erotic, can offer young women and women workers both dreams to live in and nightmares to escape. It is one of the primary means through which many young women interpret their experience. Compilations with a range of music popular offer accessible resources for beginning discussions about the complex relationship between gender, race and sexuality.

Learning About Sexuality Through 'Coming Out'

Work on the cultural construction of female sexuality – by working with the readily available resources of the popular media – can lead to difficult questions about the worker's own sexuality and sexual practice, with workers potentially very isolated and vulnerable when faced with challenging questions about their sexuality from a group of young people, and as a result potentially reacting badly. It is essential that there is some discussion in worker teams about the pressure to be personally revealing, even in the context of current employment legislation which protects people's rights to openness about their identities.

There are both advantages and disadvantages to appropriate self-disclosure, and it is certainly not helpful for workers to be more revealing to young people than they are able to be with one another. There are a number of questions which may act as triggers: 'Are you married?', 'Are you on the pill?', 'Have you ever used/seen a female condom?' But perhaps the most challenging for its implications for the rest of the work of education on female sexuality is 'Are you a lesbian?'

Teenage popular culture, like academic developmental psychology, tends to suggest that while friendship should never be rejected and must be worked at, it is inevitably subordinate to the girlfriend-boyfriend relationship. Informal education with girls and young women implicitly and explicitly challenges this sense of priority. The question of whether girls' work is inevitably concerned with work with young lesbians is one which has been widely discussed, since Mica Nava first published her essay. 'Everyone's views were just broadened' (Nava 1992).

The presence of lesbian workers at the heart of good practice in girls' work should be clearly acknowledged and recognised. Strong female friendship does offer a basis from which both girls and women workers can question 'the heterosexual presumption'. As Mica Nava pointed out, there remains, perhaps in most communities, a strong taboo against exploring the erotic dimensions of such friendships which makes discussion of lesbian identification difficult. The fear of being labelled 'lessies', with all the hostility which can still be loaded into that label, is one of the elements which can prevent young women taking part in separate girls' activities and this continues to be the case even in the period of acceptance of civil partnerships.

'Coming out' is a process which has been linked to gay identity-formation by developmental psychologists and to narratives of youth transitions by sociologists (Plummer 1995, Henderson et al. 2007). Most of the writing on this subject was preoccupied with the male experience, and most of the available accounts described strikingly similar patterns of growth and change as a mark of homosexual identity-formation. First, they emphasised the context of stigma in which gay identity has been formed. Secondly, gay identity is seen to emerge over a protracted period and to involve a number of growth points or stages. Richard R. Troiden, for example, suggested a 'four-stage model' including sensitisation, identity confusion, identity assumption and commitment. 'Coming out' therefore, can be seen as a culmination of growing pride in identity and as a highly charged process in the strengthening of gay identity. 'Coming out' in Troiden's version occurs at a number of levels and over a period of time. There is a continuum which involves 'coming out' to self, to other gay men and lesbians, to heterosexual friends, to family, to co-workers and to the public at large: from the closet to self-acceptance along an arc of progress! If only lived lives could be so comparatively straightforward.

The existence of social stigma against lesbian identity means that the process of gaining a positive lesbian identity can rarely occur in a smooth way. Young lesbians may go out with boys in a response to peer pressure and in an attempt to conform. They may indulge in promiscuous heterosexual behaviour in order to prove themselves straight, sometimes becoming pregnant. Young women involved in same-sex intimate relationships have sometimes felt they had to keep them secret. So young lesbians have had little opportunity for 'social education' in gaining a positive lesbian identity and because of the continuing impact of homophobia in schools this continues to be the case. At a time when heterosexual adolescents are learning how to socialise, young gay people may still be learning how to hide. Equally, it is very difficult for young lesbians to gain a positive sense of the place of intimate relationships in the whole of their lives. Margaret Schneider expressed this very clearly:

> Being a lesbian means being strong, secretive, non-conforming. It is full of contradictions. It means being different and simultaneously being the same. 'The most important unimportant issue' captures the ultimate contradiction in coming out: that the characteristic 'lesbian' is a private, personal issue, far

from being the mainstay of identity; yet it becomes a central focus for organising identity and life-style as the result of the need to hide, lie and to be accepted. (Schneider 1989: 219)

A woman who has confidence and strength and makes the choice to come out as a lesbian or as a bisexual at work contributes greatly to strategies for combating homophobia. In 'coming out' at work, she allows issues of sexuality to become open, including a more open-ended approach to heterosexuality, as not all heterosexual relationships and households conform to a single pattern. It is also clearly the case that the benefits for young women who are questioning heterosexuality and exploring the possibilities of same-sex relationships are enormous, because a lesbian or bisexual worker who operates as part of a team and is 'an ordinary, everyday person' offers a potential role model and a public focus for the possibility that lesbians can integrate the public and private aspects of their lives.

However, it will never be safe for lesbian and bisexual workers to be open about their identities and relationships unless the whole problem of homophobia is addressed within worker teams. 'Coming out' as a strategy needs to apply to all workers, including a 'coming out' about fears and uncertainties in relation to lesbian identification for girls. It means acknowledging a diversity of sexualities within heterosexual and lesbian identifications, and a variety of lifestyles and patterns of household. It means not privileging the two-parent, nuclear family as the best family form.

The issue of bisexuality, now recognised as a possible positive identity, rather than as a 'transition phase', needs to be discussed. It means women being prepared to locate their sexuality on a continuum, rather than in one or two opposed camps. It means everyone being aware of the impact of anti-lesbian legal processes and the social disadvantage and frequent oppression of lesbians, so that pressures and choices surrounding lesbian identification can be explored in a positive way. It means discussion about the place of sexuality and sexual uncertainty in the transition from girlhood to womanhood. It means being clear about guidelines on sex education that govern the work with young people of school age. And it involves a willingness to affirm female sexuality without reference to men. Emerging too are discussions of the places and spaces that can be offered to trans young people, and there are a number of youth groups, particularly in London and the North-west, to support trans young people. Feminine-identified trans young people may wish to access young women's groups, and undoubtedly have a right to do so, raising further issues of difference for worker teams to explore.

When it is not possible even to imagine these discussions occurring in a workplace, lesbian workers will continue to feel very threatened and unsafe when working with groups of young women, even though they are now supported by human rights legislation, including being protected against discrimination in the workplace. An alternative, more defensive, strategy has sometimes been to create a closet for everyone, so that, as a matter of principle, no workers discuss their sexuality or sexual practice, insisting that young women must set their own terms and agendas. The women workers then aim to act purely as facilitators and sharers of objective information. This is not a preferred strategy, however, as the silence about lesbian existence in what remains a strongly heteronormative culture remains unchallenged.

Support for girls who are 'coming out' can be undertaken either in the context of a young women's group or by making connections with a young lesbian group. Young lesbian groups were established in a number of areas, including a number of rural areas, despite the fears surrounding the notorious Section 28 of the Local Government Act 1988, which legislated against local authorities 'promoting homosexuality':

(1) A local authority shall not –
(a) intentionally promote homosexuality or publish material with the intention of promoting homosexuality;
(b) promote the teaching in any maintained school of the acceptability of homosexuality as a pretended family relationship by the publication of such material or otherwise.

This legislation was repealed in 2003 but according to Stonewall, it had by then affected the culture of schools to such an extent that even in 2012 many teachers still believed themselves 'not allowed' to talk about homosexuality (Batsleer 2011a *passim*, Hunt and Jensen 2007).

Suzanne, a member of the Young Lesbian Group in Manchester, described their group in the following terms:

The Young Lesbian Group has been running for three years. It's run once a fortnight on a Thursday night, it starts at seven and ends at nine. On some nights we have discussions for example about relationships and HIV and Aids. On other nights we socialise, play pool, table tennis, listen to music or have a chat about the latest gossip. Usually when new members come to the group we meet them before at six forty five. A volunteer and a member go down to meet whoever they are meeting.

The purpose of the group is to be friendly and non-prejudiced. We all tend to have a good time. (Suzanne, Manchester Young Lesbian Group)

Young lesbian groups are still irreplaceable in offering exactly the kind of opportunities for acceptance and exploration which young women who are growing up heterosexual expect to take for granted.

Learning About Sexuality Through a Civil Rights Agenda

Government guidelines about what may or may not be permitted in this area were a major inhibitor on good practice. Section 28 created a culture of fear in schools and many teachers still believe that they are not allowed to discuss homosexuality. It is very important that projects and organisations working in the informal education sector develop policy and procedures for their work, in line with current policy and practice being undertaken in schools. Same-sex relationships are now recognised legally through civil partnerships, although there remains strong resistance to calls for marriage to be open to same-sex couples and for the rights of lesbians and gay men to adopt and foster.

If lesbians and gay men are understood as a minority within society, they are clearly entitled to the rights of tolerance and protection which the human rights agenda extends to minorities. If the rights of lesbians are so little understood, this is clearly a theme for political education within young women's groups, and education about sexuality can become an education about civil liberties. The young women who shout 'We're here, we're queer and we're not going shopping' during 'Pride' are involved in a process of empowerment from which informal educators may yet have much to learn. The 'Lesbian Avengers', the direct-action movement committed to the defence of the rights of lesbians, had principles of enjoyment, being able to disagree, not making suggestions you are not able or prepared to carry out, not volunteering others and being required to come up with an alternative in the case of disagreement – principles every community project committed to taking action to defend liberties might adopt.

Female sexuality, whether directed towards women or to men as the object of desire, continues to be caught in the webs of social and political power. Access to abortion continues to be contested and debated. Safe contraceptives are not guaranteed, any more than the right to kiss another woman on the street and not be harassed for it. While this situation continues, education about sexuality will continue to be a political issue, and will continue to be, to some extent, an education in a civil rights agenda.

Lesbian, Gay, Bisexual, Queer? and the Emergence of Trans Youth Groups

Following the abolition of Section 28, the equalisation of the age of consent and the recognition of civil partnerships, there is a more active engagement with anti-homophobic politics in some mainstream schooling. This does not, however, diminish the need for lesbian youth work, most commonly found in specialist lesbian, gay and bisexual groups (Batsleer 2012). It is in this context that the work of trans youth groups is emerging, not focused on trans as a medical condition for intervention, but as a lived life. Trans young people are now being offered their own spaces and often also access young women's spaces as part of other women's groups. For example, the new Manchester group rejoices in the name Afternoon Tea (Trans Education and Action).

The thinking and work of Judith Butler – in deconstructing and 'undoing gender' and opening up conversations regarding intersex – has been immensely important in enabling these groups to emerge and thereby challenging the centrality of identity to feminist politics whilst retaining an orientation to otherness. 'Let's face it. We are all undone by the other … ' writes Butler (2004) and her ethics as developed in her recent writings such as *Precarious Life* (2006) point to the power of boundary-construction in rendering lives liveable and lives lost. Butler argues this against an individualist, liberal perspective and on behalf of populations rendered by gender politics as outside of and unnamed/able within the 'human'.

6 Poverty and Motherhood

The issue of welfare benefits is a continuing preoccupation for governments intent on reducing public expenditure. Sixteen to eighteen-year-old single parents currently receive the princely sum of just over £53 per week in Income Support (2012 figures). First, New Labour and then the Coalition Government sought to limit taxation and welfare spending, focusing attention on parenting and 'cycles of deprivation'. Parenting in the early years was addressed by the Sure Start programme under New Labour – Sure Start offered some opportunities for work with young women who were mothers, though the programme usually focused on their parenting. The Allen Review on Early Intervention (Allen, 2011) has provided an overriding point of reference for a cross-party consensus in the current period.

Although major social science studies have continued to focus on inequality rather than parenting as the source of the problems confronting people living in poverty, the power of discourses which return to focus on the deficits of young women as mothers has been consistent.

The Attack on Single Parents

In September 1993, at the height of the government's anti-single mother campaign, the BBC *Panorama* programme broadcast 'Babies on Benefit'. The National Council for One-Parent Families took their complaints about the programme to the Broadcasting Complaints Commission and won. The Broadcasting Complaints Commission found in their favour on six separate counts, including the editing of interviews with individual young mothers, and the portrayal of a young, unmarried mother of four children to two different fathers as typical. The most important political issue on which the programme focused was that of welfare benefits. The programme claimed that the birth rate in New Jersey had been halved when welfare benefits and access to housing for single mothers were cut. This was not true. On 13 September 1994, the *Independent on Sunday* published an article by Anne Spackman, Chairwoman of the National Council for One-Parent Families, entitled 'Feckless or not? The one-parent panorama. We complained and we won':

> The New Jersey Programme combined the carrot of education, work training and childcare with the stick of capping the benefits of any single mothers who had additional children while on welfare. According to the state governor, all these measures together reduced the birth rate to single mothers by 16 per cent.

It is in the context of this public debate that young women living in poverty are expected to raise children. The success of so many women in retaining a sense of purpose and worth as mothers in these conditions is nothing short of a miracle.

Nevertheless, in 2012, unemployed single parents with children aged 5 remain a target for cuts in benefit. Gingerbread (as the National Council for One-Parent Families is now called) ran a campaign in 2010 focusing on the long history of stigmatising single parents, with the strapline 'Lets lose the labels'. In 1918, when the organisation was founded, it campaigned against the 'Bastardy Act', which stigmatised children born out of wedlock. In 2010, it was fighting the same campaign. According to the 'Let's Lose the Labels' (www.gingerbread.com) campaign research on public perceptions showed an overwhelmingly negative view of teenage parents as well as a powerful misrecognition of their presence. When asked 'What proportion of girls aged under 16 get pregnant each year?', most people guessed 'about 23 per cent', when the figure is actually 0.8 per cent. The stereotype of the single mother as a pregnant teenager is undermined by the reality that about 2 per cent of single parents are teenagers. The average age of a single parent in the UK is 36.

Projects working on informal education programmes with young women often have a sense of extreme powerlessness in relation to the economic issues which affect young women's lives. It is therefore tempting to ignore the level of material oppression which affects many young women, and concentrate on other areas of work where projects seem able to have more impact. However, in working with young women, for example, in relation to issues of choice about contraception and abortion and in relation to the experience of motherhood, it is of the utmost importance that projects do not misunderstand the economic and social context in which their work is occurring.

Theorising About 'the Underclass'

In the public debate about health, welfare and motherhood, the voice and perspective of the 'underclass' theorists continues to be heard very clearly, influencing job descriptions, aims and purposes. By 'underclass theorists', I mean the group of economists and sociologists associated with the radical Right centred around the work of Charles Murray (1994). Although there are also social critics on the Left of the political spectrum, such as Frank Field, who have used the concept of the 'underclass' to draw attention to poverty and to offer a much less moralistic and pathologising anti-poverty strategy, the term on the whole is deeply pejorative and contains an analysis of poverty which blames the poor themselves for their economic position.

Charles Murray's *The Bell Curve*, returned to the old, and many had thought discredited, project of attempting to find a genetic explanation for the distribution of wealth (Herrnstein and Murray 1994). Extracts from Murray's work (which were regularly published in the *Sunday Times*) continued from the 1990s onwards to influence the thinking of policy makers and politicians who were designing the welfare programmes under which youth work is increasingly funded. Initially, many projects funded under the rubric of the Health of the Nation agenda identified as one of their targets the reduction by half of pregnancies in girls under 16 by the year 2000, whilst New Labour's Teenage Pregnancy Strategy continued this emphasis. The Coalition Government has chosen to move away from target-setting but wishes to see 'a continuing downward trend' in teenage pregnancies.

Yet the opposing perspective to that of the 'underclass' theorists – which focuses not on the culture of the poor, but on the culture of contentment and on the need to attack poverty, create employment and redistribute wealth – is voiced less clearly in this context. One current writer, Danny Dorling, has systematically attacked the basis of 'underclass theory', by attacking what he sees as the 'five new tenets of injustice':

- elitism is efficient,
- exclusion is necessary,
- prejudice is natural,
- greed is good,
- despair is inevitable.

Dorling's work (2010) shows how such beliefs can be contested whilst providing a new social geography of inequality in the United Kingdom. The 'underclass' theorists of the New Right have had a very explicit concern to re-establish traditional gender roles and there has been a strong call for a return of attention to fathering. The critique of gendered discourse here might begin by asking questions about the significance and reality of 'absent fathers' in the context of the support from wider family and friendship networks which many, though not all, single parents receive (Williams 2004). The call for fathers to take responsibility may also be a way of displacing attention to the social evils Dorling discusses.

This chapter is concerned with the work of women in projects which acknowledge the impact of poverty. It is also concerned with survival strategies for feminist practice in projects which are funded and resourced by bodies whose aims are highly consonant with a conservative political commitment to re-educate and remoralise the poor. It seeks to resist the construction of teenage single motherhood as a social problem and to focus instead on a number of positive strategies which have been developed to counteract this agenda.

The Transition to Adulthood for Girls

The transition to adulthood for both girls and boys has traditionally been understood as a transition to normal heterosexuality. For boys, this has usually been linked to the transition to adult status as a worker. For girls, the transition to adult heterosexuality has consistently been linked to adult status as a mother. Indeed, motherhood has been represented as the pinnacle of female development, the most prized female identity (Erikson 1968). This means that for young women living in poor communities – communities where there is a low level of post-16 education, where unemployment levels are high and dependence on social security benefits is common – their experience of the transition to adulthood is marked both by a lack of material resources and also by the attention of middle-class professionals, including journalists and politicians, which sees them as 'problems' when they become mothers at 'too young' an age.

It is arguable that women in poor communities become mothers at a younger age than their more affluent peers not in order to secure access to social benefits but because other routes to adulthood – such as access to employment and further education – are less available than in other European countries with lower rates of teenage pregnancy. This is now reinforced by the abolition of the Education Maintenance Allowance and other measures designed to widen participation in further and higher education. If young women in the poorest communities in the UK are to achieve adult status, their main chance of doing so is through motherhood. Sex education programmes are more contested and more difficult to implement in Britain than in the Scandinavian countries, where the rates of teenage pregnancy are comparatively low (Selman and Glendinning 1994–95, Alldred 2007).

So, in responding to the experience of both chosen and unwanted pregnancies and in responding to the experience of becoming a mother, young women make choices about ways of becoming an adult. Ann Phoenix, in her book *Young Mothers?*, argued 'Although teenage women who become mothers are often believed to constitute a social problem, it may be more accurate to view them as a group of mothers with problems – often not of their own making – who are struggling against the odds' (Phoenix 1991: 253).

Indeed, when benefit levels available to single parents are taken into consideration (the so-called 'welfare incentives' which Charles Murray believes are the problem), it is truly a miracle that there are so many young women in poor communities who achieve so much with their children.

This focus on the `problem of teenage mothers` is closely linked to discussions of the family. Poor families of all ethnicities are pathologised – as 'Negro' families were in the United States – in relation to the White, middle-class cultural norm. Some are represented as deficient in fathers: others (as with South Asian communities) as too large, controlling and ruled by 'out-dated' patriarchal norms.

The ways in which middle-class attention has defined young single mothers in poor communities as a social problem are elaborate and yet condensed into a single, powerful metaphor, in which many of the fears of middle-class culture find a home. All the ways in which young women can be seen as a problem can be expressed in the language of 'risk' and 'trouble' (Griffin 1993). Teenage mothers are seen as a problem, as at risk or in trouble, in a number of different ways. The figure of the 'Chav' (Jones 2011) contributes to their demonisation.

The problem may be seen to be a moral one: single parents have failed to enter into appropriate commitments, to wait until marriage for sexual intercourse and/or to have children only in the context of a marriage. Secondly, there is also a medical discourse about single parenthood. This is based on discussions of achieving contraceptive compliance, and the problem appears to be seen as one of stupidity or drunkenness. Third, there is a cultural discourse: the issue of dependence on welfare benefits. Here the problem is seen to be twofold: first, a moral problem of the absence of work ethic where families depend on benefit; secondly, the financial problem of costs to the welfare state, and of housing costs in particular. Finally, there is a patriarchal discourse about the responsibility of fathers. In the work of the Child Support Agency, this was largely linked to financial settlements and making fathers pay. Women claiming Income Support were threatened with benefit deductions for failing to reveal information about their children's father. The problem became mothers' inability to make fathers stay. A further development of the theme of the absent father is 'out of control' and 'criminal' sons. Mothers already perceived as inadequate are then portrayed as responsible for the delinquency and truancy of their sons, and, by association, as responsible for the rising crime rate. Lone teenage mothers cannot, according to these discourses, be relied on to socialise male children.

Having promoted the free-market economics which announced the triumph of individualism during the heyday of Thatcherism, the Institute of Economic Affairs turned its attention to the breakdown of communities – blaming family forms, in particular the feminist demand for greater economic participation and that great shibboleth 'the 1960s', for the breakdown of community and in particular the rise in crime. In *Rising Crime and the Dismembered Family*, Norman Dennis made the case very explicitly:

> The separation of impregnation from pregnancy is a fact which allows the man to escape the consequences of procreation in a way and to a degree that is quite impossible for a woman. These things have always been true in all societies. What is new about ours is that the whole project of creating and maintaining the skills and motivations of fatherhood and of imposing on men duties towards their own children that are as difficult as possible to escape are being abandoned. What is more, for the first time in history on any large scale, the lead in requiring that the project be aborted has been taken by women.
>
> Young men with a short term view of life and hedonistic values have looked on with quiet delight and can scarcely believe their luck. (Dennis 1993: 7)

Writers such as Norman Dennis and A.H. Halsey laid great stress on the importance of families in sustaining communities, and these families are conceived of in traditional fashion (see Dennis and Erdos 1993). These perspectives have re-emerged under the Coalition (in *Positive for Youth* and the *Allen Review*), particularly in calls for male role models in the context of youth work.

Within public policy in Britain, there has been a high level of consensus on the sexual politics of community, and it is a consensus which re-emphasises women's responsibility as mothers for the whole community, the importance of the family for the education of the individual, and the importance of morality. This creates a heavy burden of expectation for women, and if and when young women fail to meet those expectations, they will be focused on once more as problems. Most mothers in poor communities already have all too strong a sense of 'the duties they owe' and too little expectation of the rights they should receive. As mothers, they are in a position from which there seems no escape. Lydia Morris, citing the findings of D.J. Smith from the Policy Studies Institute, stated this very clearly:

Lone mothers define themselves out of the underclass only if they get themselves a job instead of devoting themselves to rearing their children ... they are given a choice between two evils: staying at home to look after their children, in which case they become part of an underclass; or going out to work, in which case they are failing to sustain an ideal of motherhood which others seek to impose. (Morris 1994: 120)

The Impact of Policy on 'Teenage Mothers' in Practice

At the beginning of the girls' work movement, there was a strong sense of needing to present motherhood as a problem for girls, just because becoming a mother seemed to preclude all other possibilities. In a memorable article in the *Working with Girls Newsletter*, Jill Dennis attacked what she perceived as a White, middle-class, feminist perspective on motherhood. Dennis's article, 'How dare you assume I made a mistake?', claimed that it is not the children or the young women that are the problem, but the lack of resourcing for children and the assumption that motherhood is all that girls are interested in. Jill Dennis argued that in her own West Indian community, there was a long tradition of young women becoming single mothers and surviving with the support of their own mothers. The perceived feminist attack on motherhood seemed like an attack on such communities, and on the strength of mothers within them (Dennis 1982). Now it is clearly necessary for projects working with young women in poor communities to understand motherhood as a positive option for women. Only then can its difficulties also be explored and the need to provide alternative definitions of the transition to adult status be acknowledged.

Tony Jeffs and Mark Smith have argued that the impact of social policy with a consistent identification of young people with social problems and social evils has been the development of a control culture, in which, although projects may seem to continue much as before, especially in methods, the imposition of targets via funding bodies has enormously affected the scope of youth work practice. This argument concerning targeting has been further explored in the context of the New Labour years in a series of investigations by Bernard Davies and Bryan Merton (Davies and Merton 2009). NHS agencies employed informal educators to work with young people in an area after setting targets for the reduction in the number of teenage pregnancies. Development corporations appointed community and youth workers to get young people off the street or 'slim down offending levels', Fire Services to reduce arson and false alarms, schools to improve behavioural standards and curtail truancy. City Challenge funds detached workers to cut vandalism, and housing departments to stem the flow of young homeless in a given locality.

> Workers are increasingly forced into modes of intervention located within a tradition of behaviour modification rather than education for autonomy and choice. The new managerialism, imposition of targets and an authoritarian agenda are collectively reconstructing youth related policy and informal education with young people. (Jeffs and Smith 1994: 25)

'The Look'

The culture of surveillance and scrutiny which has developed surrounding teenage parents and specifically surrounding young women in the most socio-economically deprived neighbourhoods has been increasingly discussed since the first edition of this book. The impact of well-intentioned targeting of teenage parents in order to increase their social inclusion has now been widely discussed as intensifying the stigma associated with their position. 'Being looked at' and 'being judged' have emerged as a key mechanism which also fuels practices of consumerism and problems of debt. In the face of hostile judgements (an aspect of moral regulation), young women who face such judgemental gaze from older women on the bus as well as, in a more general way, through media and policy representations, seek to show their ability to provide and care through the 'look' they can give their babies, often based on designer labels. (Arai 2009, Carabine 2007) It is important to insist that this control culture does not affect all young people and all youth work initiatives in the same way. It is very clearly and explicitly gendered, and alongside being themselves scrutinised with regard to their mothering practice, the place of girls within such control cultures is to control the boys and assist in the construction of communities better able to cope with the effects of long-term poverty. Control is, in part, to be exercised by encouraging girls to continue to care – to care about children, to care about parents and the elderly, to care about contraception, and to care for men. Such themes find expression in new programmes and new projects linked to new sources of funding, particularly from the Home Office and the Department of Health. Even when such projects employ feminist youth workers, the impact of targeted funding is to marginalise feminist thinking and practice which starts from the question of the potential of young women.

Such a process occurred with the appointment of a 'Young People's Clinic Worker – Sexual Health through Peer Group Learning' project in

Tameside. This involved a partnership between the youth service and the health authority. Each participant had identified a need for the project. The health authority had carried out a health needs assessment of primary care in family planning services, which recommended more sex education, improved information and awareness of local services, contraceptive services, counselling and support work with young people. The community education service had facilitated a young people's health network which had led to the development of peer-group education on sex and sexuality. Both of these local agendas were linked to the Health of the Nation targets to reduce the rate of conception among the under-16s by 50 per cent by the year 2000 and to reduce the incidence of gonorrhoea by 20 per cent by 1995.

On the face of it, there was ample scope within the project for autonomous, feminist work with girls and young women, and sufficient harmony of purpose to appoint a multidisciplinary team of a clinical medical officer, two family planning nurses, a reception worker and a full-time and a part-time youth worker. The overall purpose of the youth worker post was stated as 'To work within a team in providing a clinic and contribute to the planning and development of effective approaches to sexual health, i.e. design and deliver peer group learning programmes with young people'.

However, it soon became apparent that the basis on which the different services involved in the project measured effectiveness differed greatly. While the youth workers emphasised process, participation and outreach to marginalised groups, such as lesbian and gay young people, the health workers were able to assess their effectiveness in reaching their targets numerically, in relation to the number of condoms issued. Whereas the youth workers were keen to establish separate spaces for young women, including young lesbians, and to encourage them to have some say in the form the clinic was taking, the health workers wanted to encourage the young women to bring their boyfriends, as it was the boys they needed to reach if they were to meet their target of reducing sexually transmitted disease.

In the end, the health service, who had paid the pipers, called the tune, and in the second stage of the project, the youth work post was established with a specific focus on outreach to young men. In this way, the social policy aims of the Health of the Nation initiative and of 'the control culture' were established, despite the presence and best efforts of highly committed feminist workers.

The Current Economic Crisis and its Impact on Young Women

At the time of writing for the new edition (2012), the level of unemployment among 16–24 year olds – around 20 per cent – shows how the young are paying the costs of the crisis affecting the world economy. This is true both globally and in the UK, where the unemployment rate for 16–24 year olds is three times that for older workers. Overall the unemployment rate is higher for young men than for young women, but this also disguises some critical aspects of the situation.

There is a disproportionate impact of unemployment on those without a university education and particular ethnic minorities have been very badly hit. Of 16–24-year-olds without qualifications, 43.2 per cent are currently unemployed. Forty-eight per cent of Black or Black British people in this age cohort are unemployed, and 31.2 per cent Asian or Asian British people are unemployed. It is only among the group of young people with lowest qualifications that girls are most likely to outnumber boys, with an unemployment rate of 46 per cent. This is most commonly thought to be a consequence of loss of jobs in retail, hotel and catering industries, but also possible a consequence of the low absolute numbers of girls with no qualifications (<www.poverty.org.uk>).

The experience of long-term unemployment has been more frequently studied for boys or else in a way that suggests minimal effects of gender. Studies suggest that few people who experience an early period of long-term unemployment manage to make a complete recovery, and remain trapped in casual and insecure sectors of the labour market. The forms of resilience which community-based projects support are increasingly facing up to these realities (Allen and Ainley 2007).

However, women's continuing responsibility for domestic and family life means that their patterns of paid employment are being interrupted continually by their primary responsibility to support extended-family members. This means that women in the bottom end of the labour market remain most likely to be trapped in the low-pay/no-pay cycle in jobs which are insecure and which make demands of extreme flexibility which are hardly compatible with family life. This is particularly true of agency working within the health and social care system, where migrant women workers are most likely to be found (<www.lowpayunit.org>).

Low Pay Unit research suggests the continuing association of care work with low pay and with 'women's work.' Seventy-nine per cent of all employees in the bottom ten manual jobs (rated by pay) are women. Furthermore, research on social exclusion suggests that ill health– a woman's own or that of her relatives for whom she must care – is a hidden element in the stories of exclusion, especially during the critical years of schooling and education. The link between poverty and ill health becomes a very significant part of the story, which youth and community workers recognise in projects on a daily basis (Shildrick et al. 2010).

In neo-liberal policy regimes, however, the young women who experience such ill-health become 'responsibilised' and there is a strange reversal of practice in which projects are funded to tackle obesity or change the health outcomes of young women on an individual basis, whilst the overwhelming impact of increasing inequality goes unchallenged. Not only young women are blamed for their own poverty, but sometimes even more specifically feminists, and by government ministers! The *Guardian*'s headline on 1 April 2011, 'David Willets blames feminism for lack of jobs for working-men', was *not* an April Fool.

An Alternative Account of the Experience of Poverty can be Offered

There are significant alternative accounts of poverty to those put forward by the underclass theorists, but all too often, these fail to consider the nature of sexual divisions within poverty, and so the specific needs of women, once more, are not explicitly recognised. In Bob Holman's lecture to mark the 150th anniversary of the YMCA, 'Urban Youth: Not an Underclass', there is a clear, alternative account of the causes of inequality:

- economic policies which tolerate massive unemployment with its associated poverty;
- market policies which lead to low paid jobs;
- social policies which restrict welfare services, and
- tax policies which mean that since 1979, the richest 10 per cent have gained an average of £87 a week whilst the poorest have lost £1 per week. (Holman 1994–95: 72)

These points all remain very salient. It is worth considering what these mean for a young woman caught in the trap set for her, while trying to make choices about motherhood.

Young women, like young men, have been effectively removed from the benefit system between the ages of 16 and 18 and coerced into the NEETS (Not in Education, Employment or Training) system. With the abolition of the Education Maintenance Allowance, this means the perpetuation of dependency on their families for basic material needs such as food and shelter. In this situation of denial of economic independence and of structural youth unemployment, the argument of the underclass theorists that there is an economic incentive in the status of single parent takes on a quality of fantasy and farce. More resourcing of young women would offer them more choice.

Job training opportunities may not match local employment opportunities. Traditional areas of employment for women, in relatively low-paid jobs, may persist when traditional male employment has been destroyed. A young woman may expect to be both breadwinner and mother in her adult life. Economic development poses some challenging questions for community work practice with young women. Whilst wanting to open up non-traditional areas of work for women, we must not undermine more traditional roles. However, we must ask are women being offered appropriate education/ training for them to make future choices? Do secretarial courses include elements of administration, confidence building, and the idea of future routes into management?

> What sort of courses should be provided in areas of high unemployment where most of the existing jobs are low paid and unskilled? Should we train a pool of women, in for example in new technology (ICT) in the hope that ultimately such jobs will arrive? Will this build up frustration in a woman who completes such a course but can still only obtain unskilled work? Should we provide courses for community development instead? Does this have to be either/or – can courses be developed which enable women to master new technology but initially use skills in a community context? (Cole 1989: 3)

These questions are highly pertinent again now.

The Link Between Women's Employment and Motherhood: The Low Status of 'Care Work'

The impact of the restructuring of welfare and the dramatic shifts in social policy about care are a critical focus for understanding young women's experience of poverty. Young women are caught both ways. They are expected to undertake those female roles of caring for others, particularly the dependent members of their families, both young and old. If they undertake training in the 'care sector' through National Vocational Qualifications (NVQs), they will end up in low-paid jobs and remain dependent on benefits. The need to undertake unpaid caring work forces them into part-time paid work.

On the one hand, young women with children will find it impossible to take up such training opportunities as are offered because of the need to make provision for their children. Young women are also much more likely than young men to be involved in caring for their elders, particularly parents and grandparents, on a regular basis. On the other hand, women's work of caring is increasingly being accredited and certified, but with levels of pay which make economic independence a remote possibility. It is estimated, for example, that many graduates of the new degrees in Early Years will never earn enough as graduates to need to repay their student loans.

Vocational Education still remains highly sex-segregated, with the majority of placements in the social care sector being filled by girls (Cockburn 1987, Fuller, Beck and Unwin 2005). Many establishments offering nursing and other forms of care – for example, private day nurseries and residential homes for the elderly – now depend on the work of their trainees for the level of service/staffing they offer.

The establishment of National Vocational Qualifications in 'care', in youth work and community development, and of new pathways to qualification for Early Years workers is contradictory. On the one hand, what was once women's duty within families is now acknowledged as a 'skill' and is economically rewarded. On the other hand, the levels of pay associated with 'care work' remain very low – this is partly because it remains ghettoised as 'women's work'.

A number of community-based projects offer training in childcare for women, and the structure of NVQ programmes does seem to offer a basis from which women can build up confidence to approach the world of paid employment. At the same time, there is a risk of reinforcing the low valuation placed on such work by our society and of diminishing women's expectations of their own worth. It is important for community-based informal education to have good links with vocational programmes in further education, so that young women's access to non-traditional job opportunities can be promoted alongside the perhaps easier route of access to training in 'care'.

Young Mothers as Copers and Organisers

The poverty of young mothers is rooted in lack of access to a decent basic income and is often further exacerbated by the housing crisis, when there is no longer sufficient or appropriate accommodation in the parental home. Emergency accommodation to respond to the needs of young women who become homeless is still an urgent priority. However, it is important not to regard young women and young mothers as entirely victimised by these circumstances. Young women's capacity to survive and even thrive against these odds is a constant cause for amazement.

Writers like Christine Griffin take a very different view of culture from the view of the underclass theorists – they stress young women's diversity, the range of different experiences of motherhood which young women have and the range of responses that can be made, even in apparently impossible circumstances. She stresses the agency, creativity, resilience and survival which occurs among young women (Griffin 1993, 2011).

It is this kind of approach to poverty which prevents projects falling entirely back into a philanthropic model of assistance. Models of self-help and mutual aid are continually redeveloped and sustained by women in poor communities: community associations can facilitate credit unions, which mitigate the effects of loan-sharking in poor areas; food co-ops which buy in bulk can enable people to buy cheaper food); toy libraries enable the sharing of toys for children across neighbourhoods; children's clothes stores allow hardly worn clothes to be exchanged; sewing classes enable clothes to be made more cheaply; canteens in community associations allow access to cheap and nutritious cooked food. All this is women's work of community organising, and it is important that young women are involved in it. In one community association, young women organised a nappy co-op, to spread the cost of purchase of disposable nappies!

The role of the woman worker in working with young women in situations of poverty is surely to recognise and nurture such survival activity.

A good example of the networks which develop in the process of community organising is the development of the Zion Community Health and Resource Centre in Hulme, Manchester. The project originally covered HIV/AIDS and drugs, mental health, women and children, training and liaison. The Aisha Childcaring Group, which was established initially to offer training to parents, has become a childcare resource for the whole project:

> They now offer after-school club, play schemes and sessional crèche care. In the past year this has meant that the crèche has been open every week for the women's health drop-in and the women's art class. Aisha volunteers have also been developing training packages and policies to help them cope with issues such as difficult and challenging behaviour, as well as policies on assertive discipline and equal opportunities … Aisha, Homestart and Children's Services (Manchester City Council) have worked together through the Hulme Health Forum to establish a Toy Library and an Accident Prevention Home Loan scheme. (Zion Community Health and Resource Centre 1993–94)

Aisha eventually became part of The Big Life Company in Manchester.

Principles of Good Practice

Bob Holman (1994–95) suggested some essential principles for projects working in poor communities, which still stand, and I repeat them here with some modifications, because we are concerned here specifically with young women:

1. Work at the hard end. Means not turning away from young women who are most exploited and needy, and also recognising the young women who are ready to take initiatives, and building groups to support them all. It means paying attention to developing a strong project team.
2. Make sure projects are long-term. Short-term, 'targeted' funding and worker teams who come and go cannot really assist community development work with young women. Projects need time to become part of an area. Some of most successful boys' clubs have been established for more than one hundred years!
3. Make sure projects are available. The life crises associated with stress and poverty do not usually occur during project opening hours. Be prepared to employ workers during 'anti-social hours' and to employ local workers and volunteers to offer emergency support and respite.
4. Share power, and particularly information and decision making about the project with project users.
5. Be prepared to create opportunities as well as responding to difficulties.

The Class Division of Caring: Feminist Practice and the Agenda of Part-time Workers

Because young women are so often regarded as the bearers of problems and responsibilities, they must become accustomed to being seen as individuals in their own right, with their own potential to develop.

At the beginning of the girls' work movement, it was possible for Mica Nava to comment on the possibility of the shared experience of women workers and girls – the shared experience of femininity – being more important than class division.

The need to find common ground and make alliances across class positions is still of primary importance, but the significance of class divisions between women cannot be denied. Nicky Gregson and Michelle Lowe (1994) have convincingly argued that the resurgence of waged domestic labour during the 1980s represents a breakdown of the post-war cross-class identification of women in Britain with all forms of reproductive work. In other words, the re-emergence of servants means one group of women benefiting from the exploitation of other women. Many middle-class women are able to sell their labour power as 'honorary men'. They are no longer physically responsible for all forms of domestic labour. Gregson and Lowe also suggest that certain domestic tasks are becoming closely identified with women from specific classes:

> Thus, whilst the daughters of white collar lower management and secretarial labour constitute a significant facet of the reproductive labour associated with childcare in the homes of the middle classes, the messiest aspects of daily household reproduction are being transferred to working-class women. (Ibid.: 233)

Middle-class girls become nannies, working-class women become cleaners. Salaried women in full-time posts have the privilege of working all the hours that men work, in the same jobs, and paying other women to undertake aspects of 'their' housework. So, 'liberation' for some women is being bought at the cost of 'oppression' for others. Strategies of alliance will have to be created to challenge the evaluation of all kinds of caring and reproductive work.

This issue of the class division of caring, in particular as it structures the relationship between part-time, volunteer and full-time workers in informal education and in community work, must be addressed by feminist practice. Women workers with degrees and postgraduate training may find themselves able to command salaries comparable with those of other professionals, while part-time workers are accredited with NVQ-type qualifications in informal education and do most of the face-to-face work with girls and young women. Feminist-inspired work must challenge these divisions and differentials.

Feminist trade unionists in the Community and Youth Workers Union were among the first to argue the case for parity of pay and conditions between part-time and full-time workers. This case was finally acknowledged in law as a result of a judicial review in December 1994. Employment Secretary Michael Portillo announced to the House of Commons that the different qualifying conditions for part-time workers in relation to unfair dismissal and redundancy payments were to be removed. This would mean that part-time employees qualified for employment rights on exactly the same basis as full-time workers. However, this occurred in the context of an overall loss of rights and these employment rights are currently being reduced again in the context of austerity policies.

In forming alliances between part-timers and full-timers, and between volunteers and paid workers, it is essential that everyone recognises that they have something to gain as women from such alliances. Strategies for assessing good practice or proposals for bargaining and negotiating over pay and conditions were developed which revolved around the question 'How will these proposals affect the position of a low-paid, part-time woman worker who is also a single parent?' If the proposed strategy had the potential to improve her position, it could be supported as 'in the interests of women members' by the Women's Caucus, which was an autonomous group of women trade unionists within the union structures. For a time, this organisation met with some success, even though the right of women to organise autonomously was bitterly opposed by many male (and some female) trade unionists.

The insights gained into the structure of waged employment and its links to the unwaged and voluntary provision of care have the potential to transform social relations between men, women and children. It remains to be seen whether such alliances between part-time and full-time workers can survive the introduction of contract funding. Into an alliance which explores the relationship between waged work and family for women must come an understanding of the growth of self-employment and 'freelancing', as well as new forms of homeworking and 'teleworking'. Without such alliances continuing to be forged, feminist practice becomes a strictly elitist activity.

7 Independence and Dependency: The Politics of Disability

There is a cartoon which shows a social worker arriving to meet a young woman who is using a wheelchair, perhaps to prepare her for community care/independent living. The social worker says to the young woman, 'We're going to empower you ... but don't worry, if you can't manage, we'll disempower you again.'

The problem of patronising and over-protective attitudes to young women is probably felt nowhere more acutely than in the experience of young disabled women, and many of the contradictions of women's involvement with care run sharply through young disabled women's lives. Many women are supposed to occupy the contradictory position of being dependent members of households – dependent daughters or dependent wives – and at the same time be in a position to offer care to others, to meet the needs of dependants. Many of the dominant images associated with disability remove young women from one pole of the contradiction. The contradictions of femininities have become split in the representations of disabled women. That is, disabled women are permanently dependent and needy when not brave and tragic, or expected to simply carry on coping and caring for others, in their role of superheroes.

In some ways, it seems that disability overrides gender in the eyes of the dominant culture. The signs outside toilets show this graphically: men, wheelchairs, women. People who use wheelchairs are a third category. So, for young disabled women, possibly the first and most important step is to claim to be a woman in the first place, sharing in the constructions of femininity which affect women who are non-disabled too. Positioned as needy and dependent, young disabled women claim their abilities to act as women and care for others, sexually, emotionally and materially. Young disabled women also claim their rights to independence and to non-discrimination.

The perspective of young disabled women is necessary in thinking about informal education with girls and young women, both in its own right and because such a perspective sharply highlights some of the questions of

121

discrimination, of rights to counter discrimination and of the need for both independence and interdependence to inform feminist practice.

The Disabled People's Movement and the Rejection of the Medical Model

The disabled people's movement – a movement for the civil rights of disabled people – has highlighted many social practices which disable and discriminate. There have been demonstrations and direct action under the campaign slogan 'Rights not charity', media monitoring and direct action in relation to representation of disabled people by charities such as Telethon and Comic Relief, and the emergency of 'disability culture' and a 'disabled people's arts movement'. There has also been political engagement with the 'care in the community debate' from the perspective of disabled people themselves, the success of the 'Americans with Disabilities Act' (ADA) for the movement in the US, and the humiliation of the Conservative Party for its public failure to support the Disabled Persons' Civil Rights Bill, introduced as a Private Member's Motion by Dr Roger Berry MP in 1994.

In relation to professionals working in social services or in education, probably the major achievement of the disabled people's movement was to create a shift in understanding away from a medical model – 'What's wrong with you?' – towards a social understanding of disability. It is social structures which disable, far beyond the impact of particular impairments.

This, in turn, began to shift understanding away from thinking about 'special provision' for 'special needs', to thinking about how 'mainstream' provision needed to change to enable everyone to participate as citizens of the same society. Since the first edition of this book, the Disability Discrimination Act (1995 and 2005) (DDA) and the extension to the DDA which was the Special Educational Needs and Disability Act (2001) (SENDA), with their subsequent incorporation into the Equalities Act 2010, represented the substantial achievements of activists in the civil rights movement inspired disability rights campaigns. Alongside the taking seriously of children's rights and the highlighting of social exclusion under New Labour, many young people's participation projects did engage with the politics of disability and with a confident 'social model' perspective on young disabled people's rights.

The distinction between the social model and the medical model has become part of professional common sense and yet it remains unclear to what extent this can render the experience of disabled young women more visible. Jenny Morris (2001) reported that young disabled people who were in need of high levels of support identified the following significant experiences of exclusion:

- not being listened to;
- having no friends;
- finding it difficult to do the kinds of things that non-disabled young people their age do such as shopping, going to the cinema, clubbing;
- being made to feel that they have no contribution to make and that they are a burden;
- feeling unsafe; being harassed and bullied, and
- not having control over spending money and other aspects of their lives.

These experiences were accompanied by feelings of being mocked, patronised, avoided and ignored, assumed to be stupid, and treated as an inconvenience and as unfit for public view.

It is experiences such as these which a number of participation projects set out to challenge. One of the most developed accounts of this is Bill Badham's (2004) account of the Ask Us! Project. This project, led by the Children's Society, drew its strength from the engagement of the 'parks man' in the local authority and led to the creation of an integrated and accessible play space. A significant factor identified by Badham in the success of this work was the opportunity for a continuing dialogue between young people and senior officers and not a 'one off' initiative.

However, the 'gender-blindness' in the area of young people's participation and of disability politics continued to be notable. Gender-blindness is one feature of an accommodation with neo-liberalism which strongly emphasises rather than critiques work as a route to social inclusion, and neglects the traditionally female spaces of parenting, 'doing motherhood', the home and care networks, as well as leisure and sexuality: all characteristic concerns of young disabled women who face the 'Cinderella' syndrome.

It is, furthermore, possible that the social construction of 'bodiliness' associated with disability 'feminises' the whole community of activists. However, the paths to 'normalisation' so valued by activists seeking integration are the very paths criticised by feminist activists. This has led to an edgy development of 'crip activism', which like queer activism, is more interested in asking questions than producing answers and has a strong link with performance cultures as a political activism.

Coalition Building Among Disabled People

The disabled people's movement is a coalition, and there is much to learn about coalition building from its achievements. In Greater Manchester, the main campaigning body is the Greater Manchester Coalition of Disabled People, and in writing this chapter, I was very much assisted by discussion with the young women's group which met as part of the Greater Manchester Coalition of Disabled People's youth project. Workers with the project, Maureen Green, Julia Keenan and the 'trainee' worker, Tracy Yankowski, were keen to point out that while disabled people share common interests, they do not constitute a homogeneous group. Nor do disabled people, any more than any other group campaigning against oppression, miraculously shed their own socialisation in the process of campaigning for change. The young women's project, like many other young women's projects, had arisen partly in response to sexism and partly to affirm disabled young women as women and to create a trusting environment where young women can share experiences.

One of the most impressive aspects of any coalition of disabled people is the attention which needs to be directed to basic communication, to enable all participants access to the work of a group. Undoubtedly, this attention to process and to access has greatly contributed to the disabled people's movement's success in coalition-building. The women who created *With the Power of Each Breath: A Disabled Women's Anthology* expressed this clearly when they wrote:

> The complexities of doing the work in ways that maximised each of our individual strengths, and, at the same time, acknowledged our human limitations and specific disability-related needs were staggering. The material we received had to be available in several forms to be accessible to us all. We needed taped and Braille versions, as well as printed, to communicate with each other. Major fluctuations in our disabilities required us to use different media at different times. The logistics of finding and scheduling readers to tape printed information was a continuous job. But with the help of contributors and friends, tapes, Braille and the telephone, we managed. (Browne, Conners and Stern 1985: 10)

In the same way, the young women and workers who formed the young women's group at the Greater Manchester Coalition for Disabled People chose to communicate with great attention. Not everyone in the group had sight. Some members relied on lip-reading. Some members' speech was 'interpreted' by others. This slowed communication down to a level where all could participate and everyone could be heard, and, as if often the case, slowing communication down improved its quality. With the help of the youth workers, the discussion on young disabled women's perspectives focused on some important areas for consideration.

How can a Disabled Woman Achieve Adult Status?

The question of what is a 'young woman' and the transition to adulthood, is formulated slightly differently in each theme approached in this book. Does a young woman become an adult when she becomes a heterosexual? When she becomes a mother? When she gains economic independence or a house of her own?

It has been suggested that adolescence is very prolonged for a disabled woman because it is assumed that she will be unable to achieve these adult statuses. She is assumed to have no sexuality, no possibility of forming sexual relationships, and therefore to have no chance of becoming a mother. She may, as a result, remain under the protection of her parents all her adult life, retained in a state of almost perpetual childhood, or she may, perhaps well into her twenties, engage in a period of rebellion against such enforced dependency. The corollary of a long period of unexpressed sexuality may be a period of highly charged sexuality, expressed in risky and dangerous ways. If she becomes a mother, it is likely to be assumed either that this was a mistake, or that she became a mother before she was disabled, and there is likely to be scrutiny of her fitness to be a mother.

Such scrutiny is based on the perceived reversal of women's duty to be caring. How can a woman who is perceived to be in need of care, to be dependent, offer the kind of permanently available care which mothers in our kind of society are meant to offer? Will she not come to depend on her children to care for her, in ways which are disadvantaging for them? In the discussion of community care, the plight of 'young carers' – children who care for their parents – has been highlighted. Against the norms of a society in which everyone is meant to be positioned on one side or the other of a weak/strong and helper/helped divide, how can a disabled woman with children be positioned as anything other than a 'problem family'?

This roadblock of disabling assumptions in the way of young disabled women becoming adults, becoming mothers, in the ways other young women do, repays very careful scrutiny. The issues raised by the experience of women disabled from their early life who do become mothers are exciting and challenging. They have an impact on all the debate that needs to occur about how children are to be cared for, whose responsibility it is to provide that care, how children's own desire to care for others is to be nurtured but not exploited. They challenge the role our society gives to professional social workers as 'experts' in the assessment of such issues: a role which then enables everyone else to avoid the debate. Meanwhile, disabled women who do establish sexual relationships and become mothers offer an important example to young disabled women that a transition away from parents or institutions and towards independent living is possible.

The Education System as a Disabling Force

A second major area for discussion is the part played by education in 'robbing you of your rights'. Some disabled young women still experience segregated or 'special' education, and there may be a significant return to this model with the innovations of 'free schools`. The term 'special needs' is particularly disliked. It is felt to disguise the reality of young women's experience of being sheltered and protected, which leads to a lack of opportunity and the expectation that they will have menial jobs or that their impairment will prevent them from achieving. This view of the limitations of special education has been consistently upheld by Her Majesty's Inspectorate of Education, and yet progress towards integrated education provision was been painfully slow. In the mid-1990s, the TUC statement on civil rights for disabled people recorded the following:

- Reports on special schools by HMI rated accommodation and resources at best 'satisfactory' to 'downright dangerous'. Other reports have found specialist science facilities rare in the smaller special schools. Special schools often have no teachers with expertise in important subjects, especially science and maths.
- Other official reports have looked at the position of children in mainstream schools. In primary schools, most classrooms have insufficient space for children who use personal aids and equipment, and many schools do not have accessible toilets and changing rooms. In most secondary schools where there are young people with physical impairments, few adaptations have been made. In many cases, inaccessibility prevented students being able to choose major subjects at GCSE level.
- A survey of further education colleges found that fewer than a third were able to offer physical access in all teaching blocks, and more than a fifth said they might have to reject a student 'with a physical handicap' because of poor access or inadequate support. A 1990 survey of polytechnics and universities found a similar picture.

One of the young women in the Manchester disabled young women's group had been prevented from following her chosen training in caring because the nearest college which could offer her access and support to do the course was in Coventry! None of the young women in the group had expressed particularly unusual ambitions in terms of employment – a number were interested in work in the care sector, particularly with children or in social work. Others had interests in gardening and working with computers. Everyone recognised that as a result of their impairments, they might require assistance to undertake courses, or that colleges might need to make adaptations to premises and/or equipment to offer them access to the same opportunities as other young women. There was been considerable progress in the making mainstream schools as well as further and higher education accessible as a positive result of the DDA and SENDA, although the model still remained a largely diagnostic one and limitations on resources for student support can continue to make the experience of disabled learners frustrating.

The role of the women workers working with this group was clearly to build up confidence and offer a safe forum in which young women could develop the assertiveness to demand their rights to education within the society of which they are members.

Using Anger and Tackling Harassment and Discrimination

Such experience of being denied access to basic social rights, and even of being denied any expectation of such rights, inevitably leads to anger, and the manipulation of the many feelings provoked – both in disabled and non-disabled individuals – by the encounter with disability is a major source of difficulty for young women.

In our society, femininity is identified with emotionality, and being appropriately feminine means handling emotions appropriately: your own and other people's. It is probably impossible for a young disabled woman to be 'appropriately feminine', as she is so often a dumping ground for other people's fears about 'normality', weakness and pain. At the same time, she has to cope with her own feelings, both about her impairment and about the treatment she receives. As one of the young women in the Manchester group put it: 'If your confidence is battered throughout your life, you grow up very angry.' Informal education must address this anger, as it is potentially an enormous resource for change:

> Anger felt by women because of our disabilities is rarely accepted in women's communities, or anywhere else for that matter. Disabled or not, most of us grew

up with media images depicting pathetic little 'crippled' children on various telethons or blind beggars with cap in hand '(handicap') or 'brave' war heroes limping back to home where they were promptly forgotten. Such individuals' anger was never seen, and still rarely is. Instead of acknowledging the basic humanity of our often-powerful emotions, able-bodied persons tend to view us either as helpless things to be pitied, or as Super Crips, gallantly fighting to overcome insurmountable odds. (Thompson 1985: 78)

If the anger produced by such stereotyping can be acknowledged, instead of, as is so common with women, being turned inwards into despair and depression, it will become a powerful force:

Disabled women must learn to understand their own anger and to accept that it is both reasonable and justified. It is lousy to be disabled and it is perfectly healthy and normal to feel that way, at least occasionally. The trick however is to learn to control that anger so that it does not become a liability in and of itself ... Those of us who are disabled must learn to cope with the anger provoking reality that all those many barriers are not going to come tumbling down all at once, as unjust, unfair and just plain infuriating as they are. It is not easy to have to work our lives around the multitude of obstacles society has put in our way ... We need to find effective coping mechanisms to help us keep sane and strong. For some, political action may be useful. For others a support group may help. There are numerous possibilities. The important thing is to find a way to survive. (Ibid.)

The role of anger and of the emotions, especially at a point where young women recognise that their rights as independent persons are effectively being denied, is one of the most important issues in informal education with girls, and it provides one of the places where alliances between girls and women with very disparate experiences may be forged.

Another experience associated with patterns of discrimination is the experience of harassment. Young women at the Greater Manchester Coalition of Disabled People's Youth Project have described the experience of being called names and being bullied, and also the experience of being petted, pitied and talked over: 'People stroke you and feel they have a right to touch you.' For young disabled women, the experience of being touched sexually without their consent appears to be an extension of this objectification associated with disability. The young women's group provides an essential forum in which experiences of bullying and harassment can be identified and named for what they are, and in which young women can swap survival stories and tactics and be as emotional as they need to be.

It seems fairly clear that informal education projects which start from a tokenistic position of including young disabled women in 'mainstream' provision are unlikely to be able to address in the same depth the issues raised by an autonomous group of young disabled women, meeting within the framework of a campaigning voluntary organisation *of* disabled people, rather than an organisation *for* disabled people.

Integration – But On Whose Terms?

'Mainstream' projects must strive for integrated provision, but this must be done on the terms of young disabled women, and with their interests paramount. All too often, it is the need of the 'mainstream' service to be seen to be doing something that becomes paramount. Then, the development of policy and awareness can seem in inverse proportion to action taken. Disabled members of 'mainstream' projects are sometimes 'worn like a badge' of the good intentions of the non-disabled. 'Integration' or 'mixing' for their own sake can never provide a sufficient purpose and will always, in the end, fail to prioritise sufficiently the interests of the group which has been excluded. The long, and no doubt for many individuals, extremely worthwhile history of the PHAB (Physically Handicapped-Able-Bodied) clubs, seem to have done little to challenge disabled young people's exclusion. It seems better practice to support disabled workers in establishing autonomous groups and gaining appropriate qualifications, and to build up joint work, including integrated provision, with the human rights agenda in mind.

However, most of the work with young disabled women does currently occur in settings and organisations which are *for* disabled people rather than in organisations *of* disabled people. In these organisations, there is an in-built tendency for a model of charity rather than of rights to come to the fore, and it is very important that workers are aware of this. Sue Quinn, Youth Club UK's Disability Development Officer, organised a conference in Lancashire for women workers to examine their practice with young women. One of the projects which presented their working methods was Connect, a Stockport-based project which aims to 'enable disabled young people to develop their own social and leisure lives in whatever way they see fit'. The worker at the project, Caroline McPhee, stated: 'Disabled young women are affected by the same cultural influences as able-bodied young women and should be allowed to take risks and possibly make mistakes to find out what they want to do.'

Projects can gear their work to opening up new opportunities for disabled young women, particularly, perhaps, in relation to further education provision and to positive action to make up for opportunities denied through schooling.

Gill Whittle, from Merseyside Youth Association's Advocacy Project, focused on self-advocacy, described as being able to make choices and decisions, being able to express thoughts and feelings with assertiveness if necessary, having clear knowledge and information about rights, and being able to effect changes. Here, there is clearly a link to the collective campaigning work undertaken by disabled people's organisations. However, advocacy projects may have a tendency to position young people as weak and vulnerable initially, rather than starting from strength. The charity model can re-emerge in the form of mistakenly low expectations on the part of non-disabled workers.

A third workshop focused on self-defence, the development of self-confidence in young disabled women to deal with the abuse and harassment they so often face, and enabling young women to make their own definitions about personal safety, rather than simply accepting the evaluations of places and situations given them by others. When thinking such as this, alongside the necessary and more immediately graspable work of adapting buildings and resources, gains a foothold in mainstream services, the project of including disabled young women on the same terms as others is greatly strengthened.

Some young women's projects have taken positive steps to involve young disabled women in their activities. Getaway Girls in Leeds was established precisely to enable access to adventurous and outdoor activities to girls whom everyone assumes aren't interested in or can't do certain activities. The project took quite a strategic approach, particularly in taking positive action by employing a deaf woman as a trainee worker and supporting her training. This strengthened the project's existing link with deaf girls, and the project then went on to employ a sign interpreter and to offer a signing service. By 1992, the project had proposed a five-year development plan, with a strong emphasis on disability awareness training with mainstream services which discriminate against disabled people.

Self-organisation of Disabled Youth and Community Workers

Employment rights are a major focus of attention for the civil rights of disabled people, and if young disabled women are to progress with the work of coalition building, mutual support and education, greater numbers of disabled women will need to be employed in informal education and community development roles and to become qualified in a range of occupations.

And so the circle is complete. Institutions which offer training, particularly further education colleges and universities, must change their direction and policies to enable access. The desire among women who are aware of the denial of their rights to 'smash the system from the inside' is very strong. Feminist practice should give every assistance to this process. A national network of disabled youth and community workers has been established on an independent footing. It is from such an independent network of disabled workers that the essential and necessary role models for young disabled women in the future will emerge.

Finally it is important to highlight the ways in which activism in relation to mental health has drawn on the Disability Discrimination Act to begin to claim rights for those suffering 'mental illnesses' (Sayce 2000).

This follows a similar political trajectory to the one just discussed in relation to physical impairment. If a definition of distress called 'mental illness' is accepted, it is right that employers and service providers are asked not to discriminate, to make reasonable adjustments and to anticipate adjustments ahead of time. There is much emphasis on the reduction of 'stigma' associated with mental ill health and with integration into the labour market.

However, the discussion of mental health requires first of all a recognition that perhaps only 15 per cent of people with long-term mental health problems are working or ever likely to work, as well as a recognition that there is a long history of critique of the categories of madness, of psychiatric classification as a convenient way of labelling and dismissing, of rejecting and refusing to hear specifically gendered forms of distress. Much of these forms of distress relate to the body, the control of the body and the failures and indignities of the body, either in relation to physical impairment or in relation to behaviours such as those diagnosed as self-harm, depression, eating disorders. Youth work practice which opens up for enquiry the issue of how women are with our bodies remains among some of the most inspiring examples of practice. The following example – taken from Forty Second Street Young Women's Project and contributed by Tess Gregson – illuminates some of the ambivalences and dilemmas of practice.

Body Image Sessions with LGBTQ and Disabled Young People in a project for young people experiencing emotional and mental health difficulties. (contributed by Tess Gregson)

As part of a wider project around self-esteem and body image, youth workers at Forty Second Street facilitated group work with a local LGBTQ project. Forty Second Street is a specialist agency which works with young people experiencing stress or mental and emotional difficulties and has a specialist Disabilities project within it. This provided a safe space for young people to explore experiences which are often marginalised within mainstream youth work provision. Arts-based activities, group inquiry and interactive web-based resources were used to challenge assumptions and beliefs affecting body image and self-esteem from an LGBTQ perspective. The group involved two young women and three young men, with two LGBTQ identifying workers facilitating the sessions. The centre's project workers did not identify as LGBTQ, which brought interesting dynamics to discussions. Their contributions served to highlight the shared experiences between women and the particular experiences of group members, which they identified as relating explicitly to their sexuality and/or gender identity.

The group felt that pressures around body image were different for LGBTQ young people. They thought that most of their peers were affected by wider heterosexist and narrowly conceived media representation of people in terms of physical appearance, cosmetic surgery and weight loss. However, this was viewed as additional to the pressures from within the LGBTQ community. Young people were asked to create collages using 'popular interest' magazines which they felt related to body image and representation. Discussion revealed that the majority of the group felt no real connection with the people represented in the collages they had created nor did they feel it was possible to look like them. However, they identified with wanting to achieve the 'perfect body'. Youth workers posed the question 'who is excluded from these images?' Young people talked at length about the absence of LGBTQ people from the magazines and the group then went on to discuss the lack of images representing people with disabilities and the few images of Black women, other than specific US performers. Young people described the limited ways in which women were viewed in terms of their physicality and success in terms of 'beauty'. Whilst the few male figures represented were thought to rely on a stereotypical view of masculinity, young people more easily identified talents and achievements as a result of both article content and group knowledge of those figures than for women.

The magazines aimed at an LGBTQ readership raised debate around the pressures within the LGBTQ community, and the young people felt they were just as excluding and damaging to self-esteem and body image as those in the mainstream media. The group felt that gay men were subject to stereotyping and gay men in the group talked about the pressure they felt to emulate the media portrayal of gay male physicality. The magazines aimed specifically at gay men overwhelmingly depicted sexualised images, regardless of article content. One young man talked about having been on a diet. When questioned by other people, he defended this by saying that he had done it to feel better about himself. Another young man shared that he had experienced an eating disorder and said that there was a lot of pressure to be thin as a gay man. He relayed that many of his friends eat as little as possible and that this is quite normal amongst his peers. Young women in the group felt that there was an absence of lesbian and bisexual women in LGBTQ media and when asked, the group found it difficult to identify many female role models.

One of the older young women said that her feelings had changed over time and that she felt the pressure to fit into a certain lesbian stereotype had been most significant when she had first come out. She recalled going to an LGBTQ youth project and feeling a pressure to look a certain way and wear certain clothes; for her, a sense of belonging within that space was closely connected with how you represented your identity through clothes and appearance. This had been a common experience at some point for all in the group. One young person commented that this was ironic given that you had already felt different; the LGBTQ community provided a different set of rules, but there were still rules associated with belonging. One of the young women found that identifying as lesbian had meant she had the freedom to construct her identity in a different way. Her experience was that coming out had already constructed her as 'different' from her heterosexual friends and this offered her a sense of freedom to be herself on her own terms. She talked about being more confident than she was as a younger lesbian and that she could now 'ignore' language and comments such as 'you look like a man' or 'dyke'. She was now a mother and talked about how her experiences informed her parenting. She was passionate about ensuring that her son grows up with an understanding of gender and is able to benefit from some of her learning from the more difficult experiences she has had. One of the youth workers was also a lesbian and parent and this enabled a sharing of experience and strategies between the two women.

During one of the sessions, the group accessed an interactive website which shows the work of Greg Apodaca, a 'digital retoucher' who works for advertising agencies and magazines. His website offers the opportunity to view 'before and after' photographs he has been commissioned to alter. This enabled young people to recognise the extent to which bodies are digitally altered for commercial purposes. Although young people said that they knew that 'people get photo shopped', they were all, bar one, surprised at the extent of this. One young man had previously been a model and said that 'it is all fake', referring to the amount of time and post-photo retouching done to images, though he admitted that even having experienced this process first-hand, he still aimed to be thinner and look more like the images he saw. Youth workers queried the lengths to which group members might go to achieve this look, if it was viable and whether it was preferable. Most of the young people said they would alter something, if not a number of things, about their appearance. A few but still significant number of the group said they saw cosmetic surgery as an option. The young woman, who had found freedom to construct her identity as a result of perceiving herself as on the margins, was emphatic in arguing to the rest of the group that we should be recognised and valued for being ourselves. Another young woman argued that if surgery 'makes you look better' then it is ok. This developed further into a debate around the ethics of altering our bodies to fit a majority view. The group agreed that people should be valued as themselves whether that be because they are gay or the way they look, and that, in terms of the images, the women 'look like aliens; they are too symmetrical'. In exploring how financially viable it was to look like mainstream media representations of 'normal', young people rationalised that this was impossible for most people, yet the emotional drive towards such an appearance remained strong.

As part of the evaluation, the group were asked to say something they liked about themselves. Interestingly, it was equally difficult for the participating centre workers and young people to do this. Many of the statements were qualified in some way to devalue them or to refocus them on what the individual could 'do' for other people or focused on 'liking' a generally hidden body part. Youth workers raised questions around whether it felt like bragging to say something positive about yourself without undercutting it or focusing it on another person. The youth workers encouraged other group members to say what they liked about each of the people in turn. This affirming activity enabled group members to challenge negative self-beliefs in a genuine, emotionally engaged and encouraging way.

Although issues of body image may be acute for young women with mental health problems and for significant numbers of young disabled people it is clear from this case study that they currently affect all communities.

8 Violence Against Young Women

Recognising and Acknowledging Sexual Violence

The question of violence is never far away in groups of girls and women. Yet the so-called 'disclosure' of the presence of coercion in the lives of the young women is often greeted with shock. Instead of recognising that some level of coercion is, in fact, normal and everyday, this common response of shock suggests that the experience of violence is unusual. A skilful response acknowledges the presence of degrees of force and violence in the everyday reality of many girls and young women, and the differences concerning the acceptability of physical violence in different cultures, while at the same time stressing the unacceptability of violence in personal relationships.

When the particular circumstances that have led to violence are investigated, there are always ready-made explanations available in each particular case. These can easily distract attention from a common pattern. Violence seems 'alien': 'It could never happen to me.' 'It never happens to me' – or else is seen as a product of deviant individuals in deviant relationships: 'He's a bastard, but she loves him' or 'What a monster! How could they do that to their own children?' The young woman who is experiencing violence is likely to believe herself to have no connection with other women: 'It only happens to me.' Liz Kelly's important work *Surviving Sexual Violence* (1988) offered a feminist framework for understanding the connections between different kinds of violence which women experience. She identified the prevalence of a shared ideology about rape, incest/sexual abuse and domestic violence which focuses attention on the victim rather than the perpetrator. For example, in relation to the myth that 'they' (that is, women) 'tell lies/exaggerate', this may be expressed in relation to rape as 'Women make false reports for revenge, or to protect their reputation', or in relation to incest/abuse, as 'Girls fantasise about incest, or accuse men of sexual abuse to get attention.' In relation to domestic violence, it is expressed as 'It wasn't violence, only a fight. Women exaggerate to get a quick divorce.'

Liz Kelly argues that this common-sense reversal should point us to a recognition of an ideology: a powerful body of beliefs and ideas which disguise the truth, almost turn it upside down. In this case, it is an ideology which mystifies the recognition of the ways in which men's violence facilitates the social control of women. Kelly sees violence as resorted to only when other forms of control have failed, because the use of violence makes the existence of coercive power evident and so facilitates resistance: 'Male violence arises out of men's power and women's resistance to it' (ibid.: 23).

In developing her definition of violence, she begins with the recognition, found in the dictionary definition, that violence involves damage to the self, denial of the victim's will and autonomy, and that such violence may be physical, emotional, psychological. She then extends this to explore the place of sex in men's violence, and the need to include women's own account of what has happened to them in any definition: 'Sexual violence includes any physical, visual, verbal or sexual act that is experienced by the woman or girl, at the time or later, as a threat, invasion or assault, that has the effect of hurting her or degrading her and/or takes away her ability to control intimate contact' (ibid.: 41).

Unfortunately, the myths and stereotypes about sexual violence are still very prevalent and affect services offered to women experiencing or escaping violence. All too often, it seems to be the case that the impact of violence is not taken seriously and the difficulties facing women trying to leave relationships are minimised. Attention is turned to trying to get women to change their behaviour. The feminist response to this dominant welfare agenda has been the development of a network of services for women and girls who have been abused. This is largely because of the inadequacies in the response of the statutory agencies and the extent to which myths and stereotypes are reflected in their practice. From the base of these alternative services, campaigning work which challenges definitions, myths and stereotypes has been undertaken to encourage change in public attitudes. There have also been systematic initiatives to challenge practice within statutory agencies.

There have always been close contacts and connections between feminists working in Rape Crisis and Women's Aid, for example, and feminists working in community-based projects with girls and young women. The purpose of this chapter is to explore ways in which feminist understandings of violence can lead to ways of working which are not 'firefighting' or 'crisis work'. They can also enable the reality of struggle and survival to be acknowledged. Personal troubles can, over and over again, be identified as public issues. The United Nations continues to be lobbied to include domestic violence alongside torture as an abuse of human rights.

How does Sexual Violence Become Apparent to Workers?

Forms of violence which may become apparent to workers in the course of running a girls' group or a young women's group include assault, rape, sexual abuse of children by adults, physical abuse of children by adults, racial harassment and racist attacks. There are also forms of violence which are administered apparently therapeutically, for example, by doctors in the treatment of mental illness. Violence is directed against the self by young women in the form of self-harm and attempted suicide.

The experience of violence can become apparent in a number of ways. A young woman may arrive at a project displaying her bruises. She may lie about how she came by the bruises. Another young woman may organise herself to take part in a project event, only to find herself prevented from doing so as a result of threats from her partner. Sometimes, there is talk about men arriving home drunk, or of sexual encounters that got out of hand. Among a group of women, the issue of violent threats is often assumed and unspoken, or acknowledged only implicitly: 'You know what men are like, don't you?'; 'He's in a bad mood; you want to keep away from him at the moment.' The worker must then decide how and in what ways to make the issue explicit. She also has to find ways to assert the unacceptability of violence.

At other times, women's experience of violence may emerge as a result of personal conversation with a worker. She may have become desperate to break the silence and let someone know what is happening to her. Or she may have begun to internalise her angry response to violence – turning it in on herself in the form of depression or of suicide threats.

The question of the prevalence of sexual abuse, which emerged in the context of feminist movements, raised awareness of the relationship between self-directed violence and the threats of an oppressive adult exercising sexual power over a child. A child who is made to feel worthless and hateful may begin to behave in ways that reinforce this belief.

When a child or a young woman lets a worker know that she is experiencing violence from adults who are responsible for her care, the worker must be able to recognise and acknowledge her responsibilities to respond to the news she is receiving, however little she wants to hear it. It is important to recognise that girls and young women will give such information to adult women workers because they believe that the adult has more power than they have and can intervene to support them. Information shared in this way is also shared on the basis of trust, and it is essential not to break that trust. All citizens share in a duty to protect children. It is therefore essential that projects develop clear guidelines for workers, rooted in the current policy context.

In the development of feminist-inspired work in crisis projects, a number of principles for good practice have emerged.

Good Practice in Acknowledging and Responding to Women's Experience of Violence

First, it is important that any woman who begins to talk about her experiences of violence is believed. This simple step is an act of resistance to the myth that all women who report experiences of violence or harassment are liars and prone to exaggeration. It is not a matter of claiming that women and girls *never* lie or make up stories. But the act of believing allows women to make their own claims to truthfulness, to name their own experience, before perhaps having their claims subjected to the scrutiny of the courts or other 'experts'. On the whole, the ideology that women are liars or that we embroider the truth seems to lead women to disbelieve their own experience or to minimise the harm and hurt we have received, rather than to exaggerate it. There is also the important coping mechanism of forgetting. The existence of 'forgetting' as a coping mechanism and the enormous publicity given to the proponents of 'false memory syndrome' make it even more important that women's own early attempts to name their own experiences and to understand them are believed.

Secondly, it is very important to listen out for, reject and challenge ideas of self-blame, or the belief that the violence which a young woman experienced was acceptable. The belief that women provoke violence, or are able always to successfully resist if they so desire, is central to the ideology which perpetuates such violence. Some recent writers also point to the importance of acknowledging women's agency as part of the story of coping with or responding to unwanted and uninvited assault. The story of women's responsibility for the violence they experience has been internalised to some degree by everyone. Women scrutinise their own behaviour, asking themselves: 'What did I do wrong?', and it is also important to acknowledge their agency in recognising what they did as best they could. In some cases, this amounts to simply a sense of being in the wrong place at the wrong time. As Liz Kelly points out: 'That women feel they are responsible simply by "being there" demonstrates the power of the ideology that women are responsible for men's violence. That an assault happens at all becomes sufficient reason for women to feel that they might be at fault' (ibid.: 212).

Part of the role of workers is to assist young women in understanding that they are not responsible for violence committed against them. This is the beginning of a process of helping women place responsibility for violence where it belongs: with the perpetrators.

This is clearly linked to the process of building up self-respect once more. Violence often leads to a loss of self-respect, confusion, depression and breakdown. It is important for workers to be able to affirm clearly and unequivocally that violence is not an appropriate or acceptable basis for intimate relationships, that what has happened to a young woman is not acceptable, and that she does not have to accept it.

Challenging Self-blame (Contributed by Alison Healicon)

A worker had developed a supportive relationship with a young woman who accessed the service and they arranged to have some time each week to meet up in the centre. The young woman had explained to the worker that she had been dragged into her cousin's car and into a deserted field off the motorway, and had been sexually assaulted. Although it was clear to the worker that she had not been a willing participant in this incident, the young woman blamed herself for having got into the car and then not doing anything to stop her cousin when they got to the field. During their chats, the worker would reassure her that in her opinion she had done nothing to cause this situation and that it was not her fault, but it was only after the young woman was able to explain in detail what had happened that the worker could relay back to her how she had in fact done what she could to stop this situation from happening. The worker was able to put the young woman in touch with a local group to meet with other young people who had similar experiences, but remained in touch with the young woman at the centre. After a while, the young woman seemed to visibly gain confidence.

Wherever possible, workers must be prepared to offer alternatives to a young woman, and choices about how to tackle the situation as well as awareness of having exercised often self- and other-protecting agency (Warner and Reavey 2003). What kind of alternatives are available will depend very much on the age of the young woman, the statutory responsibilities this places on a worker, whether she has children who may also be at risk, and, the material resources of housing, respite accommodation and counselling available in the area. However, when a young woman can see and understand an alternative to her current situation, the pattern of self-blame and loss of self-respect can most successfully be challenged. Without such material alternatives, the work of self-recovery is greatly hampered.

Much sexual violence occurs in intimate relationships and occurs 'in the name of love'. There is a good deal a worker can do here to explore with young women their understanding of love and, without denying that their intimate relationships are indeed love relationships, to question whether love or even simply the consent to access to another person's body, inevitably involves hurt. Some groups have developed programmes of assertiveness training which enable women to clarify for themselves what they do or do not want from their relationships with others.

Finally, workers must respect the trust and confidentiality placed in them by the young women they work with, without denying the limits placed on 'in confidence' conversations by the legal responsibilities for child protection which they, in common with all adults, hold.

The Importance of Partnership

The Children Act 1989 instigated a period in which the necessary partnership between education authorities and social services departments became further reinforced as a legal duty and this was developed significantly following the Children Act 2004 (Maguire 2009). There is a duty on youth and community workers to cooperate in the implementation of the Common Assessment Framework under the leadership of Children's Services departments. Any person must assist in such enquiries if called upon to do so, unless it would be unreasonable in all the circumstances of the case. Current guidelines on partnership and safeguarding must form part of the policy framework of all youth and community work projects, and there should be no doubt in the minds of any staff employed, either in an education service, in family teams, in Children's Services, in community services, or in the health services, of their duty to refer cases of suspected abuse to locally established procedures.

It is not in the legal principles, but in the implementation of such partnership that much inter-agency discussion needs to occur. The tradition in youth work of recognising young women's rights and autonomy does not sit easily alongside the language of 'child protection'. Young women who are almost adults clearly have the ability and right to influence their own futures. It is useful, alongside recognising the general duty of child protection, to recall the important common-law 'Gillick principle', that is, 'parental right yields to the child's right to make his own decisions when he reaches a sufficient understanding and intelligence to be capable of making up his own mind on the matter requiring decision' (ibid.). This means that when girls have reached an age of sufficient understanding, they can be expected to participate in decision making which affects their care, as well as having a right to confidentiality in medical treatment.

The question of partnership between women attempting to develop feminist practice in different agencies is essential. Because the issue of violence will inevitably be present for any worker involved in informal education with girls and women, it is essential that workers are resourced and involved in inter-agency networks. Rape Crisis Centres and Women's Aid refuges are essential points of contact. There are also a number of refuges which specialise in offering support to women from diverse Black communities, although these have been pressurised by funding cuts and an approach to integration and community cohesion which marginalises such work. Members of the local social services departments (both Children's Services teams and teams working with vulnerable adults) are an essential point of reference and potential source of support. There has been a great deal of inter-professional fear and mistrust between community workers, social workers, teachers and health visitors.

The exercise of professional power in relation to young women who have experienced violence and abuse as children is fraught with difficulty, and has been defined as potentially the site of 'secondary abuse', compounding rather than counteracting the suffering that a young woman has already experienced. Social work as a profession has been expected to carry the burden of intervention for a society which believes it is right to protect children from exploitation and cruelty. The exercise of that authority can be done well or badly, in collaboration with the young woman or by ignoring her, in collaboration with other trusted adults and professionals, or in conflict and isolation. What is important is that feminists working in informal education in community settings do not isolate social workers as 'the enemy', thus potentially colluding with a persistent abuse of power in the name of retaining friendly relationships with young people.

In the statutory power of social workers to intervene, there is clearly the potential for further abuse. It is, however, also necessary to acknowledge that there is potential for alliance here, in a counter-power the law can exercise against the person perpetrating violence. In particular cases of child protection, when working through problems has not been possible on a cooperative basis, the police and the courts may have a part to play.

Young women who have a legal status as adults, through marriage, through having left the care system, or having reached the age of 18, may also choose to involve the courts and the police to ensure their own safety in cases of rape and domestic violence. At this point, the advocacy and support role of the informal educator becomes very strong. Her own need for support, the opportunity for supervision and to explore her own practice cannot be stated strongly enough.

Finding a Collective Response

When women workers become deeply involved in particular cases, it is exhausting, partly because it seems too reactive, too involved in 'Band-Aid solutions', patching women up in order to send them deeper and deeper into a war not of their own making. However, the strength of a community-based response to young women's experience of violence lies in its recognition of the prevalence and normality of violence, while continuing to stress its unacceptability.

During the process of informal education, it is possible for workers first to identify and explore the level of violence with which a particular group of women is familiar, to explore what is and is not acceptable, and to help

---

Case Study: A Young Women's Discussion and Activity Group

This is a daytime group, which has been meeting in a youth centre on an estate for about six weeks. The group is made up of young women who are all unemployed, and they are taking part in a programme of activities together and holding discussions about matters of importance to them, particularly health issues and employment issues. Ten young women attend the group, including one mixed-parentage Black woman. It is a mainly White estate.

After four weeks, one of the workers with the group notices that a particular young woman, Mary, is very subdued. She talks to Mary and finds out that she is upset. She has been told that the new baby she is expecting will automatically be very carefully monitored as a result of earlier non-accidental injuries to her first child. The worker checks this with her colleague from the 'patch' social services team, in confidence and with reference to the procedures, rather than the particular young woman involved.

The following week, Mary does not attend the group. The worker takes the opportunity to raise the question of what women expect from our relationship with men and what men expect from women, in a general way. One of the more vocal women in the group says very strongly that she never wants another man near her. Another woman mentions that perhaps Mary wouldn't want to come to the group looking a mess.

On the basis of this conversation, the worker suggests extending the programme to include some discussion of violence. Later, she becomes involved in the question of how increasing women's assertiveness in relationships can provoke a backlash from men. The group becomes a place where this 'backlash' is shared and coped with. Some silences have been challenged.

However, after the early weeks, the one Black woman who was attending the group stops coming. Much later, when the worker visits her, she finds out that it is because she has been told not to come by one of the other women in the group. Now the worker realises the need to find ways of breaking the silence about women not as coping with violence, but as perpetrators of it: in this case of racial harassment. And she can make some connections about intimidation: the experience of intimidation by male partners, and the experience of intimidation by a white majority.

As happens so often, the themes of violence and harassment became part of the group work by inclusion of young women's experience. If the experience had not been voiced by the young women, would the worker have voiced it?

young women understand the nature of the violence against them. It is also possible for workers to affirm young women's capacities for survival.

In working with a group, it is very important that a worker shows that she is able to pick up cues, and to instigate and build on conversations. It is through talking with a purpose that much of the valuable work of education occurs. Because so much of women's experience of violence has been made private and silenced, the process of finding a vocabulary and a name for what is happening becomes of the utmost importance. The case studies which follow all suggest ways, at a number of different levels, in which the process of naming and finding a voice can occur.

In another young women's project in a mainly White, working-class area, the workers identified a young Sri Lankan woman living in great isolation with a very violent English husband. In this case, the workers' strategy was to support the creation of a group including other Asian women, which she could attend. It is possible to move from identifying individual needs to establishing group processes in response.

Putting Violence on the Group Work Agenda Explicitly

Another approach is to include the issue of violence in group work from the very beginning, perhaps by including questions about the acceptability of violent behaviour in discussions about conditions for working well together. Many youth workers start working with groups by establishing 'ground rules' for work, and this often includes conditions which are understood and stated to be non-negotiable. Such conditions might include 'no discrimination', 'no personal attacks', 'no threats or intimidation'. Among many groups of girls who meet informally through community projects or youth centres, there are already well-established norms which run counter to those proposed ground rules.

Two part-time workers were working from a feminist perspective with a group of girls, both Black and White, who were members of a youth centre on an outer estate. They approached establishing a project with a group of girls by first of all paying attention to the issues that already existed among girls.

One of the workers in particular was horrified by the level of aggression and bullying that existed among the girls, and it was apparent that there was a good deal of competition for boys among them. There was, to some extent, an economic competition, particularly in relation to who could get most for least on a Friday night, both in terms of having nothing to spend financially and of 'giving away' least sexually. The workers were clear that (hetero)sexuality and money were closely linked for the young women, that the competition and aggression among the girls were tied into the sexual/economic marketplace in which boys and girls related. The girls were also strongly anti-lesbian and attacked one of the workers as a lesbian.

On the basis of their observations, the workers decided to establish a programme of discussions based on the theme of resisting rape and sexual violence. The most aggressive girls in the group found this very hard to deal with, rehearsing the view that 'girls only get raped if they ask for it' very persistently and loudly. The workers struggled with a decision about whether the group was viable, either with or without the participation of the girls who were so vocal. In the end, the problem solved itself, as the most vocal girls stopped attending. The workers then set up a residential activity weekend for girls. Evaluations of the weekend record 'I thought the idea of going in just a female group was better than a mixed group because we could relax more and the boys tend to mess about.'

In her own reflections, the worker later observed that perhaps 'she had gone in at the deep end' in trying to work on the question of 'rape' from the beginning, and that she would be able to do this much more successfully, now she had established relationships of confidence and trust with the girls, partly as a result of sharing a successful activity weekend with them. The complexities of sex and violence and context which surround rape create a challenge for group workers who need to be able to live with the complexity and ambivalence of women's own accounts (Gavey 2004).

Successful group work on the theme of violence does seem to depend on workers having a clear agenda and an intention to break the silences and collusions about violence, while at the same time working at a pace that young women themselves can be at ease with.

Violence Towards Children as a Problem for Women's Groups

Projects which attempt to establish non-violence as a basic method of working often struggle about how to respond to mothers' aggression towards their children. The Zion Community Health Centre in Hulme supported the Aisha childcaring group. In this context, project volunteers were able to develop training packages and policies to help them cope with issues such as difficult and challenging behaviour, as well as policies on assertive discipline and equal opportunities. It became possible for workers to hold discussions with mothers about the way they were treating their children, particularly in relation to smacking as a means of discipline, because the project was attending to young women's needs as a priority. In the context of a mainly Black (African-Caribbean) group, the issue of avoiding the brutalisation and criminalisation of another generation of young Black men is of great importance. Issues of how to de-escalate the level of violence which the whole community experiences are of great importance. Workers were able to relate discussions of childcare to the whole climate in which children are being raised.

The Canklow Community Project in Rotherham, Yorkshire, was established by a social services department and showed that a community-based approach to preventive work in childcare could be very successful in reducing the numbers of children on the 'at risk' register and 'in case' in a particular district:

> Better knowledge of networks and the general workings of the estate taught us more about certain families whose children had regular visits to hospital and were considered 'at risk'. The families were in fact under intense pressure with too many under-5s in the home, often with a single adult to supervise the children. Welfare rights information was instrumental in obtaining fireguards, safety gates, and where people were not entitled to these, voluntary groups were contacted for second hand items. Accessibility and the removing of worker/client barriers meant that vulnerable families came sooner with unpayable gas and electricity bills and Canklow's reputation as 'twilight city' was lessened as people did deals with the fuel suppliers on the telephone or agreed to let DHSS remove fuel payments at source. Previously some social workers had been called out in the middle of winter to unknown people with no gas or electricity, with all the resulting chaos. More than one family had been broken up by the need to receive children into care in such a situation, and the rehabilitation where possible of these families was an early priority.

> Although our building is owned by the 'welfare', it was important to welcome parents feeling under pressure from childcare, and to help residents feel that they had some control over the building. It was not always easy to dovetail this control with what management wanted from the building or the project: an on-going balancing act was required; a stroll through a minefield may have been a better analogy at times. With women's groups and a general drop-in situation, coupled with liaison from other agencies on the best methods of intervention, the numbers in both categories – on the 'at risk register' and children in care – show a steady decrease and both have been firmly established in single figures for some three years.

The Movement from 'Victim' to 'Survivor'

Workers in projects where young women are being supported after experiences of sexual violence – including projects in which young women have seen the offender punished by the judgment of a court – have stressed the importance of group work linked to counselling as a method of developing self-help (Batsleer et al. 2002, Warner and Reavey 2003).

Young women need help in expressing anger, which often turns either inwards to self-harm and depression, or outwards into aggression. Young women also need support in moving away from self-blame and to move from a 'victim' identity to a 'survivor' identity. The idea of being a 'survivor' is an important way of acknowledging that young women are still alive after having experienced life-threatening events. It acknowledges the seriousness of the suffering which many women have endured in the experience of sexual violence, and the ways that suffering is connected to killing, either in the form of the assaults suffered or in later despair, self-harm, or attempted suicide. It also acknowledges the ordinary, everyday heroism of women who survive such threats. It can, however, become another obstacle if it seems to lock young women into an identity in which the experience of violence is the defining aspect of their lives (Nicholls 1994).

Group work based in informal education can enable young women who are 'survivors' to survive by letting go and regaining a sense of everydayness in their lives.

A social support group for young women survivors of sexual violence which was established in Manchester at Forty Second Street, a resource for young people under stress, expressed the following aims in a publicity leaflet:

- to create a safe space for young women survivors of sexual violence, by validating their experience as young women and as survivors;
- to encourage mutual support and ownership of the group;
- to provide a mixture of structured and unstructured activities/ discussion topics, and
- to strive for a balance between social/fun activities, and opportunity for young women to talk about what's giving them a hard time.

Education Programmes

The most important contribution that can be made by the work of community-based informal education is the development of education programmes which shift the emphasis away from victim-blaming by exploring myths and stereotypes and encouraging young women to define and assert for themselves what is and is not acceptable behaviour in relationships. The Zero Tolerance campaign has undertaken this work of political education very effectively through an advertising campaign. Community education workers linked to Rape Crisis projects and Women's Aid have developed programmes of education and training which are appropriate both for use with girls in school in the context of personal and social education classes, and for the training of workers in community projects. They explore the basis of myths and stereotypes about sexual violence, often by instigating discussion of statements which highlight those myths including:

- 'If a girl has agreed to sex before with a boy, she can't be raped.'
- 'A lot of women enjoy a fight/a beating. They look for rough men.'
- 'If you have an arranged marriage, you can't expect to consent to sex.'
- 'If you dress in a sexy way, you can't complain if boys bother you.'
- 'She can't have been raped, because she didn't resist.'
- 'Black men have a stronger sex drive than White men.'
- 'Black women ask for it more than White women because they are more physical.'

Workers then focus on exploring attitudes through discussion and enabling young women and young men to establish and understand a non-violent code of behaviour.

'Alternatives to Violence' workshops are also being established, to explore methods of resisting the escalation of conflict in communities, and these including workshops on resisting violence against women. However, all the education and consciousness-raising and support work which continues in relation to young women's experience of violence must be set in the context of a decline in material resources which can offer positive alternatives and which can strengthen women's position relative to that of men, not only emotionally but also economically. Clearly, there is a great deal to be gained from young women sharing strategies and ideas for survival. Apparently simple features of good practice – such as creating an atmosphere of enjoyment, offering peace and quiet and respite – are all part and parcel of a commitment to affirming young women's capabilities for survival. But a safe haven is never going to be enough. Women's resistance to violence must be understood in the context of women's struggle against domination in all its forms.

Raising Awareness

It was identified amongst a group of young people that they would like to find out about different forms of oppression and a group was formed to look at issues of oppression over a number of weeks. The sessions were organised in a similar way each time and involved worker-led time and discussions focused around particular YouTube clips, newspaper articles, exercises and games. The worker would introduce the topic and provide some definitions, statistics and examples of what it feels like to experience racism, disablism, homophobia, classism and sexism, and so on, that the young people could then debate in relation to the clips and articles and to their own experiences or the experiences of someone they knew. In some sessions, guests were invited in to talk with the group about their experiences as youth work practitioners. One of the guests was a representative from a local women's organisation who works with women who have experienced sexual violence. During the session, the worker provided the legal definition of sexual violence and some statistics which demonstrated that sexual violence is perpetrated mostly by known men, and talked about the work of the organisation. The debate for this session revolved around rape myths such as 'women ask for it by their clothing, how they behave and what they say'; that 'rape occurs outside in a dark alley at night with a stranger'; 'if a woman didn't get hurt it couldn't have been rape', and 'once a man is sexually aroused he can't be stopped.'

Some of the young people were shocked to hear that most sexual violence occurs within intimate relationships or is perpetrated by someone the woman knows. Some were critical of the definitions and statistics and wanted to understand how sexual violence against men fitted into this debate. Some related the discussion to their own experiences. There was a lot of interest in the group and the debate was lively, but it was afterwards that some of the consequences of such discussion could be evidenced. The worker was approached immediately after and then in the days and weeks following the session by a few of the individuals from the group who wanted to talk about their own similar experiences of sexual violence. The session had enabled the young people to meet with a worker from a different organisation, and thereby establish a connection.

As a group, the young people were encouraged to make links between the different experiences of oppression and to consider their own experiences in order to think further than their own experiences and to identify what oppression is and how it can be challenged. In an evaluation the group expressed how much they had learnt and how valuable to them it had been in terms of changing their attitudes and prejudices about certain groups of people.

Support for Women Workers

Facing up to the presence of violence in the lives of women very often means that women workers have to face up to the presence of violence in their own lives, sometimes for the first time, and understandings may be triggered as a result of events in a group. Sometimes, women are returned to the question of violence with a fresh perception and consciousness.

It is not good practice for any woman to work solely or exclusively on issues of violence. It is certainly not work that should be sustained indefinitely. Networks of women workers can help enormously in sustaining a feminist focus and analysis. They can provide encouragement and balance to relieve some of the stress created by the work. One of the main functions of women workers' groups is to organise this kind of support activity, and it needs to be regarded as a necessity, not a luxury. Networks of feminist workers can also provide an opportunity to establish more formal links of supervision for workers, and this is essential when workers are involved in work about violence, which can be extremely emotionally demanding. It can also be extremely exhilarating, and it is important that insights gained in the process of undertaking work in this area are shared.

Feminist support networks are sustained on the basis of a recognition of connection: connection between workers, and connections between workers and the young women who are part of the groups and projects. Claiming a 'professional' identity, claiming appropriate support and developing appropriate working methods are essential and are important methods of avoiding the temptations to take on the sufferings of the world and become exhausted. It is very important that work against sexual violence is sustained and that workers are not exhausted. It is also important that the 'professional' identity does not become a barrier, a place of relative security, from which 'concern' is expressed, and not solidarity. To work as a feminist means to take the risk of acknowledging your connectedness with the violence women experience, and to develop strategies for work on that basis. In this way, 'creative support' may begin to create the conditions for change. Much of this work of support is about making it possible for certain stories to be told and heard, both by young women and by women workers.

Telling Stories

At the moment, our culture seems fascinated with the violation of childhood. A feminist account of violence must give real importance to the words which young women themselves use to explain their experience. At any point, the experience of violence may not be the most significant aspect of a young woman's position. She may be more concerned to identify immediate issues that are affecting her than to recall earlier experiences of violence – especially at the point where contact with 'professionals' makes her most vulnerable, and where forgetting may be the most effective means of coping.

In that case, it is most appropriate for workers to respond to the 'here-and-now' demands of young women. These may be for safety on the streets if they are homeless, in relation to sex with clients if they are working as prostitutes, for basic support in relation to housing needs, in access to washing and laundry facilities, and even for warmth and shelter.

There may be a danger in the focus on sexual violence, particularly when it is linked to therapeutic accounts of healing the pain of the past, recovering past pain, healing and letting go. The danger lies in the tendency of this narrative to overwhelm all other accounts, including the specific accounts offered by young women (Warner and Reavey 2003). The professional, therapeutic voice then becomes the dominant voice, rather than simply being 'one account among others'. How does this happen? First, there is a tendency – inherited from psychoanalysis – to look beyond the 'presenting problem' to a deeper structure. So, self-harm or homelessness or prostitution become the presenting problem – whereas the deep structure is a familiar pattern of male violence rooted in family forms. The account of this 'deep structure' seems more truthful than the 'surface' accounts of the present. Indeed, other accounts can then be presented as avoidances and resistances, coping strategies, which may eventually fail unless the underlying problem is faced. This in-built ability to contain other accounts is very attractive to professionals, especially as it seems to offer a clear route for individual progress and change. The transition from 'victim' to 'survivor' comes to seem manageable, achievable within the power of a small group, or even within the power of an individual. Other accounts can seem more random, even provocative. Young women explain that they cut themselves up 'because they want to', that life is a game of 'survival of the fittest' and that bullies always win, or else they are living on the street because they are homeless, and they are homeless because they were evicted and have no money.

It is also possible that the focus on sexual violence is attractive for a certain form of feminist politics. It does allow a clear attention and a particular focus for demands for change. But such political clarity will not be successful alone. And it cannot be achieved by ignoring the voices of those it most desires to represent.

Sexual violence occurs in all communities, and the expectation that it will be more prevalent in Black communities is part of the racism which Black women have encountered when attempting to tackle the experience of violence on their own terms. Alliances between Black women's refuges and White feminist groups campaigning against sexual violence have sometimes been tense, especially when, for example, White feminist groups have overlooked the racism of housing allocation policies or the assumptions of social services departments in favour of apparently rather self-indulgent 'racism awareness training' (Mama 1989, Batsleer et al. 2002).

However, the methods and principles explored in this chapter are the basis for work against violence against women in every community. When racial and sexual violence are inseparable – for example, in the context of racist attacks on Asian women within their homes, or in the practice of immigration controls which may require women to remain in violent relationships in order to secure citizenship rights – the process of making explicit and public the nature of the problem, turning cases into issues and issues into movements, is still of primary importance.

Explicitly exposing the ideologies which support racial and sexual violence is a basic education task. And the methods for supporting women who blame themselves or minimise the effect of such violence are rooted, whatever the context or the community, in an acceptance and belief that women are not to blame and are not to be blamed for the violence that is perpetrated against them, even whilst recognising women's agency in negotiating such violent encounters.

Supporting Activism

A worker at a centre had noticed a small group of young women who didn't join in with any activities and who felt themselves to be different from the rest of the group. They talked to the worker regularly about school and how their opinions were sometimes discredited by other students and some of the teachers. The worker realised that the opinions they were expressing could be regarded as feminist and when she mentioned this word to the young women they laughed and said that they weren't feminists.

After a while the worker who had links with women's organisations in the area was invited to attend a MillionWomenRise march in London for International Women's Day and she asked the young women if they would be interested in going along with her and some other women from the group. At first, the young women were reluctant but as the time got nearer to the event, four of the group decided to go. The worker explained what the march was for, why it was being held on that particular day and how it linked in with a global network. She gave them information and suggested different websites they could look at to find out more about it. On the coach, the young women met others from around the region and became involved in discussions with them. One of the groups on the coach was going to be speaking at the event in London and the young women were interested to hear what they had to say. The young women participated in the march around London and were taking note of the reactions from the bystanders. They listened to some of the speeches before deciding they wanted to go and do some sightseeing. On the coach back, they were engaged in conversations with others.

After this event, the young women decided they wanted to be involved in some way with one of the women's organisations who worked with the issue of sexual violence. A meeting was arranged with the manager of the organisation and the young women asked what the possibilities were of them being involved. Due to time constraints (the young women were studying) and the need for volunteers to take part in the organisations training, they all decided that as funding was always a priority, they would organise a fundraising activity. The manager explained some of the legalities involved in fundraising and the young women went home to consider what they wanted to do. The young women went into school and negotiated with the staff to hold a cake sale, as they thought this would be the most profitable way of raising some money for the organisation. A date was set, posters and cakes made. The young women set up their stall and had leaflets available for anyone asking what they were raising money for. Some odd comments were made, but the young women were able to raise over £50 which they presented to the organisation a week later. The group have received a formal thank-you letter from the organisation and their time was much appreciated. The young women were able to find out more about the issue which fitted with their developing opinions of the world.

9   Community, Culture and Identity

More than ever, in the context of a society struggling with attempts to assert an anti-European, anti-immigrant culture as the basis of 'Britishness', the themes of this chapter matter. There is a re-emergence of Black feminist/ womanist activism in the UK, and it is on the themes highlighted by such networks and writers that this chapter draws.

The words 'community', 'culture' and 'identity' are all difficult and complicated, capable of conveying in each case several meanings, which may be diametrically opposed. If each term is separately difficult, together they represent a nightmare for communication, so full are they of conflicted ideological resonance.

'Community', 'culture' and 'identity' are battlegrounds and girls are at the centre of the skirmishing. They are each necessary words in the discussion of the practice of informal education and community development. I have explicitly chosen these words, rather than the alternative vocabulary of 'discourse' and 'discursive practices', since they seem to me more suggestive of the link between language and meaning and the material world, without expressly privileging language. This chapter begins with an attempt to excavate some of their meanings and then focuses on current practice which explicitly addresses 'community', 'culture' and 'identity'.

Community

Like the word 'empowerment', to which it is connected, the word 'community' acts as an aerosol spray, conveying an unlikely smell of sweetness to whatever phrase it is attached. It is rarely used with a negative connotation. Yet 'community' can readily connote an authoritarian form of social relationship, with a strong emphasis on duty and a lesser emphasis on individual autonomy and rights. In Britain, during the last fifteen years, there has been an increasing sense of fragmentation and division. Margaret

Thatcher, as prime minister, espoused a political creed which placed a strong emphasis on the benefits of competitive individualism. This was not a good period for 'community education'. Now the destructive nature of competitive individualism is increasingly being acknowledged. Women, because of our role in the family, which has often been seen as the cornerstone of community, are once more looked to as bearers of community or 'the big society'.

In the context of an increasing commitment to the values of community rather than the values of individualism, the understanding of appropriate opportunities for girls to develop will be framed by shared community values. Whilst it seems likely that women will benefit when the values of mutual aid, association and cooperation are asserted, this is by no means assured, and, as Elizabeth Frazer and Nicola Lacey argued clearly in *The Politics of Community*, communitarianism, as it is currently expressed as a political theory, holds many dangers for women (Frazer and Lacey 1994).

Community and the Industrial Working Class

It is important to recall the association of the term 'community' with the history of the industrial working class and its inheritance. Current attempts to reclaim the word 'community' within Labour Party thinking on 'Blue Labour' may in part be testimony to this, and the association of the word 'community' with oppressed and exploited groups may reassert itself. Working-class culture, as it emerged in Britain, created community organisations – organisations such as the trade unions and the cooperative movement – which focused on meeting common rather than individual needs through mutual aid.

There is certainly a moral value placed on 'community' and 'sociability', and it is seen as preferable to 'selfishness'. However, the basic reference point of 'community' is not morality. It is a sense of material necessity and a historical practice of organising within workplaces and within neighbourhoods to overcome, or at least to diminish, some of the difficulties of life in industrial and urban society.

As some of the forms of life, including particular workplaces and neighbourhoods – particularly those associated with heavy manufacturing industry – have disappeared, there has been grieving and a sense of loss for earlier forms of working-class community (Williams 1989, Seabrook 1978). Alongside the grieving, there has been expressed, over and over again, a hope that women might, for the future, continue to develop and create new forms of community: often, it is recognised despite, rather than because of, the active contribution of men (Seabrook 1978, Campbell 1993).

Bea Campbell's very moving account of the experiences of young people on some of the most poverty-stricken estates in Britain, *Goliath* (1993), suggested that a gender conflict was occurring in communities which takes the form of a 'crisis of masculinity'. She depicted women as rooted in our responsibilities for kinship – for children and for older people – in relations of community support and community building. When traditional sources of honour and self-respect for men are removed, she suggested– particularly those associated with hard, waged work – it seems that only violence remains as a focus for masculinity.

The struggle which most dramatised that crisis for the white, industrial working class was the 1984–85 miners' strike. It is important to notice the essential role of women's organising in the long duration of that struggle, and the fact that, in many parts of the coalfields, it is the women's centres which were established in the aftermath of the dispute which are the strike's most enduring legacy. One of the women activists during the strike spoke of the work of the women's groups as the work of 'putting the bread on the table' and the phrase has stuck as an enduring description of women's work of community organising (Hyatt and Caulkins 1992). Informal education work with girls and young women can contribute to a process of community-building.

Community and the Life of 'Ethnic Minorities'

Girls and women are looked to at every level and across communities in a multi-ethnic society to create and sustain social bonds. But there is a danger that the term 'community' will come to have only a specialised reference to 'ethnic minority communities', as in the term, 'community relations council'.

Black communities in Britain are increasingly identified as bearers of a sense of community, of culture and identity, of cohesion, almost, it sometimes seems, on behalf of the majority and powerful society, where there is a lack of the qualities which these terms signify. There is a curious sense of envy generated within White society, as if the very cultural and community forms which have been created in the context of exploitation and oppression are not only a source of pride, but also a source of privilege in Black communities, to which White society is denied access.

It is important that youth and community workers acknowledge the sources of such community, and do not imagine that it is simply available for appropriation or copying in any setting. At the same time, second- and third-generation Black British young women have a great deal to teach about the ways new forms of community are developing; this will be explored later in this chapter.

Culture

'Culture' has been used to refer to 'the whole way of life and whole way of struggle' of a people. The term points to the connection between the material and expressive, communicative dimensions of human life.

The Rhetoric of Multiculturalism

Floya Anthias and Nira Yuval Davis have pointed out that in the rhetoric of multiculturalism in education, people are understood as connected to a community through language. They suggest that the rhetoric of multiculturalism is based on 'community' (in contrast to the way that the rhetoric of anti-racism is based on colour) (Anthias and Davis 1991, Ahmed 2004). Much positive work that is undertaken with girls and young women draws on language, meaning and culture and is thereby involved in the recognition and creation and unsettling or disruption of identities and histories.

The danger of one powerful version of a multicultural approach is that communities have been defined in opposition and antagonism to one another, as if each were indeed an island. Each community has been seen as homogeneous and with clearly identifiable male community leaders. There was no attention to class or caste divisions within particular language communities, and no attention to the dominant culture and its forms of racism, or to the class divisions within the dominant culture. In other words, there is a danger that only minority and Black cultures will be named as 'communities' in this way, leaving the communities of the White majority unexamined and in a position of silence and sometimes dominance.

In the most naïve forms of multicultural education, culture is seen as homogeneous. But on any definition, 'culture' must be understood as moving, mixed, shifting, full of antagonisms and contradictions and newness, familiar oppositions and strange, unexpected mutualities (Soni 2011).

No Culture is Fixed or Homogeneous

Paul Gilroy has done more than any other writer in Britain recently to give an account of this context. In 'One Nation Under a Groove', Gilroy contrasted racist accounts of culture with the historical emergence of new cultures in the inner cities. In a discussion of cultural racism, he wrote:

> Culture is conceived along ethnically absolute lines, not as something intrinsically fluid, changing, unstable and dynamic, but as a fixed property of social groups rather than a relational field in which they counter one another and live out social,

historical relationships. When culture is brought into contact with 'race' it is transformed into a pseudo-biological category of communal life. (Gilroy 1993: 24)

On the other hand, in the lived realities of post-war history:

It is now impossible to speak coherently of Black culture in Britain in isolation from the culture of Britain as a whole. This is particularly true as far as leisure is concerned. Black expressive culture has decisively shaped youth culture, pop culture and the culture of city life in Britain's metropolitan centres. The White working class has danced for forty years to its syncopated rhythms. There is of course no contradiction between making use of Black culture and loathing real live Black people, yet the informal, long term processes through which different groups have negotiated each other have intermittently created a 'two-tone' sensibility which celebrates its hybrid origins and has provided a significant opposition to 'common-sense' racialism. (Ibid.: 34)

Given the extent to which women are positioned as 'relationship-makers', it is not surprising that in the youth cultures of city life which Gilroy celebrated and defended, it is young women very often who are the bridge-builders, namers and source of connection. Informal education work with girls and young women from different communities needs to engage more and more with the creation and celebration of new hybridities of womanhood for the future.

Identity

In the work of community building, racism is clearly both a powerful and destructive connection between different groups as well as form of love of the self-same group which is predicated on and defined through separation from and hatred of those defined as 'other' (Ahmed 2004). The construction of identity always involves a 'cut' in the chain of meanings (Hall 2000), and what is celebrated also has its shadow-side of denigration. When racism harnesses the term 'culture' in the way Paul Gilroy suggests – producing notions of self-contained and pseudo-biological groups – it also promotes concepts of 'identity' as relying on a recognition of sameness, and an exclusion and definition of the 'other'. Identity can be built as a defensive/ aggressive shield, to ward off 'the other' and to promote the recognition of the self-same. Building up the sense of community among the English residents of an area, for example, usually means building up a climate for racist attacks on people perceived as 'foreigners'. And this can be done without categories of 'race' or 'colour' ever being mentioned (Dadzie 1997).

Community building and the strengthening of identity can, however, be undertaken in a spirit of resistance to dominant definitions and out of a desire for affiliation and connection. So, in many parts of British cities, people from local neighbourhoods have rallied to shout: 'People of Hulme ... People of Newham ... People of Bolton ... have the right, here to stay, here to fight!' These have been the themes of anti-deportation campaigns in which people deemed 'illegals' by the government have been welcomed and sustained in particular neighbourhoods. Here, an identification with a particular neighbourhood has come to mean not a closing of ranks against outsiders, but a celebration of diversity and the principle of sanctuary (Cohen 2003).

Identity as a Form of Resistance

Patricia Hill Collins, writing in a North American context, expressed the importance of building up Black women's identity and community in the process of resistance to racism. She writes of the work of bloodmothers and 'othermothers' in extending and transmitting, both in their own families and in the family of the community, an Afrocentric world view. Hill Collins writes:

> The power of Black women was the power to make culture, to transmit folkways, norms and customs, as well as to build shared ways of seeing the world that insured our survival ... This power was neither economic nor political, nor did it translate into female dominance. This culture was a culture of resistance, essential to the struggle for group survival. (Hill Collins 1991: 147)

However, Hill Collins emphasised that in developing this power of Black women, Black feminist knowledge is rooted also in a recognition of a matrix of oppression:

> Dialogue is critical to the success of this epistemological approach, the type of dialogue long extant in the Afrocentric call-and-response tradition, whereby power dynamics are fluid, everyone has a voice, but everyone must listen and respond to other voices in order to remain in the community. Sharing a common cause fosters dialogue and encourages groups to transcend their differences. (Ibid.: 237)

In the British context, West Indian women whose families faced the brunt of racism in British organisations in the late 1940s and early 1950s were instrumental in establishing numerous voluntary and self-help organisations in the cities. These included Black churches, self-help projects on health, supplementary schools for children, and housing associations (Bryan et al. 1985). Similar initiatives have occurred within

Bangladeshi and Pakistani communities, and there has been a strong, continuing connection with women and families 'at home' in Bangladesh and Pakistan, where conditions of poverty are different yet again. Sometimes, the channels for connection between communities are religious organisations and affiliations, which are then able to cross other kinds of belonging – even language, colour and nationality – in the name of faith. Aid to Bosnian Muslims and to Bosnian refugees was a good example of this kind of connection in the 1990s (Wilson 2006).

Attention to the building up of identity in the context of racism is a necessary strategy. In resisting racism, it is probably equally necessary to build up the networks, places and resources in which old exclusionary identities can be transformed and even disappear.

Identity, Culture and Community as Aspects of Resistance to Domination

As already noted, the critics of multicultural education have pointed out that attention to 'culture' and 'identity' is not sufficient to help children or adults understand or challenge racism. The phrase 'beyond saris, steel bands and samosas' has been used to indicate the necessity of developing educational strategies which promote community development and which challenge racism. It highlights the appropriation and fetishising of elements of culture and identity for the benefit of the powerful: the White Europeans who need to learn about 'difference'. When elements of a culture are fetishised and uprooted in this way, it destroys the recognition of culture as activity, of community as work. Difference becomes packaged into stereotypes, and these then prevent support services being developed which promote active participation. However, the attack on multiculturalism as an educational ideology should not be used to dismiss the importance of some of the most basic needs a community has: for food, clothing and expression.

'Putting bread on the table' is work. The teaching of a mother tongue – so basic to the constitution of culture and identity in any definition – is work. And it is women's work, whether the bread is chapatti or rice or jam sandwiches, and whether the tongue is the English of the industrial North or the Punjabi of rural Pakistan or the Sylheti of Bangladesh. Despite the fact that the languages have very different status (as does the food), such shared activity may provide a basis of connection, just as Gilroy suggests the expressive culture of Black music can.

Culture, identity and community, when they are understood as aspects of resistance to domination, can be reclaimed as sources for challenging racism. Informal education with girls and young women has an important part to play in this process. In the rest of this chapter, I will look briefly at some of the 'false starts' that were made, and then point to a number of positive directions.

The Problems of Multiculturalism and 'Race Awareness' in Youth and Community Work

It is now widely believed that the multicultural approaches and the development of 'race awareness training' which took place in youth and community work during the 1980s had a limited and even destructive potential and effect, because they failed to address the needs of Black communities and at the same time did not take account of the power of the dominant culture.

White feminist projects were one of the places where the challenge of multiculturalism and 'race awareness' was most keenly embraced. The forms which the engagement took led all too often to 'guilt-tripping' and a consequent failure to develop strategies for change. As Sivanandan noted at the time, the guilt of the privileged is a useful mechanism for appearing to acknowledge injustice while leaving existing social relationships intact. It is useful to distinguish this from 'feeling ashamed' and the movement associated with shame – a judgement against one's own standards and a desire to see them reached.

This sense of guilt certainly did exist among White feminists in the 1980s, and when the philosophy of multiculturalism was combined with a particular form of 'identity politics', as it seemed to be in the equal opportunities strategies associated particularly with the Inner London Education Authority, a pattern of provision emerged which seemed to suggest that women could only work with girls out of a sense of shared identity. It was also suggested that the most powerful basis for work with girls was a commitment to developing culture and identity.

Clara Connolly's memorable account of these processes in 'Splintered Sisterhood' (1990) is a recognisable one, when she suggested that the emphasis on culture and identity in her project led to a failure to challenge girls (perhaps White girls in particular), a failure to build alliances against specific injustices, such as violence against girls and women, or police attacks on given communities, and a failure to recognise the importance of cultural work which was forward-looking – such as the creation of Black British identities – rather than rooted in the (already-formed?) identities of adult workers. Not all multicultural work, even in London, shared these failings, and in some areas, the continuing alliances that were forged during the anti-racist movement of the 1970s re-emerged in the 1990s, only a little shaken and are much needed again (Shukra 2010). Youth workers in the London Borough of Tower Hamlets who were instrumental in establishing some of the earliest girls' and young women's groups in the 1970s were still to be found active in the 1990s in organising women to oppose the British National Party candidate on the Isle of Dogs.

In cities where the communities which have attempted to build alliances are smaller, the issue has been as much one of lack of power, policy and resources to support initiatives such as Black resource centres and Black women's centres as it has been a failure of aims and purposes, which have clearly been focused in building coalitions across communities rather than in any form of cultural separatism.

In response to the failures of a multicultural agenda, there was an attempt, within the field of youth and community work, to develop a Black perspective. The term 'Black' was understood to make reference to a political identity, forged out of resistance to imperialism, racism and White supremacy. (Various understandings of Black perspectives are found in the journal *Youth and Policy*, Summer 1995, devoted to the theme of 'Black Perspectives'.)

Optimistically, Black perspectives can be in alliance with non-racial/anti-racist perspectives which emerge from within White communities. The importance of the shift to Black perspectives was that it removes attention from the relationship between dominant and subordinate groups, rather in the way that separate and autonomous work with women removes the pressure of male dominance. It enables the work of building up intercultural alliances between Black communities to occur.

It is essential that the contribution of women to the development of Black perspectives is not marginalised, so the next part of this chapter considers some key contributions from Black women. It is also important – in the spirit of call-and-response – that the relationships between women from both Black and White communities continue to be explored, and it is with current practice in this area that the chapter ends.

The Contribution of Women to the Development of Black Perspectives

Nationality

A number of women identified the re-emergence since the 1990s, of nationality and religion as a focus for community-building among Black

British girls. Here, the new generation are seen as offering new perspectives to an older generation of educators. Although the term 'Black' is readily used as a shorthand, it is always qualified often by reference to religion or nationality. 'Yemeni', 'Pakistani', 'Bangladeshi', 'Somali' are as useful and salient as terms as are 'Muslims', 'Sikh', or 'Hindu.` These differences are recognised as differences, rather than necessarily mobilised as antagonisms within the alliance of 'Black'.

The issue of nationality and belonging is highly political, and it is also one in which the status of women as dependent on husbands or parents is clearly scrutinised. For example, the migration of young women from Pakistan, Bangladesh and India was made very difficult by the 'primary purpose rule', which made entry to Britain illegal if the primary purpose of migration was marriage (Lal and Wilson 1986). The dual claim to a right to belong in Britain and to participate without discrimination in British society as an equal citizen, and also to claim affiliation and connection with one's history and family roots/routes, is necessary for girls who wish to claim both equality and autonomy. In the North-west, there is an active tradition of community work involvement in anti-deportation campaigning, and the place of young women in these campaigns, sometimes in support of other women who have used their homes as 'sanctuaries', is of great importance (Weller 1987, Sharma and Berry 2008).

Religion

Religious faith, and particularly the increasing significance of Islam in a number of different Black communities, is also seen as having been played down by earlier generations of community educators and as needing to be reasserted. Some women workers believe that a clear understanding of Islam from a woman-centred perspective will allow the bonds between different generations of women – particularly between mothers and daughters – to be expressed, renewed and developed, so that new possibilities can emerge for women now settled in Britain. There has also been some recollection of the part which Christianity played in the development of projects in Britain rooted in the West Indian communities.

Spiritual traditions are again proving themselves to be a resource of enormous importance. Each of the major religions offers an account of the significance and value of human life that can be set against the hostility and oppression which Black communities often face in White supremacist societies (Jarret Macaulay 1996). The continued growth of the independent Black churches with their roots in the Caribbean, the significance of Islam in a number of different Black communities, both African and Asian, the traditions of Sikhism and Hinduism – each offers a resource independent of the dominant European, Christian traditions. Religion also often poses a complex challenge to women, for the patriarchal nature and continuing male control of women is a major source of the power of the faith. Sakinna Dickinson, a youth and community worker in Tameside writes:

> Religion is an active force in all areas of life (within Asian communities anyway) and there it is necessary to enable discussion and debate to take place ... This is not the same as a religious practice group. Women can only shape an Islamic personal and social framework for themselves if they are clear about their own rights and responsibilities within that framework.

A similar argument could certainly be made for women attempting to explore their relationships to other religious faiths.

It seems that the meanings of particular religious or cultural practices for women appear very different from 'inside' or 'outside' faith traditions. For example, the practice of wearing the hijab (veil), which has seemed so clearly a mark of female subordination to those outside the tradition, has become a mark of pride and self-respect for many Muslim young women. It is an assertion of individual allegiances and identity.

Particularly in relation to sexuality, religion can offer young women a way of marking a distance from the dominant commercialisation of female sexuality in capitalist societies. At the same time, all religions can produce a veil of ignorance and control of women (despite the recent apology by the Pope to all women), and what is appropriate for women is still defined by men rather than by women themselves.

Women educators working within the context of the 'appropriate' as defined by faith communities, often find themselves working at the boundaries of 'appropriateness'. There are questions about whether the women workers themselves are trustworthy, whether they can be accepted as sharing the faith even if they choose to express it differently, how they communicate a sense of respect for the older generation of women while enabling girls to make their own interpretations of the traditions the community offers. Workers find themselves needing to make clear delineations between a response to racism and issues which are issues of culture. For some women, the teachings on equality in the Koran offer a very clear basis for undertaking separate work with Muslim girls. Yet in practice, the development of Asian young women's groups, which have existed in many local authority areas, is a response to both racism and cultural requirements. Such Asian girls groups can organise events at times and with themes that are acceptable to parents and in doing so attempt to build a sense of 'women's space' across generations, in a society that has little understanding of the strength and resource of Asian women, and thereby to enable both young women and their own community to develop with pride. It is hoped that this will strengthen women in dealing both with conflicts with men within their own communities, and with the pathological view of Asian girls and women as passive victims, which is still the dominant view in British society.

For example, the Asian Girls' Drama Project in Leeds linked with youth workers to promote drama projects with Asian young women. Asian girls' groups in Leeds at present offer a safe space for women to meet and talk and work confidentially. For some of the young women the group is one – and perhaps the only – place where they can voice their ideas and beliefs without fear of judgement. Some issues young women have been keen to explore are racism, sexism, HIV/AIDS, arranged marriages, domestic violence, families and infanticide. Many of these issues are seen as taboo within Black (and White) communities.

The Importance of the Body

Skin colour and hair emerge once more – and not at all surprisingly – as an experience to be talked about by young women. 'What do you mean, Black?' one young woman asked her community worker, 'Do you mean Black like me or Black like you?' – and in fact that conversation, the whole question of difference, heterogeneity and yet the importance of there 'being a mirror' in which Black girls can recognise themselves is revealed. To young women who want to talk about their experience of femininity being lived in their skins, to talk of Black as a political colour seems obvious in relation to the recognition of how racism operates, but it also seems to deny the reality of skin colour and its meanings in a racist society: 'Black is not a political choice; Black is what you are.'

The celebration of Black images of beauty has been a necessary working strategy in all Black young women's groups. The presence of a range of images of Black women is of the utmost importance. The absence of representation and the presence of racist representations, usually linked to a representation of sexual 'otherness' and availability, has been the focus of much important feminist writing which can form a resource for the development of practice (hooks 1992).

Working Across Communities and Cultures, and Identifying Diversity Within Communities

Projects which have worked with second- and third-generation Black British women from well-established communities often find themselves in a strong position to offer support to new migrants and to refugees. This is partly because the experience of migration is never far away, even in relatively settled communities, and also because such projects have a strong commitment to work which crosses boundaries and makes links between different communities (Imam and Bowler 2010).

Workers at the GAP Centre in Sheffield worked as a 'racially'-mixed team from very early on in the life of the project, working with West Indian, Pakistani and Yemeni working-class communities in Sheffield, as well as with White working-class girls. The established Somali community in Sheffield has grown as a result of the arrival of refugees from the war in Somalia. Not surprisingly, given their recent experiences, the daughters of the community are highly protected by their parents, but there was a recognition among the workers at the GAP project that this protectiveness was proving difficult for the girls, who sometimes reacted by taking very serious risks and seeming to show little regard for their own safety. GAP workers used funding available for crime prevention to establish a forum for the discussion of young women's safety. Together with young women from different communities, the workers established an agenda of themes in relation to 'risk' for young women, with a particular emphasis on the question of independence and the question of sexual harassment/ exploitation. Young women then facilitated a conference, attended by teachers, police officers, health visitors and social workers, at which these themes were developed.

The GAP project workers' ability to work across communities and to build alliances across communities has also facilitated the development of a Black Women's Resource Centre in Sheffield.

There are many lessons for coalition-building in the experience of Black women workers. Jill Dennis, a worker at GAP, identified a number of aspects to her work which have enabled her to make alliances. The first is the ability to continue to work and have links and connections at grass-roots level. Black women workers often continue to be very closely identified with the communities they are working in.

Secondly, the worker needs to be able to identify sources of funding and fight for them on behalf of a coalition of groups which are often excluded from the bidding process. In this way, a Black woman worker often experiences herself as the bridge who forges the coalition, stretched between marginalised communities and funding agencies, attempting to build up resources for young women. The experience of Black women often raises the question of 'on whose terms' alliances and coalitions are to be built. Black women have a great deal of experience of slowing down processes of agenda-setting that are taking place in White funding bodies, in order to create a forum for Black as well as White voices to be heard.

Third, the experience of building alliances between different Black communities is not based on an abstract principle of 'the need to build alliances', but on very specific and possibly narrow shared concerns – such as the need for safety and protection, and the parent-daughter issues this raises. It is also based on a recognition of important, shared experiences of migration and settlement, and of the hostilities of racism. Similarities of experience can be glimpsed and a connection can be made, first in imagination and then in reality.

The forms taken by cross-cultural alliances clearly depend on the power relationships at stake. It may be easier to build alliances among girls from a number of different marginalised communities than to cross barriers where major political power is at stake. Here, the experience of girls' work in Northern Ireland is very instructive: 'cross-community projects' have tended to be dominated by boys, and yet girls have also experienced the restriction of living in a divided society, particularly the restrictions on mobility (Morgan and McCardle 2009). Once cross-community projects from a local youth centre were established, it clearly became much easier for girls to visit and make contact than it was for boys.

As the Northern Ireland Association of Youth Clubs report (Trimbell 1990) pointed out, the sense that 'it's different for girls' has both positive and negative aspects. It is harder for young men to make visits to areas of 'the opposite religion' because of the expectation that they will be aggressive. However, the pressures on young women not to form relationships across the divide are very strong, and a young woman who does so is strongly censured by her own community. Again, the importance of having a focus for connection which is separate from the fact of connection is very strong.

Youth work with Black young women is also enabling the experience of diversity within communities to be explored. In 'Making Youth Work Accessible to Black Women in the North East of England', Yasmin Kutub (1995) wrote about the benefits which arose from the establishment of a specific training course for Black women:

> During the first session, some of the students began to talk about their own experiences of racism, which ranged from institutional forms, in relation to employment (or the lack of it), housing and education, to more insidious forms such as harassment on the streets, vandalism of homes and cars and even some assaults ... For some it felt like the first time they had been able to do this in a supportive environment, and others felt they had been denied this opportunity on other courses.

Kutub went on to explain how the course facilitated the exploration of diversity:

> Usually, in relation to equal opportunity issues, there is an expectation that Black women will only be concerned with responding to issues of race and

gender. However, one of the main focuses of the course was to acknowledge the diversity that exists within communities of Black women, and to shatter the myth (which is often internalised by us) that we are one homogeneous group. By examining other forms of oppression, and drawing analogies with the students' own experiences of oppression via racism and sexism, we gave the students the opportunity to explore issues such as lesbianism within the Black communities, and class issues as they affect Black people. (Kutub 1995: 88)

For many projects rooted in Black communities, and for work with girls in Northern Ireland, it has been international work which has offered a vehicle for continuing to build connections.

Internationalism

In many cities, the celebration of International Women's Day has become a focus for the work of women's projects and young women's groups. International Women's Day, on 8 March, became a focus for women's politics in the early years of the twentieth century and was first commemorated to mark the beginning of a strike of garment workers, who were demanding equal pay. The celebration of International Women's Day was revived in the 1960s and became a focus for demonstrations on subjects such as equal pay and childcare.

In the 1980s and for the girls' work movement, an increasingly cultural focus for the work was developed, and to some extent there was a decline in the political and international focus. This has been revived in projects which work across different communities, particularly by Black workers. In such projects, although International Women's Day remains a focus for celebrating women's friendships and for offering non-traditional opportunities to young women, there is also the dimension of informing and educating ourselves about women's struggles internationally. The events might include drama, dance, fashion shows and sharing food. They also include a celebration of the success and achievements of women, and celebrities are often invited. Other methods of sharing information and promoting education include showing films, hosting real-time video links, organising bookstalls and inviting speakers, followed by a discussion. In some cities, conferences are held with international links and there is a major civic focus on International Women's Day which local projects connect with.

Global Youth Work

Global education, as it has developed in schools, enables young people to make links with wider development agendas and these very often take young women as their focus. The strategies of global youth work may draw on many of the informal education strategies discussed earlier, with a focus on matters of everyday significance to young people and extending the discussion into a wider framework (Adams 2003). Food and textiles have often been important starting-points for conversations which open up a sense of global connectedness; for some youth projects, there has been a strong commitment to continue this work through the development of international exchanges and visits, quite often but not exclusively with countries where members already have connections. The 'girl effect' is a major development campaign currently being led by the Nike Foundation which is discussed in the final chapter of this new edition.

The overseas student community offers a point of connection, and where there are shared interests in development, projects such as *Southern Voices*, which aim to link the experience of people from the South with the work of development agencies based in the North can offer inspiration.

International work can also take young women/s projects beyond a narrowly European focus in the opportunities for international exchange work. The Commonwealth Institute and British Council have facilitated visits and exchanges with Commonwealth countries. International work can explore cultural forms such as writing, film and video to explore how women are dealing with the issues of rights and responsibilities 'back home' and before visits and exchanges are undertaken (Soni 2011).

Call and Response: Can White Women Listen?

If it is true to say that questions of material survival – 'putting bread on the table' – and questions of communication – 'teaching the mother tongue' – are constructed as women's work, then it may be that connections between Black women's projects and community organisations run by White working-class women will be effectively based on questions of economics and questions of communication.

In West Yorkshire, the Low Pay Unit has provided a forum for meetings between women workers in the textile industry internationally. Castleford Women's Centre, which arose from the work of a miners' wives' support group during the miners' strike of 1984–85, focused both on opportunities for employment for women and on the development of educational opportunities. The connections between women in different centres in West

Yorkshire are potentially strong, and young women across communities need resourcing and encouraging to make those connections.

One of the strongest political alliances – although an unsuccessful one at the time – was that between miners' organisations and the inner-city Black communities, and much of this alliance-building was facilitated by women. Paul Gilroy noted:

> During that industrial dispute highly dissimilar groups were able to connect their fates across the divisions of 'race'; ethnicity, region and language. For a brief period, inner city populations and the vanguard of the orthodox industrial proletariat shrank the world to the size of their immediate communities and began, in concert, to act politically on that basis. In doing so, they supplied a preliminary but nonetheless concrete answer to the decisive political questions of our age: how do we act locally and yet think globally? How do we connect the local and immediate across the earthworks erected by the division of labour? (Gilroy 1993: 46)

When women's work of community-building in White working-class communities was undertaken in a spirit of resistance and struggle, it became much more evident that the traditional narrownesses and chauvinisms associated with Englishness in some working-class communities could be broken down. Where White women workers see analysis of and resistance to racism as necessary to feminist politics, rather than as a diversion, alliances can more readily be built. Some White feminists have undertaken joint work with Black workers, male and female, to offer educational programmes about racism in predominantly White communities, and to offer support and development opportunities to Black young people, who are often intensely isolated in such areas.

The most concrete basis for alliance and solidarity seems to be where there are survival issues at stake, where the social existence of groups is in jeopardy. It is also likely that women will be among those most strongly insisting on alliance. Within that context, there is a need to explore that the question of the autonomy of women, perhaps especially young women, and women's need to develop their own goals are not lost in the process of developing support for the extended community.

In order to avoid the clear danger of community being established on the basis of the subordination of women's own potentials and goals, perhaps the surest basis for alliance between Black women and White women of diverse communities is mutual pleasure and enjoyment. It is to the unexpected friendships between girls and young women in the 'hybrid cultures' of our cities that feminist education with girls and young women should look, in anticipation of receiving an accurate, informal education.

Intersectionality

In academic terms, this discussion of connection, hybridity and alliance moves towards 'intersectionality', the interconnections of many flows of power, which constrain and enable young women and resistance to any forms of 'essentialism' which make women carry the 'problem' for what are already represented or constructed as 'problematic cultures'. In 2012, it is Muslim women who wear non-western dress who above all are positioned as bearers of problems Other women who are literally positioned at an edge of belonging/not belonging and often experiencing destitution, precariousness and acute uncertainty about their rights are women who are asylum seekers, alongside other vulnerable migrants, such as women who may have outstayed the terms of their visas and 'disappeared'. Such people are subject to a regime of truth which treats all their statements as by definition incredible and which renders them automatically suspect as 'bogus'. This applies also to those who arrive in the UK as children, who are subject to age assessment, and who are entitled to support until the age of 18 and subsequently lose all their rights.

Finally, Roma communities are newly established in the UK and subject to scrutiny and hostility as well as offers of engagement in ways which make the situation of young women in those communities highly visible. The new genres of TV and of personal memoirs, for example, 'Gypsy Boy' and 'My Big Fat Gypsy Wedding', demonstrate rhetorical tropes of child-snatching, amorality and violence which have long been attached to the nomadic Roma people across Europe and have led to their immiseration.

Youth workers responding to young women in these communities and offering association, friendship and fun are likely to find themselves working with specialist agencies as part of their everyday work. These include important mutual aid networks such as WAST (Women Asylum Seekers Together); specialist education outreach teams such as the International Arrivals and Supplementary Schools Team run by Manchester City Council, and campaigning groups supporting women to challenge the rulings of the Border Agency, many of which are supported by the National Coalition of Anti-Deportation Campaigns. In engaging in such work, practitioners see their engaging in informal learning as border-crossing. (Coburn 2011, Batsleer 2008, Soni 2011)

Responding to Lives, not Events

In the UK, the Muslim Youth Work Foundation has provided a platform for the exploration of youth work responses and Gill Cressey's important paper 'The Ultimate Separatist Cage? Youth Work with Muslim Young Women' (2007) remains a very important starting-point. Cressey's argument against making assumptions about the meanings of practices such as wearing the hijab is an essential starting-point for work which recognises that faith identity for Muslim young people has, in M.G. Khan's words, 'become increasingly positive and equally painful to negotiate in a context that makes them vulnerable to acts of violence and discrimination by being labelled as the "enemy within"' (Khan 2006b). For many, the Preventing Violence Extremism (PVE) agenda positions them as Potential Violent Extremists. The fear generated in the policy climate of the first decade of the twenty-first century has suggested that beneath every 'veiled woman' may be a knife or a bomb.

At the same time, images communicated globally of women who are resisting emerging patriarchal controls in the democratic revolutions of the Arab Spring inspire hope in communities in the UK that change is possible and convey an alternative set of meanings for traditional Muslim dress for women, messages associated with dignity and respect.

The levels of attack, suspicion and violation faced by Black women and by women across minoritised communities are such that particular attention needs to be paid to supporting women's own survival strategies in communities and paying due regard to the needs for sustenance, nurture and support. This has led to an increasing attention to the politics of diversity in youth work and to the particular skills and strategies involved in working transversally and in diverse staff teams. In this context, the development of culturally specific as well as gender-specific youth work is always a part of a network of provision which is addressing questions of inequality and injustice, and which is strongly associated with community education and activism. Informal education for young women cannot occur apart from their specific community contexts, as their community networks may be both their source of survival and their immediate place of conflict (Shukra 2010).

The Politicisation of Religion

The salience of religion in youth and community work has re-emerged in the first decade of the twenty-first century after a period of strong secularisation of practice. The necessity to negotiate the meanings of being a girl and becoming a woman in the context of faith traditions needs to be recognised in new ways and many faith-based youth work practitioners are able to draw on women-centred readings of their own traditions which, in the face of patriarchal traditions of leadership, affirm and assert the dignity of women.

However, alongside the new recognition of the resources of faith traditions and the place of women in them, of building community and inspiring mutual support, needs to be placed a clear evaluation of the politicisation of fundamentalist religion globally, which, across all faith communities, is inscribing practices which constrain and regulate women's bodies and sexualities, rendering them normatively subordinate to the husband and father in families and to male leaders in churches, mosques and synagogues. The campaigning group Women Against Fundamentalism defines fundamentalism in this way:

> Fundamentalism is a modern political movement that uses religion to gain power. It is found in all major religions throughout the world sometimes holding state power sometimes in opposition to it – and sometimes working within the confines of the secular state to control minority communities. Fundamentalism is not a matter of religious observance which we see as a matter of individual choice.

> Fundamentalists set out to perpetuate women's role as the upholders of the supposedly unchanging morals and traditions of the whole community. Women who refuse this role may be demonised, outcast from their own community, subjected to physical violence and even killed.

> Control of women's minds and bodies is at the heart of the fundamentalist agenda.www.womenagainstfundamentalism.org.uk

Such conservative thinking is present in abstinence education programmes currently being promoted in the UK by Challenge and the Romance Academy.

Many religious people do not see religious observance, or perhaps more significantly, belonging to a faith community, as a matter of 'individual choice'. Faith identity (with Butler 2004) can be seen as a place where we are undone by the other, rather than where we are constructed as liberal individuals. It therefore remains possible and necessary to affirm a place of being woman in faith communities in ways which deny and problematise the fundamentalist agendas rather than othering, denying and controlling young women.

10 Feminist Work with Girls: Professional Formation and Community-based Practice

Youth policy during the New Labour Years created a new framework for youth and community work. As the new additions throughout this book have shown, the reorganisation of Children and Young People's Services into Integrated Teams, and the targeting of resources towards those deemed most vulnerable led to a renewed focus on sexual health, pregnancy and parenthood, or obesity and healthy eating, and to an abandonment of the association with 'community' as a contested source of practice. This changed the focus of practice in many youth services and led to the loss of older approaches based on models of curriculum development and programme planning which were negotiated and group-led. Such shifts in resourcing and funding of youth work have been widely discussed and it is not the intention to repeat this analysis here.

The policy paper 'Resourcing Excellent Youth Services' (REYS) DfES, 2002) led to a strong emphasis on 'recorded and accredited outcomes' in youth work. Some practitioners saw this as supporting the development of educational purpose in the otherwise *laissez-faire* free association of youth work, whilst others saw it as a means of constraining the open curriculum processes of youth work even further and rendering the practice closer and closer to formal education (Davies and Merton 2009). UK Youth was a key player in offering accredited programmes such as those offered through ASDAN, a curriculum development and awarding body that offered basic level qualifications in the area of personal development and skills for life. The offer of policy-orientated short courses came to predominate in local authority youth work too, contributing to the development of a form of 'liquid youth work' (Batsleer 2010b), consonant with the records of achievement and personalised learning being developed in schools.

One aspect of being a girl in late modernity – one aspect of femininity, it has been argued – is to be flexible and well-adapted to negotiation in a complex labour market in which traditionally 'feminine' soft skills are valued more highly than the skills of traditional working-class masculinity (Harris 2004). Thus girls' work may be thought to have returned to an

175

agenda more conservative than feminist, of adaptation for work considered suitable for working-class girls.

One strand of activity, however, in which girls have outnumbered boys has been in the development of youth work as participation and active citizenship (Percy-Smith and Thomas 2010). Young women have outnumbered young men on school councils, in youth forums and in the youth parliament. Again this represents a commitment to traditional female roles as volunteers and in community-building, whether in projects such as V Inspired or in the role of advocate for other young people's search for transformation, whether of transport systems or media representations (Hill and Russell 2009).

The emphasis on youth voice developed in proximity with an emphasis on 'pupil voice' in schools and 'student voice' in universities. Again, the question of what languages can be spoken and what agendas created through 'youth voice' work has been much debated and, as already discussed, it has become evident over time how far an emphasis on 'voice and choice' can be corralled into neo-liberal agendas, with its entire focus being not on young people as co-creators of an informal education process, but on consumerist or managerialist models in which young people 'assess' or 'inspect' services almost before they have engaged and participated in them (Batsleer 2012, Podd 2010). Volunteering, furthermore, draws on an aspect of traditional femininity – that of altruism, of caring for others more than oneself, of service and of creating community. In turning once again to community – as distinct from the institutional or the corporate aspects of youth work – it will be important not to overlook the kinds of historically accepted limitations and 'burdens of care' which this places on women.

Definitions of Youth and Community Work

Students undertaking initial training courses in youth and community work are often asked, as part of the assessment of their professional practice, how their work differs from that of a social worker or a teacher. They very often reply that they, unlike the others, start from young people's own agenda. They may also reply that youth work or informal education is characterised more by method than by content. Such professional boundary-marking disguises as much as it reveals, and in the case of youth and community work, it certainly has a compensatory flavour. Unlike social workers and teachers, youth workers exercise absolutely no statutory authority. The compensation for this lack of authority is a whole sphere of influence, exercised through voluntary relationships and enjoyment. No wonder relationships between professionals from these different disciplines can be difficult.

Following the establishment of the first training courses for professional, full-time youth and community workers, there was a period of protracted debate and definition of the professional role. This process of debate and definition is still continuing, and feminist practice has much to contribute. However, it is important to recognise from the outset that this long period of professionalisation created a number of shared understandings and agreements about the nature of good practice in informal social education and the linked practice of community work. Despite this process of professional role clarification, youth and community work has historically suffered from a lack of funding and of appropriate resourcing. Much of the resource consists of buildings which constantly require repairs, are difficult to staff, need caretaking, and which seem to lend themselves to activities more appropriate to the social containment of boys than to the social and political education of girls or boys. Staff working in such buildings find themselves policing the building rather than forming educative relationships with young people. There has thankfully been a period of new building under the 'My Place' initiative and other regeneration programmes, of large new youth centres and there has been some practice of involving young people in their design.

Such inherent difficulties have led to a lack of understanding both from the formal sector of schooling and from the statutory casework-orientated social services, and which have, until recently, made relationships between feminists working in these different sectors more difficult than they need be.

Statements of Professional Values and Activity

In the context of developing appropriate training for both full-time and part-time youth workers, alongside the professionalisation of community work, there were a number of codifications of the values and activities which have informed good practice. Statements of shared principles and values and of the key functions undertaken by youth and community workers were first usefully synthesised by Dr Michael Erault and Dennis Kelly of the University of Sussex in a report commissioned by the National Youth Agency and the Department of Employment.

Erault and Kelly offered an initial summary of core values as follows:

- valuing and respecting all individuals, groups and communities – their work, their abilities, their rights, their contributions to society and their cultural resources;
- valuing oneself;
- autonomy of individuals and groups;

- justice and equality;
- the right to participate in decisions and actions where one is a stakeholder;
- moral accountability towards those affected by one's actions;
- the obligation to monitor and regularly review one's own behaviour, practice and relationships, and
- lifelong learning and development for all.

They went on to suggest seven core areas in which competences in youth and community work might be defined:

1. self-awareness, self-management, self-evaluation and self-development;
2. establishing relationships of trust with individuals, groups and communities;
3. involving groups and communities in participative approaches to learning;
4. working with individuals to promote personal and social development;
5. working in teams for organisations and in association with other agencies;
6. planning and evaluation in consultation with stakeholders, and
7. organisation and management of people and resources (Erault and Kelly 1994).

This account built on a number of statements of the core skills involved in community work and youth work and was broadly connected to similar processes of definition taking place in community care and in counselling and psychotherapy. Erault and Kelly claimed to have consulted these discussions in other disciplines when drawing up the statement for youth and community work.

There was and is a continuing debate about the definition of practice as an accumulation of skills. However, it is important to notice that it is on this basis that a good deal of agreement was reached about the role of youth and community workers.

Discussions such as the one above led to the development of the National Occupational Standards (for Youth Work, and for Community Development) first published in 2002 and the subsequent development of the QAA Subject Benchmark in Youth and Community Work. These drew on a wide range of statements which had been developed across the four nations of the British Isles. For example, the NYA's statement of values and principles for *Ethical Conduct in Youth Work* (NYA 2000) directed professionals to engage with (young) people with respect and avoid negative discrimination; respect and promote (young) people's rights to make their own decisions and choices (unless the rights of others are negatively threatened); promote the safety and well-being of young people without preventing them from learning through undertaking challenging activities, and contribute to the promotion of social justice among young people and in society generally, honouring diversity, yet identifying and challenging discrimination. The 2009 QAA Subject Benchmark in Youth and Community Work developed this further:

> Such principles as these require that undergraduates learn to recognise the links between the interpersonal, the intrapersonal and the cultural and structural aspects of the power relationships in which people's lives are embedded. They will understand the impact of injustice and inequality and of oppressive or limiting social relationships, and offer constructive challenges to social injustice in its personal, cultural, institutional and structural dimensions. They will support people in creating open, critical and safe spaces for learning and in maintaining control of their own agendas for learning and development, limited only by concern for their own and others' safety, well-being and rights. They will create respectful alliances across socially constructed differences, divisions and inequality, and work in partnership with young people and adult community groups in order to effect change.

> Programmes of study should encourage students to develop inclusive and anti-oppressive practice in their own settings as well as in the wider social context of education. They should equip students with the ability to deal with complex ethical issues through sound moral reasoning, including an understanding of how values are explored and expressed in informal contexts. They should aim to draw on and extend current thinking and practice in relation to the development of knowledge and understanding, skills and abilities, and personal values and commitment, both in graduate professionals and in other graduates who achieve non-profession The educational principles underpinning practice can be characterised as follows(the definition of each term is open to contestation and debate): **appreciative enquiry**: the educational process starts from recognition of the strengths and potential of participants rather than from an appraisal of deficits and pathologies; **holistic**: educational practice aims to engage body, mind, heart and spirit; **democratic and participatory**: the curriculum of education is drawn from the real world and context of the group of participants, and is developed in discussion with them. Learning is active and experiential; **associative**: the educational process values the small group as a resource for development and learning. It also values small group learning as an aspect of citizenship with many potential (and potentially conflicting) contributions to political democracy; **critical collaborative enquiry**: the educational process draws on the strength of group collaboration to enable new questions to be posed and new understandings developed. It is an open-ended process of questioning received ideas and settled social contexts and norms; **voluntary/free**: people

are engaged in this practice on the basis of informed choice and consent. They take part because they want to and can leave without penalty. This principle underpins the democratic nature of the curriculum; **reflective**: professionals and those involved as 'learners' or 'activists' are engaged in systematic reflection on their learning; **emancipatory**: the education process is committed to personal, social and political empowerment/change. (QAA 2009)

However the professionalisation process in youth work has brought losses as well as gains. In the immediate post-Albemarle period, until the early 1980s, there was a strong sense of community work as associated with political movements which challenged existing social relations between the people and the power bloc, that is, associated with collective struggle for transformation. This connection supported the development of feminist-inspired practice in youth work and it is this which became less visible as the work became professionalised. There is an ever-present danger that work with other professionals, in partnerships, replaces the orientation to the neighbourhood or community where the practice of youth and community work is rooted.

The Work of Informal Education

From being perceived as glorified caretakers of buildings or as 'soft cops' with the gift of 'keeping young people off the streets' and quelling riots, the specific educational style and focus of youth and community work became sought after by other professionals from the 1990s and in the subsequent New Labour period. As the role of teachers became much more tightly defined in terms of the National Curriculum, at the same time, schools were held much more closely responsible for aspects of the social life of pupils. Schools became publicly accountable for their record on school attendance, for example. These contradictory demands left teachers in a highly contradictory role, and the skills of youth and community workers became particularly valued at this point because they attend to aspects of the social education curriculum and to educational processes which had been squeezed to the margins of schooling. The inclusion of a discussion of the role of youth workers in the 'Nuffield Review of 14–19 Education' is testimony to this. and opened a continuing, wider, dialogue between youth work and education (Tiffany 2009).

Following Conservative reforms of education, in the subsequent New Labour period, there was enormous pressure to redefine the skills of informal educators as skills in the management and delivery of services. Much of the impetus to define the role and analyse the skills of youth and community workers has come from professional associations and trade unions. Such bodies have been keen to value the group work, networking and work with individuals undertaken by their members, rather than allow this work to be undervalued in comparison to equally necessary work of fundraising, budgeting, staff appointment, team-building, report-writing, project evaluation, staff appraisal, which are valued in the context of the new managerialism (Ord 2011a).

The Resources of the Woman Educator

A woman educator always works at a number of boundaries. She draws on her personal resources enormously. Many women youth and community workers, when asked where they derive their strength to continue with the work, make reference to their friends and families, particularly their mothers and their children, as a source of love, strength and support. Women educators also draw on their political analysis of the position of girls and women within the communities they are working with. Here she may draw on a history of involvement with campaigns, on reading and study, and on shared reflection with others, inside and outside the profession, with whom she can make common cause. She may also draw on a professional network of resources, including opportunities for staff development, for training and for supervision of her practice. In all her interventions, personal, political and professional elements are drawn on. Each may contribute to her success or difficulty in undertaking the work.

Some existing accounts did stress the part played by the personality and character of the worker in the success of their work, for example, one very attractive account by Fred Milson. Milson was already arguing in 1970 that 'In the matter of personal qualities, one wonders if the pendulum has not swung too far in the direction of a detached and "professional" attitude' (Milson 1970: 78). He went on to say: 'The successful operator uses rather than suppresses his personality whilst checking any tendency to be subjective in his judgements or to be unconsciously satisfying of his own needs rather than the needs of young people in his efforts' (ibid.).

He identified three qualities found to be rewarding for the processes of social education: (1) imagination, linked to 'that undiscourageable faith in people's possibilities which is the mark of the true educator'; (2) the ability to work as a member of a team, and (3) 'the ability to grow as people with the work we are doing' (ibid.: 78–9). The authors of *The Management of Detached Work* suggested that an appropriate match between the worker's personality and the nature of the project is a key both to success in detached work and some of the characteristic difficulties of managing it (Arnold et al. 1981).

Most recent writing sets out a professional code of practice with an explicit set of professional values. Such writing is usually relatively depersonalised and it also curiously unsituated, making little reference to its own historical context. It is almost as if all the developments in community-based work with young people were leading up to this point of professional clarity, from which there can now be little movement. So, Mark Smith, whose excellent accounts of informal and local education have done much to establish a consensus about the profession, suggested that the key question to be asked of any youth work intervention is 'Does it facilitate learning?' (Smith 1988). And the major question to be asked by interviewers focusing on a task-based and skills-based approach to practice is 'Does this person show evidence of possessing the appropriate knowledge, skills and values to perform the work that has been identified?'

There have also been occasional attempts to develop definitions of the worker's role in which a social/political or theological/religious analysis offers the guiding framework for intervention. These can take both a conservative and a progressive form. The goals of practice are then both highly specific and of global and trans-historical importance: 'to do my duty to God and the queen', 'Black community development', 'liberation', 'socialist character-building' (Chauhan 1989, Taylor 1987).

The Distinctiveness of Feminist Practice

Given that approaches to practice have either emphasised the personality of the worker or the professional code or the political goals of the work, the distinctiveness of feminist-inspired practice lies in an ability and desire to connect all these aspects of the work and to draw on them critically. Such practice can look to a whole body of thinking, professional work, political practice and personal transformation that grew from the slogan 'The personal is political.' So, feminist workers would reject the commonly held view that there are people who show 'natural gifts' as educators – and would, for example, recognise that being 'naturally a good listener' (in the case of a woman), or a 'natural leader' (in the case of a man) is in fact a profoundly social creation of the gender system. Yet, like Fred Milson, a feminist perspective would place a strong emphasis on the person. 'Professional skills' and 'political analysis' cannot be detached from the person of the worker. Unlike Fred Milson (at least he was writing in 1970), feminists know that persons can be women.

There is an important sense of *being* as well as *doing* in feminist practice. Who a woman is, as well as how she acts, the whole history conscious and unconscious, of how she has become a woman: this all matters in the form of education she can offer. This is not to claim that identity is the sole source of good practice in education and certainly not to claim that shared identity is the basis of good practice. However, it does mean that she actively consults her own sense of herself and her own agenda in any work she undertakes. For example, becoming a mother clearly changes the way women workers work with young women's groups. Black women may decide their resources are best used in working with other Black women and building coalitions across different Black communities. A worker who is questioning her own sexuality may decide not to work on issues about sexuality with a group at that point. Or it may seem the right moment to do so. There is no formula for 'the conscious use of self in relation to other', but there is a history and archaeology of the self on which our practice draws as a source of collective knowing. In this, feminist educators draw on a humanist tradition of ethics, with a stress on an attention to particular people in particular moments, rather than on precepts or maxims as a substitute for this attention.

So, one of the characteristics of feminist practice is the way a woman worker can draw on her own resources as a person, and is supported to do that, within the context of a professional code, and always with the aim of extending the learning and development of the young women as her priority. There has been a great emphasis on the importance of supervision as a place where the links with the personal can be explored. This leads to a reintegration of the personal within the context of professional/ political discussions. It means that her own learning and development is not counterposed to the learning of the young women she is working with. As Fred Milson remarked, youth work provides a fine liberal education. At the same time, the issue of developing appropriate professional boundaries is of the utmost importance. It is important, although difficult, both to acknowledge the mutuality of the learning process and to maintain a distinction from friendship.

Feminist practice has something to contribute to all these debates, and discussions. The aim here is to show how some of the terms that have come to form a 'professional common sense' can be criticised and extended from within feminist debate, and how insights from feminist practice can be useful to the whole profession. One of the critical issues is the way in which professionalisation led to a technicist emphasis on reflection and reflexivity as an aspect of professional practice which contributed to a narrowing vision of the practice of youth and community work.

Case Study: Feminism and Reflective Practice

'The model of cross-generational learning that Feminist Webs embodies is not individual but shared and collective. Many models of reflection are intensely individualised and promote problem-solving. The experience of Feminist Webs reinforces the idea that reflection can move beyond this, as has been suggested by writers in critical management studies who have suggested that 'critical reflection' is concerned with questioning assumptions, focused on the social not the individual, paying particular attention to the analysis of power relationships and concerned with democracy.

The experience of Feminist Webs suggests that the situated knowledges of professionals might be understood in terms of a bigger picture. 'Professional identities' are formed in ways that are always interacting with the other aspects of biographies, both personal and political. While models of collective learning which draw on ideas of 'communities of practice' may assist with understanding political learning which may occur in organisations, some critical management theorists also point to group relations conferences as sources for understanding the conscious and unconscious processes at work in organisations and networks which release energy for change, or undermine it or both

The model of learning in Feminist Webs, while it is collective, is not yet institutionalised. The model of learning through communities of practice which operate on the edge of and across the boundaries of institutions offers a fruitful basis for understanding this. Wenger's (1998) components of learning in communities of practice – meaning, practice, community and identity – can be used to analyse this:

- Meanings – of what it means to be a woman, as well as what it means to espouse feminism – are investigated and exchanged.
- Practice – that opens up the historical resources of informal social education that is youth work, of which girls' work is one strand.
- Community – that affirms through the public production of memories and the sharing of stories that such efforts are worthwhile and valuable and that we can grow in competence in negotiating an unequal world as a result of them.
- Identity ('learning as becoming') – so that the learning that occurs through involvement with Feminist Webs has the potential to shape, affirm and change our sense of who we are in

the context of being a woman, within the feminist communities reflected in feminist webs and in our roles as women in a range of communities. (Batsleer,2010a).

Working as a community-based professional, or working as an activist alongside others to define and develop struggles offer distinct relations to 'community', movement and struggle. Yet there are inescapable marks of the Gramscian politics of developing counter-hegemonic alliances, challenging common sense and developing good sense that form a critical element of the inheritance of feminist-inspired practitioners in community and youth work. According to Mary Issit (2000):

Reflective practice involves group discussion through feminist/womanist and other networks and may feature as an important part of different cultures. One African Caribbean woman likened reflective practice to the act of 'reasoning' that takes place among Jamaican people when you: 'Check out the position you are coming from, think about the position other people are coming from, does it hold water … if not, why not? … and that starts from within your family and through your friends … it's a whole that informs and influences the position that you take.

Perhaps the most important element of a Gramscian-inspired feminist approach is the capacity to develop reflection on practice in dialogue primarily with different women's struggles, stories and agendas, as they arise in specific communities, rather than primarily in dialogue with policy makers, however powerful they may seem.

(Batsleer, 2010a)

11 Established Patterns, New Directions: The Organisational Context of Work with Girls and Young Women

Although the places in which informal education work with girls and young women occurs do change, with marked shifts as a consequence of the Conservative and subsequent New Labour restructuring of local education authorities, it is important to begin by recognising the role of a tiny department within most LEAs known as 'The Youth Service'. The work of Youth Services developed in partnership with voluntary organisations such as the Young Women's Christian Association (now called Platform 51) and the Girls' Friendly Society, which have the promotion of the welfare of girls and young women as a major aim. There has also been a connected partnership with the uniformed voluntary organisations such as the 'Guides' and other faith-based organisations.

Starting in 1945, youth services and other voluntary organisations offered an apparently open space in which social educational work with young people could be developed. This seemed to be in contrast with more explicitly regulated areas of work, such as social work (where issues of child protection are among the statutory responsibilities held by workers), or the probation service and Youth Offending Teams (regulated directly by the criminal justice system), or schooling (regulated by the demands of the National Curriculum and the examination system).

From the beginning of the establishment of professional training courses in the field of youth and community work, the literature stressed the 'voluntary principle' and 'the principle of association', and there has been a stress on participation, alongside a developing understanding of the aims and purposes of social education and advocacy. However, as a number of writers have pointed out, the absence of statutory control does not mean the absence of regulation. There are now a number of analyses of the regulation of girls and of women workers by the informal domination of boys and men and by the dominance of the 'male agenda' (Sawbridge and Spence 1991). But wherever there is domination there is also resistance, and it was the contradiction between the explicit commitments to openness of 'youth service' organisations and their failure to respond to the needs of girls and young women from different communities, which created the space for feminist and woman-centred practice from the 1970s onwards. Youth service-based work included both important initiatives from national and regional organisations (such as the Girls' Work Unit of the National Organisation of Youth Clubs) and local projects and events.

Patterns of Separate Provision

Separate provision for autonomous work with girls occurs in different settings and has been made available in a number of different ways. In some local authorities, girls' clubs and young women's activity groups were given their own time slots within the context of mixed clubs and projects. This was usually determined by the male-dominated patterns of the mixed projects, rather than any consideration of the needs or expectations of young women – in more than one Northern city, all the girls' nights ran to coincide with the weekday evening when local football matches are played.

In another pattern, women workers were nominated to undertake 'separate work with girls' in the context of busy, mixed club sessions. This was really an impossible pattern of tokenism. Fair and equal treatment of boys and girls is important in mixed sessions, and working out strategies to promote this way of working is the responsibility of all staff. This may well form a complementary strategy to promote separate and autonomous work, but one should not be used to substitute for the other.

Another pattern was to establish separate young women's centres. These were sometimes city-centre-based or borough/city-wide resource centres and meeting places. In other cases, young women's centres were to be found in flats or houses on council housing estates. Another pattern was to allocate a set of rooms within a larger building.

'Separate provision' encompassed outreach projects and detached work, and such projects usually focus on the needs of young women who are perceived to be particularly 'marginal' or 'vulnerable'. The information, support and advocacy aspects of social education practice can be seen at their strongest in such work, which includes work with homeless young women, work with disabled young women who have been segregated from 'mainstream' provision, and work with young women who are working as prostitutes. A great deal of the innovation associated with detached youth work and outreach work has been found in the voluntary sector – both in the 'old' voluntary sector, with its roots in nineteenth-century philanthropy, and the new voluntary sector with its roots in the 'New Left' community politics of the post-1968 generation. However, even in the apparently radical approach of detached work, male perspectives still dominated. The model of street-based work was challenged by women workers who pointed out that:

1. Young women tend to have more domestic commitments and tasks than young men.
2. Parental pressure to be at home is exercised more with young women than young men.
3. Women are more vulnerable on the streets than men, especially at night. (Youth Work Unit 1983: 4)

Women workers, such as those who created the document *Looking Beyond Street Level* from which the statements above come, transformed the understanding of detached work. Within the practice of feminist work with girls, detached work and outreach work can be understood as an essential aspect of all informal education, which must constantly be returned to and which links to group-building and to the development of projects and organisations in a spiral of working methods, rather than as a completely separate form of work.

The links between feminist approaches and the detached youth work traditions of working with young people on their own terms and on their own agendas in their own places are strong. But when young people's own places are the bedroom rather than the streets, as is often the case with girls, new insights about 'starting where young people are' have to be developed. The challenge of creating girl-friendly spaces where society provides none must be accepted, and this is a collaborative activity between girls and young women and women youth workers. It cannot be undertaken solely 'on young women's own terms'.

Older organisations, such as the YWCA (now Platform 51), the Guides and the Girls' Friendly Society, have sometimes been willing to support new work, and there are links – personal, professional and political – between work in the voluntary-sector youth organisations and the new 'feminist voluntary sector', which includes Women's Aid, Rape Crisis Centres, Lesbian Line and projects responding to the needs of survivors of sexual abuse. A good example of this kind of coalition in the voluntary sector was the work being undertaken by Manchester Survivors' Project, which drew on feminist insights, the strengths of trained social workers, counsellors and youth and community workers, and the resources of a partnership between the local authority and the Richmond Fellowship, an established voluntary organisation in the mental health field.

It will be apparent that these patterns of provision, which have their roots in the Youth Service, are not exclusive to it. Partnership projects came to dominate youth services from 1997 onwards, drawing on the health agenda, and crime prevention, anti-social behaviour and community safety agendas, as well as the 'child protection' agenda and based on the 'Five Outcomes' of Every Child Matters with the mantra: Be healthy; stay safe; enjoy and achieve; make a positive contribution, and achieve economic well-being. Skills, practices and principles developed in the crucible of youth work were necessary to the development of new partnerships. Health authorities establishing young women's health centres, social work teams looking for ways of offering support to young mothers, counsellors considering different methods of support to survivors of abuse, schools looking for ways to encourage and enable young women from a variety of backgrounds and communities to develop their potential have all drawn on the principles of informal education with young women and girls.

Work with Asian Girls has been Represented as 'Other'

A division between work with girls (usually meaning work with white girls and African-Caribbean girls) and work with Asian girls had existed from the very beginning of the girls' work movement. From an anti-racist perspective, it is clear that White feminists have sometimes been able to open up or prevent the allocation of resources to Black women's groups. Although White feminist work originates in a resistance to the malestream, it can occupy a remarkably strong 'gatekeeping' role – able to influence the policy and sometimes resourcing in key areas, and able to deny access to Black women's groups or promote participation of Black women's groups in wider forums. These inequalities in access to the power structures make alliance-building a very difficult process.

A great deal of the work in Black women's projects has drawn on voluntary initiatives from within the communities themselves, from the grass-roots level – organisations such as the Palace Youth Project in Leeds and Abasindi in Manchester provided supplementary education from an African perspective for children who have their histories and experiences denied in the curriculum of White schools. Similarly, within Bangladeshi and Pakistani communities, much informal education work builds on already-existing women's networks. However, there is often an absence of connection between women's groups based in different communities, which can be attributed to the workings out of racism within service provision. Black women workers consistently report a sense that their work is dismissed, ignored, or simply not valued. The working party which reported to the DES on girls' work in 1989 had the following comments to make:

> In some cases, especially in voluntary organisations, work with young Black women is exciting, positive and evidently meeting their needs. It is purposefully separate and autonomous. In other cases however the existence of separate groups amounted to their having been virtually abandoned by the Youth Service management. One group of 27 Asian girls had never been visited by a Youth Officer. (DES, WO and NACYS 1989: 12)

Particularly in relation to work with Asian girls, where convenient and destructive myths about the complete 'otherness' of language and culture still prevail, separate provision can become a vehicle for sustaining the fear and ignorance of a racist culture as much as a positive basis for work. So the pioneering cross-cultural work which occurs in many projects is never acknowledged, valued and learned from at the level of management structures, and workers are denied appropriate support to develop purposeful, autonomous work. This lack of support is a danger throughout the field in relation to work with girls. When this is combined with racism, it makes it far too easy for the work to be undermined and discredited, and individual women workers can carry a very heavy burden.

Some local authorities developed positive action projects in which Black women found themselves promoted as a result of the 'two for the price of one' syndrome – a rather cynical phrase which encapsulated the perception that may be held by the women themselves or by people around them, that is, that they were promoted because they were Black and because they were women. Very often, they found themselves unsupported and expected to deliver, usually on the back of a postage stamp, a whole range of informal education provision to communities whose needs are neither recognised nor acknowledged within White structures. Language and support work – in the form of posts within education authorities, and in posts in social services and health authorities – has been a major area of work for women workers from Asian communities.

Again, it seems to be in the area of detached and outreach work that some of the most woman-centred work has been able to take place. It seems that Black women have worked creatively with the 'crumbs' dropped in the form of positive action strategies from the 'White man's table'. Projects focusing on Black women's health needs, on relationship issues, on ways of resisting racism and providing advice on immigration and nationality, mother-tongue projects and welfare projects, and Black women's refuges all emerged, as well as young women's projects which offered the opportunity to young women to build up their own strong positive identity. As will always be the case among the most oppressed communities, the basic questions of welfare and the questions of educational development combined.

The argument for separate and autonomous work with girls has been well established, but it is clear that the contexts in which such work can occur have changed and will continue to change.

The Importance of Partnership in Provision

It is clear, too, that informal education work will no longer be primarily Youth Service-based, but will occur in a number of different settings, particularly perhaps in the voluntary sector and in the partnership provision which is being encouraged by patterns of funding based on contracts for specific services. The authors of *The Youth Work Curriculum* (Newman and Ingram 1989) identified a range of organisations in contact with youth workers. These included community organisations such as sports clubs, religious organisations, Rotary Clubs and trades councils; educational agencies such as schools, the careers service, basic education, adult education, training agencies, further education colleges and outdoor education centres; local government departments, and caring agencies such as probation, social services, intermediate treatment, health departments, substance abuse agencies, family planning, Relate, Shelter and St John Ambulance. The authors of this document include 'race relations' and 'Equal Opportunities Commission' under caring organisations. The kinds of contact that might exist between youth workers and such a range of organisations would range from referral of young people to other services, to partnership projects and joint working.

Given that most of these organisations are male-dominated or have a male-dominated agenda, it is likely that the partnerships which will emerge in this context will once more prioritise boys, and that issues concerning a wide range of different groups of girls and young women will be pushed to the edge unless there is a clearly articulated strategy to counter this process.

There is therefore a need to explore a number of aspects of 'difference' and to consider ways of rebuilding alliances or making them anew in the competitive marketplace in which organisations supporting girls' work now exist.

There is also a need to consider the ways in which older commitments and methods can be renewed with the next generation of young women. The issue of how work is shared across generations is very important. Linked to this are questions of the definition of youth with which this book has been, in part, preoccupied. In relation to a long-standing discourse concerned with 'risk' and 'protection', young women are again being infantilised and seen as children. The question of how to sustain a critique of this discourse while retaining resources and funding is very important. What kind of national and international forums are necessary to sustain a feminist approach to informal education with girls and young women is also a critical question. These may be supported by newly emerging 'girlhood studies' networks in the social sciences internationally.

Association Across Diversity, Not Problems as False Unities

There is a need to recognise and acknowledge the plurality of practice in autonomous work with girls and young women. There is no automatic focus of unity in seeking to build solidarity among women. It is also clear that although 'youthfulness' as a social construction does render girls vulnerable and position them in similar ways – in ways distinct from, say, middle-aged and old women – being young is not, on its own, a basis for connection. How does a young woman whose primary focus of attention is the need to leave an oppressive family connect with a girl of a similar age who is going to have a baby and needs the support of her mother? Is there the possibility of discussion between a young woman who wants to be heterosexually active and needs support in obtaining and using appropriate contraception, another who finds herself in love with her best friend and yet another who is planning to marry someone approved of by her parents? It is now absolutely essential to recognise that the basis on which workers promote association among young women will not be simply, if it can be at all, on the basis of shared assumptions about what it means to be a woman.

In some areas and in some projects, it is possible to make the development of association across diversity a very explicit aim. At other times, the arguments for, and the promotion of, separate and autonomous work are likely to be couched in terms of young women's experience of risk or young women as problematic. Such definitions produce false unities which project workers then have to work very hard to undo and they are closely associated with the institutional and organisational location of practice. Histories of professional and client group definition cut across attempts to state shared political values and aims. Funding of projects sets aims and purposes for work which are not easily disconnected. So a major question which currently confronts practice is about the kind of institutional and organisational settings that are re-emerging which will allow the work to continue. A number of new frameworks and coalitions seem to be emerging, including an alliance with workers in play work, adult education and community development. There have also new proposals for the accreditation and validation of community work professionals. The impact of curriculum changes and the development of the National Curriculum in formal schooling have meant that there is now a clear place for the role and work of informal educators in promoting person-centred educational processes in schools.

Informal education, of the kind described in this book, will increasingly struggle for space in places where the agenda of education and development work is already very heavily directed from elsewhere. One of the major tasks of youth and community workers will be to define their work in relation to a multidisciplinary team and to continue to assert, within projects which may well have a very different focus, the need for autonomous work which proceeds from agendas set by young women themselves.

These are all essentially organisational questions, so in the rest of this chapter, I will indicate the debates that emerged in the 1990s and which pointed to a direction for the future.

Difference and Alliance Between Professionals

New patterns of funding through partnership arrangements required new kinds of interdisciplinary networks and cross-professional working. It became increasingly common for women trained in informal education as youth workers and community workers to be working as members of staff teams alongside counsellors, social workers, teachers, midwives and health visitors. The challenge for feminist practice is to be able to cross these disciplinary boundaries and work in ways which promote the recognition of the rights and potential of young women. Much of the current experience of interdisciplinary working tends to be in areas where young women's behaviour has been defined as risky or problematic. Feminist practice in informal education, which is taking place in the context of a multidisciplinary team, must negotiate both the demands of interdisciplinary working and the formulation of an agenda for work which is not problem-centred.

An interesting example of interdisciplinary working can be found in the pupil support services, especially Pupil Referral Units, for children who experience emotional and behavioural difficulties. The Peacock Centre in Manchester adopted an innovative approach to work in this area, and offered both separate and autonomous work with girls, in groups and individually. The Peacock Centre employed both teachers and youth workers, and worked with clinical psychologists and social workers in making an assessment of young women's needs. The psychological services do not have a method of assessing young women's needs which might focus on the gender issues involved, and while many of the young women involved in the Peacock Centre may have experienced sexual abuse, the impetus to establish separate girls' groups came from the teaching and youth work staff associated with the centre.

In relation to working with young women who are escaping abusive relationships, the teachers and youth workers in the pupil support team had to work hard to establish their credibility to work in this area, particularly with social workers, who had themselves undertaken a specific training and possessed a specific expertise. It was both the commitment of the educators and the willingness of the social workers to set aside assumptions about expertise which allowed the shared work to develop. The fact that the City Council had adopted a policy for women which itself promoted interdisciplinary working also helped. Key members of the group which developed the work on child protection had met as members of a domestic violence working party. In this way, organisational structures and policy commitments at the level of the city council enabled women workers from different professional backgrounds with a history of mutual suspicion to recognise shared values and develop effective working relationships.

The fact that the pupil support services straddle the social work/ education divide also makes it possible for work with girls, which is rooted in the assessment of risk – still, all too often, associated with 'promiscuity' – to take on a role which, through educational work, challenges the conditions which create the difficulties. Work can focus on the transition from primary to secondary school, a transition in which the assertiveness and self-esteem of girls can take a severe knocking. Within the curriculum of personal and social education, teachers from the pupil support service have promoted the idea of 'a child protection curriculum'. This enables the establishment of girls' groups which work on assertiveness, developing ways of talking about feelings and emotions, the place of secrets in our lives, and the relationship between trust and touch. Within the National Curriculum for schools, it has proved possible to incorporate the aims of 'the child protection curriculum' within the targets for attainment in speaking and listening, for example.

It is interesting that the staff involved in the Peacock Centre who trained initially as teachers come from subject backgrounds which are often seen as marginal to the school curriculum: from PE and domestic science, for example. Perhaps these disciplines lend themselves to the building of relationships and cooperative working which are identified as essential to interdisciplinary team-building. All the women involved in the pupil support services identify themselves as strong women and as offering potential role models to young women, though not all would use the word 'feminist' to describe themselves. There was a strongly female organisational culture, and work with girls has strong support from the management group. This, in its turn, gave both youth workers and teachers the confidence to work alongside social workers and clinical psychologists, while retaining a sense of expertise.

Other examples of projects which have successfully established alliances across professional boundaries can be found in the voluntary sector, where partnership funding and the development of contracts for the provision of specific services have led to the creation of new forums for inter-professional discussion. At Forty Second Street in Manchester, projects have drawn on funding from the NHS, the Mental Health Foundation, and from local authority joint funding (which includes a contribution from the social services department) and from many charitable sources including the National Lottery. There has been little input of funding from education-based sources. The project draws explicitly on an agenda which is concerned with empowerment in relation to the mental health system and employs workers from a number of different backgrounds to staff its projects. The fact that staff may identify as feminists and share a similar political agenda for the empowerment of women in relation to the mental health system does not mean, for example, that the tensions between a counselling-based approach to work with young women under stress and a community action-based approach will disappear.

These inter-professional alliances are creative and necessary and may offer the only resource base for some time to come. Partnership funding has also extended to work with the police force and work with the probation service, for example, in addressing issues of young women's safety. At the same time, it is very apparent that the perspectives of informal education will be quite marginal within inter-professional alliances, because it comes with no money, as the poor relation to most projects. It is important that a separate organisational and funding base is retained for informal education/ community education.

When professional partnerships are entered into, it is also absolutely necessary that there is clarity about the aims, curriculum and methods of informal education, and the distinctive emphasis which feminist youth workers and community workers can bring to a coalition. In the absence of a great deal of financial power, the power of clarity of purpose and commitment to certain aspects will have to be drawn on.

Inter-professional alliances are sometimes envisaged at a 'high-level strategy' meeting. For example, prior to the recent merger of the two departments, there were consultations between the Department of Employment and the Department for Education about the form of training for work in the fields of informal education and community care. Feminist agendas have occasionally had a voice at national level in the civil service. The recommendations of an early working party on *Youth Work with Girls and Young Women* (DES, WO and NACYS 1989) remain worth considering:

1. Voluntary organisations concerned with provisions for girls and young women and local authorities should formulate a policy for youth service provision and make girls' work-central to this policy.
2. Providers of the youth service should develop an action programme for the development of work with girls and young women.
3. Alongside recommendations 1 and 2, an analysis should be made of the allocation of financial resources for youth work, to identify comparative amounts spent on work from which young women directly benefit, and to set financial targets to redress any imbalance.
4. A fresh look should be taken at meeting accommodation needs, to secure more appropriate premises for the development of the work.
5. Voluntary organisations and local authorities should additionally show how they have addressed and are meeting the needs of specific groups of young women.
6. Positive action should be taken to increase the number and seniority of women in the youth service.
7. A review of access to training courses should take place to ensure that women are not disadvantaged.
8. A unit or units should be set up for the development of girls' work nationally.

The National Youth Agency – which acted on behalf of the government in coordinating youth work-based initiatives – has a governing body elected by a number of different constituencies. One of the constituencies is the women and girls' organisations, which includes representation of the Guides and Girls' Friendly Society. The demise of the National Organisation for Work with Girls and Young Women left a significant gap where autonomous work with girls from a feminist perspective was represented at the level of the National Youth Agency.

At a regional and metropolitan level, local authorities can still provide a forum for feminists to make alliances across professional disciplines within public services. Such alliances can be facilitated by senior managers and by elected councillors. They may take the form of consultation forums and working parties – such as the successful domestic violence working parties which have been established by chief executives' departments in a number of councils, or curriculum development groups within education authorities. It is in these apparently unpromising places that networking may occur which can achieve shifts of resource and emphasis in the direction of empowering work with young women. The presence of some women at middle-management level in organisations is certainly essential to the development of these forums. Women managers – especially those with their roots in community-based initiatives or who have made explicit feminist commitments – need to be regarded as allies and actively supported and encouraged to facilitate the development of feminist practice.

Alliance Across Difference: The Different Voluntary Sectors and the Contract Culture

Cutting across the difficulties and possibilities of partnerships between professionals is the problem of the poisonous meeting between a Thatcherite project of privatisation and the introduction of market principles into the provision of education and welfare services on the one hand, and the fragmentation of the 'new social movements' on the other. Many of the projects which came to form the 'new voluntary sector' during the 1970s – including the girls' work projects with which this book is concerned – are founded in the self-help principles and resistance to State control associated with both a libertarian left agenda and with liberal community politics.

The 1980s saw a convergence between the agenda of the government and the ideology of much of the 'new voluntary sector' in a resistance to State control. Resourcing new projects happens through a quasi-market-based system of achieving contracts for particular aspects of service provision. This is thought to make service provision more efficient and able to remain closer to the agendas of service users/clients/customers.

However, the hidden hand of the market seems as unlikely as it has always done to distribute its largesse equally. Somehow, even with the freedom and the creativity of the market at work, established hierarchies re-establish themselves. Services geared to the needs of boys are more easily funded. Provision for girls all too readily becomes provision for girls who already have access to resources: young women's projects which have never had a voice or representation in funding bodies struggle to establish a presence at all in the funding game. Competition for resources favours those who already have access to resources, and even among the habitual losers there is a scramble for advantage which can easily destroy earlier attempts at coalitions.

The Inheritance of 'Identity Politics'

If one side of the difficulties which girls' work faced came from the divisiveness and competitiveness of the contract culture, the other comes from the problems of 'identity politics' created in the forums of equal opportunities strategies in the 1980s. The impact of a liberal equal opportunities agenda has now been carefully explored and subjected to critique (for example, Baker 1987).

In the context of declining resources, the potential for groupings based on apparently exclusive identities to compete with one another for the crumbs has been intense. There has been a tendency in this context for a feminist agenda or a 'women's agenda' to be perceived as a White agenda (with the diverse needs of women from different Black communities subsumed under a 'race' agenda), or to be perceived as a heterosexual agenda (with the needs of lesbians and bisexual women subsumed in a 'gay' or 'queer' agenda). Further, the needs of women as mothers and carers seem to have been most actively addressed as part of a 'children's agenda', leaving the women's agenda for those who do not have children. The women's agenda becomes a disappearing space. There is a lack. It was in part as a result of these pressures that the National Organisation for Work with Girls and Young Women disappeared and will have to be created again in a new form which recognises the diversity and complexity of organising as women.

In this context, it is vital that any organisation of women is anti-separatist in its orientation and prepared to ally, for example, with others who seek to challenge exclusion. In the 1990s, the National Organisation of Lesbian and Gay Workers, the National Organisation of Disabled Youth and Community Workers, the National Black Workers' Conference and Sia, the National Development Agency for the Black Voluntary Sector, were all potential allies. Networks of projects based in poor communities – such as the Outer Estates Network funded by Church Action on Poverty – were also an essential point of contact for work with women which is about empowerment. Most of these networks, however, disappeared in the New Labour years and became refocused on specific targeted groups. Without specific networks of these kinds, work with women and girls will exclude all too many perspectives, and feminist practice will again become a code word for White, middle-class practice. Women who work in positions and in forums where decisions are made, particularly about funding and resourcing, need to work in ways that are actively counter-cultural. Timetables for consultation need to be realistic; programmes for bids to be made need to be drawn up in ways which encourage all groups to participate, and notice needs to be taken of the groups which are absent from the decision-making process. Women's groups which find themselves in competition for funding need to find ways to collaborate, and potential conflicts between mainly White women's groups and Black groups need to be attended to very carefully.

Alliances can only be made to work if they are undertaken with the involvement and support of organisations. They cannot rely solely on the good relationships between individuals. Once these patterns of organisational coalitions are in place, then the long-term work of exploring the points of difference and the points of commonality can be undertaken. At present, this is often undertaken at the level of avowed principles, shared values and aims. There may exist shared commitments to, for example, anti-oppressive practice. Unfortunately, stating a set of principles is not usually the problem. It is at the point of perceived failure to act according to apparently shared principles that coalitions break down.

Tackling the Ideological Agendas of Danger and Safety

Reading the work of Maude Stanley again in the current climate and then referring to the archives of material from the girls' work movement of the 1970s and 1980s, it is hard not to conclude that work with girls and young women is closer in spirit and preoccupations to the agenda of the 1890s than it is to the exhilarating, libertarian agendas of the much more recent past. Part of the impact of the shifts in funding was to refocus the agenda of concern around issues of the protection of girls and young women. There was also a renewed concern with motherhood as the place from which women's contribution to society is most frequently assessed. From the point of view of a feminist practice which challenges the subordination of women, this is a profoundly conservative agenda, which reinforces the sense of girls and young women as victims or as existing to nurture and to meet the needs of others. It infantilises young women and promotes a continuing state of dependency. It suggests a false unity among girls and young women: a unit which seems to derive from either the presence of threats and the need for protection, or, failing all else, a unity which derives from the capacity to bear children.

The commitment to self-activity and self-definition which characterised the early initiatives of the girls' work movement was not alone strong enough to prevent this agenda from re-emerging. It is also difficult to believe the protestations of youth workers that the use of such discourse in funding proposals is merely a convenience and that empowering practice continues, despite the framing of work by very conservative language. Methods which involve the assessment of project success in terms of the attainment of key outcomes and targets clearly mean that the language of funding bodies has its impact. It does not take long to establish itself in our own thinking. Perhaps the persistence of these ideologies of risk and protection and of motherhood suggest the need for a very long-term feminist strategy, capable of persisting as a counter-discourse over generations, capable of becoming an alternative 'common sense' which can achieve the adherence of more than one generation of women.

As well as celebrating diversity and self-activity, it will continue to be necessary to offer alternative accounts of what it means to be a mother and of the nature of female sexuality. The discourse of women's rights and women's potential clearly has staying power. We also need to keep creating and sharing alternative imaginings in which independence and motherhood, pleasure and risk, sexuality and safety are not in opposition to one another. Informal education with girls and young women could ally itself with feminist intellectual work again, including work which is taking place in women's studies. It must certainly ally itself with feminist work in the mass media, where much of the creation of meanings about femininity takes place. It must also value and connect with the work of film-makers, musicians, artists, novelists and poets who resource the imagination.

Working Across Generations?

A number of strategies have been adopted, and there is clearly a commitment and recognition of the need for a variety of responses. The most commonly mentioned are the following:

- There is a perceived need for more women to take their concerns and commitments into senior management positions where the allocation of resources and the formulation of policies can be influenced in the interests of girls and young women. There has been a tendency for women who seek to occupy such senior positions to be seen as 'selling out'. Perhaps the tendencies which create them as 'token women in bureaucracies' or as 'honorary men' need to be addressed instead. An organisational strategy which is explicit about the relationships between feminists who occupy different roles and positions of power in organisations needs to be addressed. Networking among women managers is obviously important, but equally obviously, it is less important than networking between women managers and their subordinates.
- The role of staff development and training has been identified for a number of years as critical to the continuing strength of feminist work. Again, a number of strategies have been adopted, ranging from those which focus on enabling women workers, whether part-time or full-time, to develop their own understandings of their position as women, through to strategies to ensure the development of feminist competence through to staff appraisal schemes! As long ago as 1984, the working group which produced the document *Starting from Strengths* (Bolger, S and Scott D. 1984) commissioned an extensive report on women, training and change which made the following observations in its conclusions.

- Women are not a homogenous group whose needs can be met if only 'the one right formula' is found. What is important is that women can choose and that their right to choose is respected by those who are responsible for ensuring that women part-time and voluntary workers have the training and support they deserve.

- Some women do derive a tremendous amount of support and learning from meeting together in small, women-only groups, where work and personal feelings concerning work are discussed and shared. This will maintain the momentum for change within the roles and opportunities open to women and girls. (Lacey and Sprent 1984: 8)

- Women identified the need for more explicitly-acknowledged mentor relationships which have the purpose of valuing work and of allowing expertise and understandings to be shared. Mentoring involves a one-to-one relationship in which there is an explicit commitment to the development of individuals within the workplace, and even within the career structure. It has been developed as an alternative to managerial supervision and has its roots in traditions of supervision and support which are based on non-hierarchical relationships. However, it also enables a recognition of the place of sponsorship within hierarchies and the need for those who are not part of the traditions of the '(White) men only culture' to find ways of counteracting the tendencies of White, male-dominated organisations simply to reproduce themselves. The practice of mentoring is becoming particularly important for Black professionals, and Black women have much to gain from such a process.

- Women identified the need for networking at all levels, and between women working at all levels in the system and with different levels of experience. Networking needs to occur purposefully and explicitly. It should not be merely a reproduction of social support networks, which may, by their very nature, be fairly homogeneous and exclusive. It is also important to clarify the kind of support women can expect from one another in workplace or professional settings. Just as the boundaries between friendship and work may need to be clarified with young women, so women workers need to be very explicit about what their expectations are of one another in relation to giving and receiving professional support. There is a demonstrable need for support systems for strong, experienced and competent women workers. All too often, professional support is offered only to those who are perceived to be weak or inexperienced or incompetent in some way.

Feminism Across Generations

It should be clear from the argument of this book (and many others) that the transition from being a girl to being a woman is not a natural one. It is socially marked by motherhood, by the acceptance of adult responsibilities for care of dependants and by negotiation of a relationship to heterosexuality. It may also be marked by a relation of economic and social independence from parents and by release from compulsory schooling.

This social and economic independence is not absolute. Dependence on parents and parent substitutes may well be exchanged for dependence on benefits or dependence on a male partner. All the negotiations which occur in this transition are potentially the subject matter of informal education; they form the contested landscape of femininities.

If women are to become a group asserting a political agenda in relation to rights, sexuality and motherhood, the form that the transition from girlhood to womanhood takes will be an essential part of that agenda. It is clear that such a political grouping calling itself feminist, will be characterised by its positive commitment to diversity and the recognition and acknowledgement of difference.

Within feminist writings and discussions, the issue of negotiations about the meaning of the term 'feminism' across generations has paid some attention to the difficulties and potentials of the mother-daughter relationship as a political issue for feminism. It seems very important to me that feminist politics can be identified with the difficult and obstreperous daughters, if it comes to a fight between them and the controlling good-enough mothers. At the same time, feminist politics needs to be able to embrace the power of motherhood and offer alternative forms of adult womanhood including motherhood, to young women.

Informal education with girls and young women in community settings has something to offer to this process of feminist politics, because its starting-point is always future-orientated. It is about girls looking into the future (and changing the world on the way).

The 'gender-mainstreaming' of the New Labour Years, in which Integrated Children's Services and Integrated Youth Support Services were established in local authorities in the UK led to a consequent focus on 'targeted' work which led to a decline of open-access youth work; although open-access work had never been especially hospitable to girls, much autonomous girls' work had developed in this context, which had meant that girls' work could retain an open and developmental, community-based feel rather than develop as a 'social work intervention' for girls at risk, which is where much work with girls has been located in the New Labour period.

The Youth and Policy conference of 2009, 'Thinking Seriously about Work with Girls and Young Women', brought together women to reflect on the position of youth work with girls, and there were many explorations of the constraints and possibilities created by such targeted work. In the new context of austerity politics, it seems likely that youth workers wanting to develop feminist-inspired work with girls and young women will need to develop partnerships which support this work, including partnerships with organisations and networks promoting an open agenda for single-sex work with boys. The exciting re-emergence of political discourses of feminism will do much to support this work. Youth Services in Local Authorities – where they still exist – cannot be relied on to provide the sole infrastructure and it is possible that the development of regional consortia – such as the Regional Working with Girls and Young Women in the North West of England – are likely to provide the most significant platforms for practice in future.

In an evaluation of Feminist Webs conducted in April and May 2009 for National Equality Partnership case studies, one contributor spoke about how the network was operating:

> There are not specific roles in Feminist Webs, we support and energise each other … we did a lot of talking about the structure for Feminist Webs and identified that it's fluidity that's its great strength. We went down the road of discussing a committee structure – but no-one wants to impose a structure so we are trying to think about it in a creative way about how it should operate. Women can identify with it in the way they want to – a different way – organising is needed but we don't know what it is yet. It needs to be loose and fluid.

There is a great desire to remain connected, to be part of the flow and movement of change and transformation, and yet to evade wherever possible the constraints and compliance associated with marketisation and regulation. Nevertheless, organisational and financial support is necessary and Feminist Webs has also been hosted by ICA: UK (Institute of Cultural Affairs), it has been supported by a range of small and medium sized grants from the Heritage Lottery Fund, from Manchester Metropolitan University, from the Big Lottery, from V for Volunteering, from Awards for All and from ROSA, the UK fund for women and girls.

12 The Politics of Globalisation

Unemployment levels in the UK have once again been announced as having reached their highest levels, putting the future of an entire generation at risk, and, according to one analysis of the most recent increase, eight out of ten people who lost their jobs between November 2011 and March 2012 were women, mainly older women ('The female unemployment crisis' http://www. guardian.co.uk/society/2012/feb/20/female-unemployment-crisis-women).

It is uncertain what form services for young people will take in the future in the UK. In Scotland, Wales and Northern Ireland, there appears to be a continuing commitment to direct public service provision whereas in England, the development of a marketised form of public services is at the heart of what is proposed as the basis for any 'youth offer' in the future. Publicly funded services are likely to be required to demonstrate their social impact in order to attract social investment which can generate either savings for the public purse or some new market with profit for the investor. This cock-eyed reasoning will lead to requirements for forms of metrics and accountability which promote a deepening psychologisation of services, relying as they do for their 'well-being indicators' on a variety of scales and measures rooted in psychology as a discipline. Youth work with girls which espouses feminism and which seeks to provoke feminist questioning will have to navigate and negotiate and, whenever possible, steer clear of this terrain.

However, on 10 March 2012, an exhibition opened in celebration of International Women's Day, at the People's History Museum in Manchester, representing the work of the Feminist Webs project presenting both the oral history archive and the current arts projects by young women exploring the themes of women's strength and resilience. The exhibits included banners, photos, cartoons, even love letters of a kind. There was a washing line for pegging out super-powers like resilience and survival which girls currently wish for and a heart of wicker, where the leaves and pages written by young women participants are for healing and dreaming.

It is in such tension between what is dying as a result of the global financial and economic crisis (the provision of public services) and what is still being born (the creation of mutual networks of support such as Feminist Webs represents) that enquiry into the present happens. In 2012's winter of economic crisis and the spring of the democratic uprisings, it is necessary to attend to and enquire about the kinds of transformation these crises might engender. Sylvia Walby has argued that the analysis of the gendered nature of the current crisis might lead to a deeper understanding of new directions for the planet. Walby (2009) has claimed:

> There is no recognition of the role of gender inequality in creating the crisis, as in the absence of women from financial governance. And thus no mention of the benefits to financial governance from the inclusion of women in the reformed financial institutions. There is no mention of the gender-specific impact of the crisis. There is no mention of potential improvements in the position of women in the new economy that could be helped to arise from the ashes of the old via recovery plans.

She has pointed out that the problems in the world financial system were brought into being by an overwhelmingly masculine elite, such as gathers regularly at Davos, suggesting that the 'herd mentality' which prevailed to provoke the financial crisis might have been mitigated by the presence of women. In contrast, the damaging effect of the austerity measures which have been imposed globally has been experienced above all by women. This is a direct consequence of the gendered segregation of labour, where in the workforce, women are still strongly represented in public services which are being demolished or, in the world's poorest nations, in export industries which are under threat. Furthermore, because women still anchor the domestic economy, sustaining (in Iris Marian Young's (1994) formulation) compulsory heterosexuality and the care of babies and bodies, they are occupying positions and spaces globally, which finds them repairing and mending when public services have been withdrawn. Women's time and labour, overwhelmingly though not exclusively, is called on to bridge the gaps left by the withdrawal of public support (Colley 2003). A discussion on such themes was instigated by Fazana Shain at the Gender and Education Association 2012 seedcorn event at Brunel University on 'Modern Girlhoods'.

Walby has further argued that in relation to the current crisis, it is not possible to move the world in a more sustainable direction without women and girls being actively involved in shaping the response to the current crisis. In the words of the old slogan, 'The future is female.' However, this theme has nowhere been taken up with more effect than by the Nike Foundation, in a powerful example of ways in which the corporate sector is able to appropriate and reshape radical analysis and action. 'The Girl

Effect' has a series of campaigning adverts which propose the power of the education of girls to change the world, especially as a means of challenging poverty. This example of philanthropy is what is termed by Bill Gates 'creative capitalism'; the harnessing of both altruism and self-interest to set agendas and retain the capacity of the rich 1 per cent to continue in their wealth needs careful analysis. Such analyses have already been commenced by postcolonial feminist scholars. Lindsay Hayhurst (2009), for example, is drawing attention to the prevalence of sports programmes which both depend on and secure brand recognition.

The sequence of moves in 'The Girl Effect' videos spell out an argument which might at first view indicate a feminist project of 'empowerment': 'The world needs a good kick up the pants' 'Agree/Disagree'. We are then presented, for example, with a 'ticking clock' reminiscent of images of the 'population explosion' which supposedly threatens the world. Then, there are two different cartoon stories about a girl who lives in poverty. In the first, 'her future is clear': 'In the eyes of many she is already a woman. No, really. She is. Married at 14, pregnant at 15, if she survives childbirth she may well need to sell her body, she is likely to contract AIDS.' Alternatively, at 12, happy and healthy, she visits a doctor regularly, stays at school where she's safe, and uses her education to call the shots. After 18, she marries when she chooses, has children when she chooses and this goes on from generation to generation: 'We call this "The Girl Effect": the unique potential of 600 million girls to end poverty for themselves and for the world'.

The difficulty with this powerful campaigning video is that, just as in the UK and the policy about teenage pregnancy, there is globally contested evidence of the truth of claims that levels of adolescent fertility are related to poverty. In fact, levels of adolescent fertility in Rwanda (where 'Girl Effect' projects are underway), Vietnam and Pakistan, for example, are similar to those in the United States, from where this campaign has been launched. Drawing on the United Nations 15-Year Review of the Beijing Platform for Action and the claim that 'empowered girls will 'marry later, delay childbearing, have healthier children and even better incomes that will benefit themselves, their families and their communities', the images of the campaign support a liberal feminist project and, to reprise the old African saying, 'Educate a man and you educate an individual. Educate a woman and you educate a nation.' Yet they present a strongly colonial relationship between the 'helpers' and the 'helped.'

The powerful series of 'Girl Effect' videos reprise a number of themes which make them deeply problematic and obviously colonial, from the point of view of solidarity between women. Whilst appearing to offer a connection based on solidarity and the offering of 'help' which might become self-help, the suggestion is plain that forms of family among the poor are inherently problematic compared to those among the rich (in particular in relation to the 'breeding' habits of the poor), and that the reconstruction of communities through education in readiness for the labour-market needs of global companies is empowering, especially into a consumer society with purchasing power to spare for the Nike trainers.

Whilst the Nike Foundation promote the 'Girl Effect', Nike Sportswear manufacturers are among the companies exposed in War on Want's report *Race to the Bottom: Olympic Sportswear Companies exploitation of Bangladeshi workers* (www.waronwant.org/olympics). This report, which is supported by the National Garment Workers Federation of Bangladesh, shows that women workers for the company face routine sexual harassment, forced unpaid overtime, low wages and the sacking of pregnant workers.

Clearly, the impact on the ground of the 'Girl Effect' is likely to be much more complex and negotiated than its advertising campaign suggests. Nevertheless, it offers a vivid illustration of the capture of the term 'empowerment', as has been discussed throughout this book. A neo-liberal version of empowerment emphasises the rights of girls and young women as individuals, whilst neglecting any attention to the social connectedness which women have created in all societies. Such a 'monetised' version of rights and empowerment means that both bodies and rights are seen as legal entities to be protected, whilst 'voice' and 'choice' are linked to models of democracy based on the ability to consume, whether it be goods or services that are to be chosen. If 'empowerment' is to be retained as a goal of feminist education, it needs to reconnect with practices of sustainability, community, cooperation and struggle. It needs to be part of an 'education otherwise', 'otherwise' than the directions shown by the philanthropic agendas of wealthy corporations.

There are a number of implications of this for youth work with women and girls. It means resisting the pull of mentoring, role modelling and 'one-to-one' relationship as the sole or dominant method of working and continuing, against all the pressures, to value association and group work. It also means that feminist practice must make explicit the assumption that there is a grave problem with the current global economic and financial system which is creating deepening inequalities and forms of coercion and which could be changed. There are alternative visual and political representations of solidarity and struggle in relation to global justice. Kum Kum Bhavnani's film 'The Shape of Water' (2006) suggests some ways in which solidarities can be built. It starts from the politics and agendas of women's campaigns in the global South. It depicts women as collective activists on their own behalves and shows how the flows of energy and activism, like the shape of flowing water and its power, move and shape new possibilities. In doing so, the film recognises and acknowledges complexity, ambivalence and difference as aspects of women's collective political agency.

Difference

'Difference' has been another significant theme of this book. Feminist work with girls, as well as acknowledging and prioritising connectedness, will also continue to open out from difference, from the presence of many histories and communities, and from the presence in each woman of becoming and change.

According to Luce Irigaray (2004), acceptance of difference whilst living on common ground involves at least the following:

- A non-reducible commitment to the expression of difference within the human and across the boundaries of the human with the animal and the human with the machine;
- A recognition of the non-reducibility of 'the other' to the 'the same' and at the same time a recognition that it is in this way that speech comes to be possible;
- A foregrounding of a process of becoming subject in relation to others, rather than a training of the subject by means of knowledge;
- A respect for life and the existing universe rather than an education in the rule of the subject over the world;
- The learning of life in community rather than the acquisition of skills, and
- Construction of a liveable and more cultured future rather than submission to a tradition.

As Irigaray argues:

> A change of perspectives of this sort leads to respecting women as mature citizens and to the enrichment of the community with values which it needs: the practice of intersubjectivity, the sense of the concrete, concern for the future; and to enabling co-existence between women and men, not only on the instinctual level- with all the forms of violence which the institution of the family modestly conceals – but on the level of civilisation.' (Irigaray, 2004)

Such thinking offers a framework for an educational vision of social education which may be a sustainable vision not only for youth work as a counter-practice but also for the development of education systems more widely. It surely involves:

- An unsettling of assumptions about the values in a youth project of playing with cars, working in a motor vehicle workshop, or tending to the horses or chickens on an urban farm, an openness to exploration of what difference might mean and a playfulness in challenging existing boundaries.

- A genuine openness to diversity of projects and experiential learning and to the speaking of a range of different languages within the process of relationship building: not just in terms of the multi-lingual contexts of the contemporary urban setting but in terms of emerging languages and cultural expressions of the young, graffiti projects and Facebook spaces, as well as Roma-Somali football teams.
- Relationship – rather than mastery of knowledge and facts to be passed on – the core and the sense of equality in relationship must be genuine and not feigned for the purposes of 'fitting people in' to existing and designated social categories. An image of community is of groups of young people and adults walking and talking together, whether in the countryside or the city streets.
- Respect for life rather than mastery and rule – a building up of community. Can we rethink the goals of autonomy so that women can learn to respect their own lives and men can learn to value interdependence? Can we reinvent the traditions of the general meeting and the open space in ways that prevent them being dominated by a few very powerful voices?
- A sense that education is a here-and-now and co-created event rather than a fixed body of knowledge which the young must learn. Arts-based creative activity is a fundamental necessity of this practice.
- A non-violent ethic will be fundamental to the work and the stories that are told will foster a more creative future. How then do rules and structures work in youth work? And how are they to be negotiated?

Rosi Braidotti (2004) – building in part on the Irigarayan perspectives – has argued that all this involves an attention to the narratives of becoming-subject within the social imaginary. According to Braidotti, narrativity is 'the crucial binding force' between the material and semiotic conditions, the institutional rules and regulations and the forms of cultural regulation that sustain them. Within this narrativity – the shared cultural process of contributing to and making myths, and operational fictions, significant stories – power both negative (prohibiting and constraining) and positive (empowering and enabling) – flows and it is in this domain that counter-practices and counter-narratives which embrace difference are being made.

Up Against the Positive

In the UK, some of the forms of practice against and in the fissures of which such a practice will develop are clear from the policy document 'Positive for Youth'(DFE, 2011). Whilst this is clearly not a document which will stand the test of time, it reiterates some well-worn themes.

The first rhetorical move is to put young people first, appearing to position the document against deficit models, whilst at the same time rendering young people as responsible for their own position, above all in the labour market. Like the 'empowerment' of the 'Girl Effect', this recognition of young people's agency seems to relieve all other social actors and most especially the Government, as the least responsible – a useful position for a Government policy paper in a period of austerity. The document opens: 'Young People – taking responsibility, making the most of every opportunity available, and speaking up on issues they care most about.' For the more than 50 per cent of young people in the lowest socio-economic groups who are Not in Education Employment or Training (NEET), the Government is offering the 'Youth Contract', for 16–24-year-olds to enable them to participate in learning and work. This is a version of work-related experience which is designed to keep young people 'in the system' without challenging their status at the very bottom of the heap when it comes to the minimum wage and to conditions of employment. Using the 'payment by results' system to youth contract providers creates an incentive to shunt young people into any available opportunities and to work with those young people easiest to reach, rather than challenge either the 'low-pay, no-pay cycle', or the gender segregation of work opportunities.

A second significant development is the development of the National Citizen Service (NCS). This, along with the Cadets, is the only youth organisation currently listed on the UK DfE website. The NCS is an eight-week programme offered to 16-year-olds across the country; it includes outdoor education, community service and a residential, and encourages the 'social mixing' of young people. At the Budget proposed for the National Citizen Service has been widely reported as almost equivalent to the funding lost from Local Authority year-round youth services as a result of austerity measures, if half of those eligible took up the scheme Whilst the opportunities on offer through the National Citizen Service are very much in the personal and social development traditions of youth work, the programme is haunted by a desire for 'oneness' in a nation becoming ever more deeply divided by class. It has historically never been straightforward to communicate what is meant by citizenship in an English(or British) context, where the status of the people remains that of subjects of the Crown rather than of rights-bearing citizens. Set against attempts to teach the meaning of 'Britishness' through a school curriculum in a didactic fashion, the emphasis on implicit and experiential learning of core values in the NCS is strong. Memories of 'all pulling together' and images of the Blitz are still readily culturally available, especially in a London context, but the war-time reference is perhaps more recent, closer to hand and more traumatic than can be easily be spoken.

If 'Britishness' and even 'Englishness' cannot be taught didactically, there is nevertheless a version of Englishness which is promoted as powerfully to be desired in this scheme. The ideal of 'social mixing' is in fact necessarily underpinned by a strongly felt hierarchy of classes and perhaps of rank, of officers and men. One side of this mix which will create 'Englishness' or perhaps more accurately 'Britishness' is a sense of 'noblesse oblige' among the privileged classes. But the 'lower classes' also contribute to the mix. Paul Oginsky – the front man for the NCS and a man of impeccably humble origins – worked previously with Simon Weston, a veteran of the Falklands War, and together they established Weston Spirit, which was inspired by Weston's recovery after multiple burn injuries during that war. Apocryphally, Simon Weston, when wished 'Get Well Soon' by Prince Andrew, is reported to have replied 'Yes, sir, I will.' That 'yes, sir' sums up an approach to authority which is integrative, drawing on shared experience between officers and men, but which is also profoundly anti-democratic.

It is a model with a clear preference for the masculine, with citizen service conceived primarily as physical challenge and discipline. Strongly assimilationist, the prospectus of 'service' for the more advantaged participants is surely a preparedness to take part in the scheme at all and therefore potentially to mix, for a few weeks of their lives, with the 'lower orders'. Sixteen-year-olds, of all backgrounds, who are ready to take part in this scheme are then marshalled – ideologically – against 'the enemy within': now recognised, after the riots in British cities in the summer of 2011, as 'those sections of our society not broken but sick' against whom 'a fightback' is underway. Specifically addressing the riots, the British Youth Council's 'Not in Our Name' campaign followed this prime ministerial rhetoric, positioning the 'respectable' against the 'rough' once more. Those (among the poor) who do not or will not share the aspiration for mixing with those of 'other ranks', who prefer their own spaces however confined and who seek to mark their difference, through Islamic dress for example, whilst holding a UK passport, are the problem (Binnie et al 2006). It is therefore against such young people from the poorest communities that the seemingly friendly 'Dad's Army' sub-text of the 'nation pulling together in wartime' is in fact addressed.

Given the anti-democratic spirit which imbues the youth work of the National Citizen Service (de St Croix 2011), it is useful to track the networks of private philanthropy, business and faith which are informing the developments. The Christian philanthropist Steve Chalke leads the Challenge Trust which has been the major provider of National Citizen Service programmes,prior to the involvement of the company SERCO in the 2012 bidding round. Nat Wei, David Cameron's key adviser on the 'Big Society', was founder of the Teach First Charity and of the Shaftesbury Partnership. In taking Lord Shaftesbury, the great nineteenth-century evangelical philanthropist as his model, Wei, the state-school educated, Hong-Kong born Christian, aligns himself clearly with the charitable traditions of the English elite. It is no surprise, therefore, that alongside a conservative model of philanthropy should be found a return to ideals of masculinity, muscular Christianity and discipline founded in military traditions. Alongside the current encouragement of staff leaving the armed forces to enter teaching as a career, there is encouragement of and funding for Cadet Corps in schools, especially state schools, as a form of youth engagement and proposals for military academies as a response to so-called riot-torn areas. This is accompanied by a return to 'boot-camp' style interventions, to boxing as the basis for 'anti-gang' strategies and by a renewed emphasis on 'role models' – again, especially for young men – who are seen to lack positive role models in poor communities.

In this context, in which attention flows both to the problematic and the potential of boys first and above all, the chief focus on girls is once more in relation to sexuality and especially to forms of dress. The Bailey Report (2011) – *Letting Children be Children*, by Reg Bailey of the Mothers Union – is the chief source of a commitment in Positive for Youth to address the commercialisation and sexualisation of childhood. This report seems to have ignored a widespread academic discussion and critique of the very notion of 'sexualisation' in favour of focusing simplistically on the purchasing power of working-class families to offer a style of clothing to girls which encourages them to emulate a particular (dis-approved) form of adult femininity from a young age. The Bailey Report deliberately marginalises discussions of gender stereotyping and 'pinkification' of products and focuses instead on the prevailing current concern with 'sexualisation' (Barker and Duchinsky 2012). There is no discussion of what 'growing up' or 'developing sexuality' might mean in this day and age, for boys or girls, or that for girls, this period of growing into adulthood seems, once more, to be full of danger conceived as risk rather than as adventure. There is no 'Dangerous Book for Girls' to accompany the widely circulated *Dangerous Book for Boys*. There is no discussion of the pleasures and possibilities of sexuality conceived as part of adult life, or of the variety of consensual expressions it may have, for girls as well as boys. Crop-tops and lipstick for little girls, no way. However, in relation to the commercial exploitation and 'pinkification' of childhood, and the targeting of children as consumers, nothing is said. Pink plastic kitchen sets, and 'Star Wars' computer games, it seems, still rule OK.

Delivery Models: What the New Labour/Con-Dems Ordered?

The favoured method through which this socially conservative youth work is to be delivered is through the marketisation process. Although there is some slight 'nod' towards the development of cooperatives and mutuals, it is through ideas of social enterprise, the development of social impact investment and the 'monetising' of impact measures that the Government believes youth work can be delivered. As Stephen Ball (2007) puts it in his analysis *Education plc*, privatisation, philanthropy and peripheralisation go hand in hand. Models of the Big Society, that is, a society which is governed by the power of a market economy with little countervailing pressure and regulation from the state (which is seen only as imposing unnecessary inefficiencies through regulation) may seem attractive at first sight to community development practitioners who have long argued and developed practice in conflict with the bureaucratic structures of local government. Big Society thinking can appear to hand 'power to the people' in the form of creative and responsive voluntary-sector organisations which replace those led by local authorities. However, local authorities still commission services and in this context they are demanding 'more bangs for the buck' (more excitement for their money? More what exactly for their money? The connotations of sexual exploitation here are inescapable to my ears!)

At the beginning of discussions of the Big Society, Anna Coote, director of social policy at the New Economics Foundation (http://neweconomics. org) argued for ten ways to make the Big Society work:

1. Make Social Justice the main goal.
2. Build a broader economy: involving reform of the banking system including access to credit for all.
3. Build a bigger democracy, based on participatory democratic models.
4. Make sure everyone can participate: not just knowledge, skills and confidence, but also the material means, especially in relation to IT and new communication technologies.
5. Make co-production the standard way to get things done. Blur the distinctions between users and providers whenever possible.
6. Transform the role of professionals and other providers. Help them see their place in partnerships and in whole systems approaches.
7. Redistribute paid and unpaid time. The report proposes a move towards a standard 21-hour working week.
8. Make it sustainable. This involves supporting initiatives that work to create and sustain a low-carbon economy.

9. Measure what matters. This is the direct opposite of the 'monetising' of impact currently proposed. It builds on local understandings and long-term narratives.
10. Be part of a great transition to a bigger society and a bigger democracy.

Ideas such as these, with their roots in social democracy, offer strength to the image of youth work rooted in democratic alliances rather than in 'bidding consortia'. If there is to be a burgeoning of cooperative initiatives in youth work, such ideas of social enterprise within an independent cooperative sector will deserve attention and development, linking with the development of other cooperative educational and social welfare initiatives, such as cooperative community schools.

Democratic practice will build on what has been learned through long histories of participation and association in youth work and will have an emphasis on the individual-in-relationship and on association in practice. Democratic and radical experiments in schooling as well as wider cooperative and community-based intergenerational education will continue to offer the basis for future partnership working, if we are not to require informal educators to become 'impossible subjects' attempting critical practice in conditions which render it impossible. The contradictions implicit in critical practice in the increasingly conservative context are now widely discussed and the importance of mutual support and care of staff has never been greater. Many staff who are employed full time will find themselves working in services geared to young people with needs for specialist services or for those who have been targeted as part of the '120,000 families with complex needs'. They will necessarily be pulled towards practices of case work intervention.

The impact of the structural and material conditions such as those imposed by austerity budgets and the development of the practice of social investment leads to a stronger and stronger sense of compromised subjectivity among youth and community work practitioners, as the contradiction between the aspiration to contribute to a radical democratic practice and the actual conditions of labour becomes ever more acute. Helen Colley's work (2003) has pointed to the ways in which the emotional and ethical labour of staff – often in relatively low-paid and para-professional roles in welfare and education – is exploited in order to sustain a network of social relations which is being neglected and marginalised in the global economy. The espousal of ideologies concerning 'role modelling' and 'mentoring' and the development of pathways to success does little to ameliorate the deteriorating conditions in which such work takes place, leading to the creation of impossible subject positions for staff. In these conditions too, staff are likely themselves to reiterate stigmatising discourses about young people, sometimes as a means of shoring up their own self-identities.

The processes whereby youth work staff themselves adopt discourses concerning a 'lack of role models' or a 'cycle of violence' in relations to the 'threat of gang involvement' for example, reiterating, reworking and sometimes resisting prevailing discourses is certainly too little researched and understood (Parkes and Connolly 2011). Youth workers can be both angry at the stigmatising of young people and neighbourhoods and yet more than able to replicate it in their own talk, positioning themselves as heroes and rescuers.

It is only if practitioners are able to associate with one another and with traditions of practice which go beyond and beneath the economistic requirements of social investment and 'monetising' that critical work will have a chance of being sustained and practitioners will be enabled to live with and think and imagine beyond and against the contradictions which the current situation imposes. Recent work on the significance of developmental group work with girls and young women's groups has been undertaken in the context of schooling (Cruddas and Haddock 2003) and recent writing on schools – such as the Nuffield Review on 14–19 education – has positively welcomed the inclusion of youth work-based traditions such as detached youth work in the education network (Pring 2009).

Fielding and Moss (2011) have suggested a number of characteristics of a practice which embodies this radical democratic tradition, discussed earlier. These include:

- a proclaimed democratic vitality;
- insistent affirmation of possibility;
- the centrality of dialogue and co-creation of knowledge as a pedagogic practice;
- the importance of inter-generational working;
- positional restlessness and the ability to experiment with democratic forms and relations of authority including an exploration of the role of school meetings in this process, and
- a sense of connection with the regional, national and global.

Feminist work with girls needs to be located clearly in the democratic tradition and needs to embrace a willingness to experiment with and enquire into the inherited forms of democracy and authority which have continued to enshrine patriarchal authority even when it is seen as fraternal rather than fatherly. Recent EU guidance on multicultural practice in youth work suggested the following modalities for practice: Break Down Walls, Remove Barriers, Build Bridges, Share Spaces (Grattan 2010), and these will remain significant guides for the future direction of radical democratic education.

However, for some time yet, experimentation with all these things, within the enclosed space and sometimes admittedly high walls of separate work with girls and young women may enable conversations to flourish which can contribute to the challenge to the tyranny of the gaze and the symbolic violence enacted in all young people's lives. In the face of the takeover of the term 'empowerment' by global companies and their philanthropic institutions, in neo-liberal governance and by the beauty industry, and in order to enable real engagement with the complexity of the multicultural question in young women's lives, community-based feminist youth work in young women's spaces (though connected to the common conversation supported by a common school or neighbourhood network) continues to offer vital unsettling possibilities through informal education.

Thirty years after it first opened, the Young Women's Night at the Water Adventure Centre at Droylsden, Greater Manchester was still offering 'a weekly session, providing a safe space for young women to explore the issues that affect their lives. Regular activities have included rafts, poetry, canoeing, discussions, health education, volunteering, applying for grants, International Women's Week events, trips out and residentials!' But even this long-established project is threatened by closure in 2012, as this work is seen as less important than provision targeted at families with complex needs. Many of the displays about resilience made by young women's projects in the North-west on display in the People's History Museum spoke of love as a super-power. 'All you need is love' was a common theme. But in order for that power to be realised, it may be necessary for some time yet to remember, in the face of the devastations being wrought by the loss of public services and the waste of young women's potential this implies, the place of anger and collective organising in the work of love, and the role of risk, danger and shared adventure as essential elements of feminist-inspired informal education.

Appendix 1 Every Girl Matters! Young Women Matter! A Feminist Comment

During the consultation period for the 'Youth Matters!' Green Paper (DfE 2005), I was invited to join a consultation seminar organised by the YWCA. This is a slightly extended version of the paper I gave at that seminar, seeking to address the historical and theoretical roots of the case for gender specific work. Thirty years after the passing of the Sex Discrimination Act, the absence of any discussion of gender in the Green Paper is startling.

Catching the wave of organising for 'women's liberation' in the 1970s and riding it right up to the mid-1980s transformed the lives of many women who were part of the youth and community work scene, and transformed the lives of many of the girls and young women we worked with. These were girls who in the punk rock era wore tampons for earrings. They were also the girls who, by the end of the 1980s, marching against Section 28 of the Local Government Act, chanted 'We're here, we're queer and we're not going shopping.' They (and we) took part in motorbike workshops, ran girls' football teams and leagues, took apprenticeships in the manual trades, set up sexual health clinics even before the AIDS epidemic made this a cruel necessity (the one in Manchester was called YWait), created and managed more than two hundred refuges for women leaving violent relationships (there was no Women's Aid Federation at the beginning of the 'second wave'), ran cultural events, made music, films, plays, rituals, wrote stories and poems which formed an enormous resource for the movement, printed newsletters on inky machines called Gestetners, networked before the term 'network' referred to computers … It is hard at my age not to become nostalgic.

There have been enormous transformations in gender and our understanding of gender in the last 25 years, but there are also some persistent patterns. One of the achievements of the 'second wave' has been to make gender visible in ways in which it was invisible before. Pre-feminism, 'youth' means boys: writing and thinking about 'youth' was thinking about boys and if, occasionally, girls were mentioned, it was as a source of embarrassment and problems for group dynamics. Short sections of long studies of group work or experiential learning mentioned the problem of 'The girl in the club'. And, now in the period some call 'post-feminist', the dominant reference of the word 'youth' is once more to a highly visible and troublesome population, most if not all of whom are male.

'Separate work' with women and girls and with boys and men was seen – from the period in which the YWCA and other girls' organisations were founded – as natural and right. Based in the doctrine of 'separate spheres', separate youth work offered the opportunity to teach appropriate feminine virtues to girls (particularly those concerned with cooking, cleaning and domestic labour) and to teach appropriate masculine virtues to boys (drill, survival, the outdoors and ropework). Second-wave feminists saw it differently. For us, separate work was very hotly debated. The Sex Discrimination Act had just been passed and there was a real need to challenge practices and organisations which excluded women, from maths class onwards. It certainly did not always seem a sensible tactic to be excluding men, but the place of separate small groups as a sphere of empowerment for women, of what was called 'consciousness raising', was established early on. By making common cause with other women who shared our predicament, we could see our 'femininity', if you like, more clearly and open it up to change, see what needed to change. And if this made sense for us as young adult women workers, it made sense too for the young women we worked with. 'Girls' Nights' and 'Girls' Weekends' and 'Girls' Days' opened (with much opposition) all around the country. 'What about the boys?' was the cry which greeted these initiatives 'Don't they need something too?' The response of feminist workers was stubborn: why *not* give young women the space to ask questions about what was on offer to them, in their relationships, in their working lives, as mothers, as women from Black and minority communities? Why *not* give them space to explore what they had in common and what divided them? To ask for themselves the question that had always been asked and answered for them. 'What do women want?' So the rationale for separate work shifted away from the idea of 'separate spheres' and became more political. Small-group work with girls was about change: identifying and then changing 'what was within our grasp, and what was outside our power'.

What happened? Why did this practice disappear, as it seems to have done, from the mid-1980s? Was it discredited? There was certainly a decline in resources. There was also an attack on 'feminists' while retaining a rhetoric of equality. Or were we more successful than we realised, many of our goals achieved? Certainly some of our goals were achieved, but many patterns persist. The Family Planning Association, in its 'Beyond Barbie' work, still promotes separate advice and guidance for young women and young men, as well as mixed gender work and culturally specific work in order to reach both young women and young men. The Surestart Plus evaluation of work with teenage mothers and fathers recommends separate personal advisers or 'lead professionals' for young mothers and young fathers, and makes the case that this supports both the mother and the father in their negotiation of their relationship, partly because of the persistent problem of domestic violence. The Equal Opportunities Commission recommends two work experience placements for young men and young women in secondary school, at least one in a non-traditional setting, to counter the labour market segregation which results in three-quarters of young women finding work in catering, cleaning, clerical, cashiering, or caring employment.

However, the rationale for separate work seems to have changed, post-feminism. More often than not, separate work seems to exist because of some perceived 'lack' in girls. Lack of confidence and lack of self-esteem are mentioned a lot. Or else it is justified because of some 'risk' against which girls need special protection, particularly the 'risk' of unplanned pregnancy. Separate work is also sometimes argued for because of some 'other' culturally specific practice which requires separate meeting spaces and places for males and females. This is usually presented as a conforming to a condition of patriarchal culture (young women and young men are not allowed to mix socially). The source of such cultural norms may not be well understood and is rarely explicitly engaged with critically or as a source of inter-cultural learning. This explains the persistence of 'Asian girls groups' in areas where all the others have ceased to exist.

I think, however, the feminist case for separate work remains. I think it would look different now from the way it looked in the 1970s and 1980s. It would involve much more rapid changes in patterns, more permeable boundaries, the exploration of difference as much as commonality, and the investigation of masculinity as well as femininity. 'What about the boys? Don't they need something too?' If the failure to respond adequately to that challenge was understandable, tactically, in the earlier movement, it could not and would not be right to repeat that failure now. There is more openness now than there ever was then to the exploration of masculinity. Separate work with boys, that isn't just about playing football, is a real possibility now. And perhaps the new concern for boys – especially in relation to mental health and suicide – and the renewed crime and disorder agenda which affects boys disproportionately – can be seen not as a threat to girls but as an opportunity to press once again for a vision of work with young people that takes gender dynamics seriously and that treats boys and girls, young men and young women equally.

This is not, of course, the language of 'Youth Matters!'. It is striking how invisible the presence of 'difference' is, not only gender difference, but all those 'differences' which can be understood as the signs of inequality, documentation and domination. In the language of 'Youth Matters!', we are already 'one nation', with but one dividing line, between those who deserve help and support and those who, as a result of their anti-social behaviour, do not. This cannot detain us for long here although it is a serious and significant matter. When pressed, the drafters of Green Papers will always acknowledge the importance of 'equality and diversity', and yet the discourses which have been developed in the last thirty years which enable both the analysis of discrimination and the challenge to it are missing from youth policy. Institutionalised racism, sexual harassment, homophobic bullying, disability discrimination: this is not the lexicon of 'Youth Matters!'. Still, this must not put a stop to conversation. What are the themes of 'Youth Matters!' that have potential for those of us who still do not speak with those words?

Things to Do and Places to Go

Shall we say, girl-friendly places to go? Girl friendly, girl-challenging things to do? What might this mean now, for feminists? Some themes remain from earlier times. To what extent are girls still more likely to be found in the 'private sphere' gathering in small numbers in one another's bedrooms rather than on the streets, bowling alone, or in parks and other public spaces? What sort of places to meet can offer the security and warmth of that private space? Young women in the YWCA's consultation groups emphasised the importance of clean, attractive, warm, secure and well-lit meeting places in contrast with far too much youth provision. Femininity is certainly about creating spaces and making them beautiful still – 'gilding the lily' it used to be called – so can we expect to see girls and young women taking an active and creative part in the making of these 'places to go'? I hope so.

Places to go also need to be places where consenting adult relationships can be explored, with one another or with boys. Youth work has long had a commitment to the development (in theory, if not always in practice) of safe spaces. Of course, this can be a protective move, a move to close down risk. But it can also be an empowering one: a practice that enables women and girls to name what they will and won't put up with. There was no word for sexual harassment before second-wave feminism. It was called 'having a laugh'. There are words now, and young women will create new ones if they have the opportunity to do so.

'Things to do' need to be things you want to do, and things you might never have thought of doing until someone gave you a chance, and things you aren't really supposed to do but would like to try. Running around the football field still? A women-only music night? Playing the bass guitar? Pointing the camera?

Opportunities

Part of the inheritance of the earlier girls' work movement is the emphasis on breaking down isolation and also competitiveness between girls and women. 'Better together' might have been a slogan for all our work. The image of the isolated individual wielding a credit card as he skilfully navigates the fluid opportunities of liquid modernity is a long way from either the reality or the aspirations of most young women in the poorest communities, where survival depends again and again on the quality of the network of relationships on which they can draw and to which they contribute. Youth work is about working with the strengths of peer groups and networks, the strengths that can come from association to create new opportunities for young women and for young men. Choice isn't only about being an effective consumer. The most important opportunities do not depend on having a plastic card. Choice in the feminist lexicon is about non-negotiable rights, far more than about responsibilities. Choice is created by the informing and accompanying process that informs informed consent, and it is about an inherent motivation for involvement in the negotiated processes and opportunities youth work offers. It is about raising new and greater expectations, creating opportunities where they haven't existed yet, or haven't been sustained. Youth work is about young people being creators of the future, not only inheritors of the past and two hours' PE a week. Sports, arts, music, even politics are all vehicles of youth work, even if the Olympic Games are the focus. If we put the word 'equal' in front of the word 'opportunities', let's hear it for dancing and aerobics, for women's football, women's cricket, women's and men's netball, and for everyone to have the chance to learn to abseil. Though perhaps it is better not to remind MPs of the places where abseiling has been put to good effect.

Citizenship

Citizenship has been the focus of feminist work with girls and women for many decades. After the vote was won, the National Union of Societies for Women's Suffrage became the National Union of Women's Societies for Equal Citizenship. But what is citizenship in the twenty-first century, where the tearing apart of war and the global inequalities of wealth are driving huge waves of refugees and transforming our sense of national borders? And what is women's citizenship, and how are we to talk to young women about it in a world which makes them (still) as women far more aware of their responsibilities than of their rights? The volunteering programmes which are so important currently are very important to young women, and probably remain more attractive to them than to boys. A good woman still puts others before self. At the same time, mothering and motherhood provides the stumbling block for an image of citizenship that emphasises autonomy and contribution to society through participation in the labour market. And yet it remains the 'most important thing', but we can never get the timing right. Too young? Or else too old? Women as mothers are also women as citizens and our image of inclusion needs to change to include the unpaid labours of love, as well as the bread-winning of the labour market, whether it is men or women who undertake those labours. And equal citizenship between men and women means an equal voice for these aspects of the life of the national and the world.

It is important to make sure that young women's voices are heard right through the process of consultation on which governments now depend. Gender audits of local political participation are discovering (again!) the gendered pattern of community involvement: women organising at local level, men at the strategic partnership board, male speech at meetings outweighing female speech by many times. We could start by doing a number count of young men and young women in the consultation process. And we can go beyond that to deliberately seek out the voices of young women whose experience may be especially marginalised. I am thinking, in particular, of asylum-seeking young women whose experiences and stories are so often demanded and then disbelieved, but there are many others. Citizenship in the twenty-first century is more and more about voice, and in the wonderful words of Arundhati Roy: 'There is no such thing as the voiceless. There are only the deliberately silenced or the persistently misheard.' Our job remains that of enabling young women to break silences, particularly perhaps the self-imposed ones, to come to speech, and to participate as equals in the thousand big and small conversations which are shaping the future.

Originally published in *Youth and Policy* 90 (2006).

Appendix 2 Questionnaire Based on Pearl Jephcott's questionnaire in *Girls Growing Up* (1942)

Youth workers were asked to use the following prompts which are largely those used by Pearl Jephcott with occasional updating:

- Date
- Age
- Self-identification (in terms of nation, ethnicity, sexuality, disability, gender, or anything else)
- Post Code

Favourites

- What is your favourite outfit/item of clothing at the moment?
- Do you buy your own clothes with your own money or do you have support from parents/carers?
- How many pairs of shoes do you have?
- What is your favourite magazine?
- Do you buy it?
- Are you reading any books at the moment? If so, what?
- What is your favourite TV programme?
- Do you have a favourite radio programme?
- What is your favourite music?
- Do you have a best friend who is a girl? How old is she?
- Do you have a best friend who is a boy? How old is he?
- Do you go around mainly with a) a group of girls? Or b) a group of boys and girls? Or d) a group of boys?
- What is your favourite pastime?
- What is your most treasured possession? How did you come to have it?

- Your favourite volunteering work and/or charity (if any?)

Jobs

- Do you have a job or jobs?
- What are they?
- What hours do you work?
- Do you get any breaks?
- Are you studying at all? Do you learn anything linked to your work?
- Are your jobs easy, hard, or monotonous?
- What wages are paid?
- Do your parents/carers give you money?
- What holidays do you have each year?
- Do you belong to a trade union? Which one?
- Would you like to do a job with children?

Home

- Do you have a garden where you live?
- Are there any parks or open spaces where you live? How near are they?
- Do you have any pets?
- What did you have today for breakfast?
- For your main meal?
- What is the main job done by your parents/carers?
- Who else lives in your house?
- What rooms do you have in your house?
- Did you do any housework yesterday?
- Have you been to the doctor this year?
- Have you been to the dentist this year?
- Have you ever slept away from home?
- Have you done any of these in the last seven days? Been dancing? Been to the cinema? Watched a DVD? Cycling, the gym, walking, swimming or other exercise? Been to a bar or club? Taken part in a social, music, or cultural group, and if yes, which one? Been to a lecture or class?
- Finally, a 2010 addition: what social issues do you think are important to you as a young woman today?

References

Adams, P. (2003) 'Social Exclusion and Citizenship in a Global Society', *Youth and Policy*, Summer 2003.

Aggleton, P., Rivers, K. and Warwick, I. (1990) *AVERT/AIDS: Working with Young People*, Horsham: AVERT.

Ahmed, S. (2004) *The Cultural Politics of Emotion*, Edinburgh: Edinburgh University Press.

Alinsky, S. (1971) *Rules for Radicals. A Pragmatic Primer for Realistic Radicals*, New York: Random House.

Alldred, P. (2007) *Get Real About Sex: The Politics and Practice of Sex Education*, Maidenhead: Open University Press.

Allen, G. (2011) *Early Intervention: The Next Steps*, An Independent Report to Her Majesty's Government..., London: HMG.

Allen, L. (2004) 'Beyond the Birds and the Bees: constituting a discourse of erotics in sexuality education', *Gender and Education*, 16: 151–67.

Allen, M. and Ainley, P. (2007) *Education Makes You Thick, Innit*, London: Tufnell Press.

Anthias, F. and Davis, N.Y. (1991) *Racialised Boundaries: Race, nation, gender, colour and class in the antiracist struggle*, London: Routledge.

Arai, L. (2009) *Teenage Pregnancy The Making and Unmaking of a Problem*, Bristol: Policy.

Arendt, H. (1986) 'Communicative Power', in Lukes, S. (ed.) *Power*, Oxford: Basil Blackwell.

Arnold, J., Askins, D., Davies, R., Evans, S., Rogers, A. and Taylor, T. (1981) *The Management of Detached Work: How and Why*, Leicester: NAYC Publications.

Ashby, A. (1994) 'Asian young women act it out', *Youth Clubs*, April.

Back, L., Keith, M., Khan, A., Shukra, K. and Solomos, J. (2002) 'New Labour's White heart: politics, multiculturalism and the return of assimilation', *The Political Quarterly* 73(4): 445–54.

Badham, B.(2004) 'Participation for a Change. Disabled Young People Lead the Way', *Children and Society* 18(4) April: 143–54.

Bailey, R. (2011) *Letting Children Be Children* (Department of Education report), London: HMSO.

Baker, J. (1987) *Arguing for Equality*, London: Verso.

Ball, S. (2007) *Education plc: Understanding Private Sector Participation in Public Sector Education*, London: Routledge.

Banks, S. (ed.) (2010) *Ethical Issues in Youth Work*, London; Routledge.

Banyard, K. (2010) *The Equality Illusion*, London: Faber.

Barker, M. and Duchinsky, R. (2012) 'Sexualisation's Four Faces. Sexualisation and Gender Stereotypes in the Bailey review' <www.academia.edu>.

Batsleer, J. (1986) *Project Report*, Wakefield Youth Service.

_____ (2008) *Informal Learning in Youth Work*, London: Sage.

_____ (2010a) 'Feminist Webs: A Case Study of the Personal Political and Professional in Youth Work', in Robb, M. and Thomson, R. (2010) (eds) *Critical Practice with Children and Young People*, Bristol: Policy Press, 217–33.

_____ (2010b) 'Youth Work Futures?', in Batsleer, J. and Davies, B. (eds) *What is Youth Work?* Exeter: Learning Matters.

_____ (2011a) 'The History of Youth Work with Girls in the UK. Targets from Below?', in Coussée, F., Verschelden, G. and Williamson, H. (eds) *The History of Youth Work in Europe and its Relevance for Youth Policy Today*. Vol. 3. Strasbourg: Council of Europe Publishing.

_____ (2011b) 'Voices from An Edge? Unsettling the Practices of Youth Voice and Participation: Arts-based practice in The Blue Room, Manchester', *Pedagogy, Culture and Society* 19(3): 419–34.

_____ (2012) 'Dangerous Spaces, Dangerous Memories, Dangerous Emotions: Informal Education and Heteronormativity. A Manchester Youth Work Vignette', *Discourse: Studies in the Cultural Politics of Education*. vol 33 no 3, 345-361

_____ and Davies, B. (eds) (2010) *What is Youth Work?* Exeter: Learning Matters.

_____, Hanbury, A. and Lee, A. (2010) 'Youth Work with Girls. A Feminist Perspective', in Batsleer, J. et al. (2002) 'Domestic Violence and Minoritization. Supporting Women to Independence', Manchester: European Social Fund and Manchester Metropolitan University.

Beetham, D. (1991) *The Legitimation of Power*, London: Macmillan.

Beetham, M. (1996) *A Magazine of Her Own? Domesticity and Desire in the Woman's Magazine 1800–1914*, London: Routledge.

Benhabib, S. (ed.) (1995) *Feminist Contentions: A Philosophical Exchange*, New York and London: Routledge.

Berry, H. and Oyteza, C. (2007) 'Not Seen and Not Heard: Gender, Community Participation and Representation', Oxfam, A Re-Gender Briefing Paper.

Binnie, J. et al. (2006) *Cosmopolitan Urbanism*, Abingdon and New York: Routledge.

Bolger, S. and Scott, D. (1984) *Starting from Strengths*, Leicester: National Youth Bureau.

Braidotti, R. (2002) *Metamorphoses. Towards a Materialist Theory of Becoming.* Cambridge: Polity.

Browne, S.E., Connors, D. and Stern, N. (1985) *With the Power of Each Breath: A Disabled Women's Anthology*, Pittsburgh, PA: Cleis Press.

Bryan, B., Dadzie, S. and Scafe, S. (1985) *The Heart of the Race*, London: Virago.

Burman, E. (2008a) *Deconstructing Developmental Psychology*, London: Routledge.

_____ (2008b) *Child, Image, Nation*, London: Routledge.

Butler, J. (1989) *Gender Trouble: Feminism and the Subversion of Identity*, New York: Routledge.

_____ (2004) *Undoing Gender*, London and New York: Routledge.

_____ (2006) *Precarious Life The Powers of Mourning and Violence*, London: Verso.

Butler, S. and Wintram, C. (1991) *Feminist Groupwork*, London: Sage.

Campbell, B. (1993) *Goliath: Britain's Dangerous Places*, London: Methuen.

Carabine, J.(2007) 'New Labour's Teenage Pregnancy Policy', *Cultural Studies* 21(6): 952–73.

Carpenter, V., and Young, K. (1986) *Coming in from the Margins: Youth Work with Girls and Young Women*, Leicester: National Association of Youth Clubs.

Chauhan, V. (1989) *Beyond Steel Bands n Samosas*, Leicester: National Youth Bureau.

Coburn, A. (2011)', 'Building social and cultural capital through learning about equality in youth work.' *Journal of Youth Studies* 14: 4, 475–491.

Cockburn, C. (1987) *Two-track Training: Sex Inequalities and the Y.T.S*, Basingstoke: Macmillan.

Cohen, S. (2003) *No-one is Illegal*, Stoke on Trent: Trentham Books.

Cole, P. (1989) 'Northern College, Barnsley and Wakefield Partnership', *Replan Bulletin* 3, Summer.

Colley, H. (2003) *Mentoring for Social Inclusion: A Critical Approach to Nurturing MentorRelationships*, London and New York: Routledge Falmer.

Connolly, C. (1990) 'Splintered Sisterhood: Anti-Racism in a Young Women's Project', *Feminist Review* 36, Autumn.

Coward, R. (1984) *Female Desire*, London: Paladin.

Cressey, G. (2007) *The Ultimate Separatist Cage? Youth Work with Muslim Young Women*, Leicester: NYA.

Cruddas, L. and Haddock, L. (2003) *Girls' Voices. Supporting Girls' Learning and Emotional Development*, Stoke on Trent: Trentham Books.

Dadzie, S. (1997) *Blood, Sweat and Tears*, Leicester: Youth Work Press.

Davies, B. (1986) *Threatening Youth: Towards a National Youth Policy*, Milton Keynes: Open University Press.

_____ (2008) *The New Labour Years. A History of the Youth Service in England Vol. III 1997–2007*. Leicester: NYA.

_____ and Merton, B. (2009) 'Squaring the Circle? A Modest Enquiry into the State of Youth Work Practice in a Changing Policy Environment', Leicester: De Montfort University.

De St Croix, T. (2011) 'Struggles and Silences: Policy, Youth Work and the National Citizen Service', *Youth and Policy* 106: 46–59.

Dennis, J. (1982) 'How dare you assume I made a mistake? Young Black Women with Children', *Working with Girls Newsletter*, 9, May/June.

Dennis, N. (1993) *Rising Crime and the Dismembered Family*, London: Institute of Economic Affairs Health and Welfare Unit.

_____ and Erdos, G. (1993) *Families without Fatherhood* (Foreword by A.H. Halsey), London: Health and Welfare Unit.

Department for Children, Schools and Families (DCFS) (2007), *The Children's Plan: Building Brighter Futures* Cm 7280. London: HMSO.

Department for Education (2011) *Positive for Youth. A New Approach to Cross-Government Policy for Young People aged 13-19*. London, DFE.

DES, WO and NACYS (Department of Education and Science, Welsh Office and National Advisory Council for the Youth Service) (1989) *Youth Work with Girls and Young Women*, January, London: HMSO.

DfE (Department for Education) (1994) *Education Act 1993: Sex Education in Schools*, Circular No. 5/94.

Department for Education and Skills (DfES)(2003) *Every Child Matter*, London: DfES.

_____(2001) *Transforming Youth Work: Developing Youth Work for Young People*, Nottingham: DfES.

_____(2002) *Transforming Youth Work: Resourcing Excellent Youth Services*, London: DfES.

_____ (2005) *'Youth Matters'* Green Paper (Cm 6629), London: HMSO.

DHSS and WO (Department of Health and Social Security and Welsh Office) (1988) *Working Together: A Guide to Interagency Co-operation for the Protection of Children from Abuse*, London: HMSO.

DoH (Department of Health) (1992) *The Health of the Nation: A Strategy for Health in England*, London: HMSO.

Dorling,D.(2010) *Injustice: Why Social Inequality Persists*, Bristol: Policy Press.

Dickinson, S. (1995) personal correspondence with author.

Dominelli, L. and McLeod, E. (1989) *Feminist Social Work*, Basingstoke: Macmillan.

Driver, E. and Droisen, A. (1989) *Child Sexual Abuse: Feminist Perspectives*, Basingstoke: Macmillan.

Duncan, C., Alexander, C. and Edwards, R. (2010) *Teenage Motherhood. What's the Problem?* London: Tufnell Press.

Eastham, D. (1990) 'Plan It or Suck It and See? A Personal View of the Canklow Community Project', in Darvill, G. and Smale, G. (eds) *Partners in Empowerment: Networks of Innovation in Social Work*, London: National Institute for Social Work.

Ellsworth, E. (1992) 'Why doesn't this feel empowering? Working through the repressive myths of critical pedagogy', in Luke, C. and Gore, J. (eds) *Feminism and Critical Pedagogy*, New York: Routledge.

Erault, M. and Kelly, D. (1994) *Preparatory Study to Explore the Scope for Developing N.V.Q. Standards for Youth and Community Work*, Brighton: University of Sussex.

Erikson, E. (1968) *Identity, Youth, and Crisis*, New York: Norton.

Fielding, M. and Moss, P. (2011) *Radical Education and the Common School: A Democratic Alternative*, London: Routledge.

Foucault, M. (1980) *Power/Knowledge: Selected Interviews and Other Writings*, New York and London: Harvester Wheatsheaf.

Frazer, E. and Lacey, N. (1994) *The Politics of Community*, Hemel Hempstead: Harvester Wheatsheaf.

Freire, P. (1972) *The Pedagogy of the Oppressed*, London: Penguin.

Fuller, A, Beck, V. and Unwin, L. (2005) *Employers, Young People and Gender Segregation (England)*, Manchester: EOC and University of Leicester.

Gavey, A. (2004) *Just Sex? The Cultural Scaffolding of Rape*, London: Routledge.

George,R.(2007a) *Urban Girls' Friendships Complexities and Controversies*, Rotterdam: Sense Publications.

_____ (2007b) *Girls in a Goldfish Bowl Moral Regulation,Ritual and the Use of Power Amongst Inner City Girls,*,Rotterdam: Sense Publications.

Gewirz, S. (2002) *The Managerial School. Post Welfarism and Social Justice in Education*, London: Routledge.

Gill, R. and Scharff, C. (eds) (2011) *New Femininities? Postfeminism, Neo-liberalism and Subjectivity*, London: Palgrave Macmillan.

Gilroy, P. (1993) 'One Nation Under a Groove' in *Small Acts: Thoughts on the Politics of Black Culture*, London: Serpent's Tail.

Gratton, A. and McMullen, M. (2010) *The Role of Youth Work in Supporting Interculturalism*, OfSted Youth Action Occasional Paper, Belfast: Youth Action Northern Ireland.

Green, M. and Christian, C (1998) *Accompanying Young People on their Spiritual Quest*, London Church House Publishing.

Gregson, N. and Lowe, M. (1994) *Servicing the Middle Classes: Class, Gender and Waged Domestic Labour in Britain*, London: Routledge.

Griffin, C. (1993) *Representations of Youth: The Study of Youth and Adolescence in Britain and America*, Cambridge: Polity.

_____ (2011) 'The Trouble with Class: Researching Youth, Class and Culture Beyond the "Birmingham School"', *Journal of Youth Studies* 14(3): 245–59.

Hall, S. (2000) 'Conclusion: The Multicultural Question', in Hesse, B (ed.) *Un/Settled Multicuturalisms*, London: Zed Books.

Hampshire, G.K. and Frith, H. (2004) 'Pretty in Pink: Young Women Presenting Mature Sexual Identities', in Harris, A. (ed) (2004) *All About the Girl Culture Power and Identity*, London: Routledge.

Hansford, L. (1993) 'Student Placement Report', Manchester Metropolitan University, unpublished.

Haraway, D. (1991) 'Reading Buci Emecheta: Contests for Women's Experience in Women's Studies' in *Simians, Cyborgs and Women: The Re-invention of Nature*, London: Free Association Books.

Haritaworn, J. (2011) 'Reckoning with Prostitutes: Performing Thai Femininity', in Gill, R. and Scharff, C. (eds) *New Femininities? Postfeminism, Neo-liberalism and Subjectivity*, London: Palgrave Macmillan.

Harris, A. (2004) *Future Girl: Gender and Education Young Women in the Twenty First Century*, New York: Routledge.

_____ (ed.) (2004) *All About the Girl: Culture Power and Identity*, London: Routledge.

Hayhurst, L.M.C. (2009) 'The Corporatization of Sport, Gender and Development: Postcolonial Feminisms, Transnational Private Governance and Global Corporate Social Engagement', Munk School of Global Affairs Working Papers 2009–10.

Hemmings, S. (ed.) (1982) *Girls are Powerful: Young Women's Writings from Spare Rib*, London: Sheba.

Henderson, S. et al. (2007) *Inventing Adulthoods: A Biographical Approach to Youth Transitions*, London: Sage.

Herbert, C. (1992) *Sexual Harassment in Schools*, London: David Fulton.

Herman, D. (1994) *Rights of Passage: Struggles for Lesbian and Gay Equality*, Toronto: University of Toronto Press.

Herrnstein, R. and Murray, C. (1994) *The Bell Curve: Intelligence and Class Structure in American Life*, New York and London: Free Press.

Hetrick, E. and Martin, D. (1984) 'Egodystonic homosexuality: A developmental view', in — — and Stein, T. (eds) *Innovations in Psychotherapy with Homosexuals*, Washington, DC: American Psychiatric Press.

Hill, M. and Russell, J. (2009) *Young People, Youth Projects and Volunteering A Rapid Review of Recent Evidence*, London: National Centre for Social Research.

Hill Collins, P. (1991) *Black Feminist Thought: Knowledge, Consciousness and the Politics of Empowerment*, New York: Routledge.

Holland, J., Ramazanoglu, C., Sharpe, S. and Thomson, R. (1994) 'Power and Desire: The Embodiment of Female Sexuality', *Feminist Review* 46, Spring.

Holman, B. (1994–95) 'Urban Youth: Not an Underclass', *Youth and Policy* 47, Winter.

hooks, b. (1984) *Feminist Theory: From Margin to Center*, Boston, MA: South End Press.

_____ (1989) 'Feminism: A transformational politic' in *Talking Back: Thinking Feminist, Thinking Black*, London: Sheba.

_____ (1992) 'Selling Hot Pussy' in *Black Looks: Race and Representation*, London: Turnaround.

_____ (1994) *Teaching to Transgress: Education as the Practice of Freedom*, London: Routledge.

_____ (2003) *Teaching Community: A Pedagogy of Hope*, London: Routledge.

Hudson, A. (forthcoming) *Troublesome Girls?* Basingstoke: Macmillan.

Hulme Girls' Project (1984) *Young Women with Children Report 1981–4*, Manchester: Hulme Girls' Project.

Humm, M. (1992) *Feminisms: A Reader*, Hemel Hempstead: Harvester Wheatsheaf.

Hunt, R. and Jensen, J. (2007) *The School Report. The Experience of Young Gay People in Britain's Schools*, Stonewall. London.

Hussain, R. (1994) *Student Placement Report*, Manchester Metropolitan University.

Hyatt, S.B. with Caulkins, D. (1992) *'Putting bread on the table', The Women's Work of Community Activism*, Occasional Paper No. 6, Bradford: Work and Gender Research Unit, University of Bradford.

Imam, F.U. and Bowler, R. (2010) 'Youth Workers as Critical Interpreters as Mediators: Ethical Issues in Working with Black Young People', in Banks, S. (2010) *Ethical Issues in Youth Work*, London: Routledge.

Ingham, R. (2005) 'We didn't cover that at school': Education Against Pleasure or Education for Pleasure', *Sex Education* 5(4): 375–88.

Irigaray, L. (1980) 'When Our Lips Speak Together', *Signs: Journal of Women in Culture and Society* 6(1).

_____ (2000) *Democracry Begins Between Two*, London: Athlone Press.

_____ (2004) *Key Writings*, London and New York: Continuum.

Issit, M. (2000) 'Critical Professionals and Reflective Practice: The Experience of Women Professionals in Health Welfare and Education', in Batsleer, J. and Humphries, B. (eds) *Welfare, Exclusion and Political Agency*, London and New York: Routledge.

Jackson, C., Paechter, C, and Renold, E.(eds) (2010) *Girls and Education,3-16. Continuing Concerns,New Agendas*, Maidenhead, Open University Press.

Jamdagni, L. (1980) *Hamari Rangili Zindagi: Our Colourful Lives, A Report by Laxmi Jamdagni of Her Work with Asian Girls in the Midlands*, Leicester: NAYC Publications Special Report Series.

Jarret Macaulay, D. (1996) *Reconstructing Womanhood, Reconstructing Feminism: Writings on Black Women*, London and New York: Routledge.

Jeffs, T. and Smith, M.K. (1994) 'Getting the Job Done: Training for Youth Work, Past Present and Future', *Youth and Policy*, Spring.

_____ (2005) *Informal Education Conversation, Democracy and Learning*, Nottingham: Education Heretics Press.

Jephcott, A.P. (1942) *Girls Growing Up*, London: Faber and Faber.

Jones, C. and Mahoney, P. (1989) *Learning our Lines: Sexuality and Social Control in Education*, London: Women's Press.

Jones,O.(2011) *Chavs! The demonization of the working-class*, London: Verso.

Jordan, J. (1989) 'Report from the Bahamas' in *Moving Towards Home: Political Essays*, London: Virago.

Kelly, L. (1988) *Surviving Sexual Violence*, Cambridge: Polity.

Khan, M.G. (2006a) 'Making a Place for Muslim Youth Work in British Youth Work', *Youth and Policy* 92, Summer.

_____ (2006b) 'Responding to Lives, Not Events', *Youth and Policy* 92, Summer.

Kinsey, A. (1948, and 1953 edn) *Sexual Behaviour in the Human Male*, Philadelphia, PA: W.B. Saunders.

Kutub, Y. (1995) 'Making Youth Work Accessible to Black Women in the North East of England', *Youth and Policy* 49, Summer.

Lacey, F. and Sprent, S. (1984) *Women, Training and Change Patterns for Development*, Extension Report No. 4, Leicester: National Youth Bureau.

Lal, S. and Wilson, A. (1986) *But My Cows Aren't Going to England: A Study of how Families are Divided*, Manchester: Manchester Law Centre.

Lather, P. (1991) *Getting Smart. Feminist Research and Pedagogy with/in the Postmodern*. New York: Routledge.

Ledwith, M. (2011) *Community Development: A Critical Approach*, Bristol: Policy Press.

Lee, A. and Withers, D. (2012) *The Exciting Life of Being a Woman – A Handbook for Women and Girls*, Manchester: Hammeron Press.

Lees, S. (1986) 'A New Approach to the Study of Girls', *Youth and Policy* 16.

Levy, A. (2005) *Female Chauvinist Pigs. Women and the Rise of Raunch Culture*, New York and London: Free Press.

Lorde, A. (1984) 'Uses of the Erotic: The Erotic as Power', in *Sister Outsider*, Freedom, CA: Crossing Press.

Lukes, S. (ed.) (1986) *Power*, Oxford: Basil Blackwell.

MacKinnon, C. (1982) 'Feminism, Marxism, Method and the State: An Agenda for Theory', in Keohane, N.O., Rosaldo, M. and Gelph, B.C. (eds) *Feminist Theory: A Critique of Ideology*, Brighton: Harvester Wheatsheaf.

Maguire, M. (2009) *Law and Youth Work*, Exeter: Learning Matters.

Mama, A. (1989) *The Hidden Struggle: Statutory and Voluntary Sector Responses to Violence Against Black Women in the Home*, London: Race and Housing Research Unit.

Manchester Young Lesbian Group (1992) *The First Three Years*, Manchester: Shades City Centre Project.

McCabe, T. and McRobbie, A. (1981) *Feminism for Girls: An Adventure Story*, London: Routledge and Kegan Paul.

McFadyean, M. (1986) 'Youth in Distress: Letters to Just Seventeen', *Health Education Journal* 45(1).

McIntosh, M. (1993) 'Queer Theory and the War of the Sexes', in Bristow, J. and Wilson, A. (eds) *Activating Theory*, London: Lawrence and Wishart.

Mies, M. and Shiva, V. (1993) *Ecofeminism*, London: Zed Books.

Milbourne, L. (2009) 'Valuing Difference and or Securing Compliance. Working to Involve Young People in Community Settings', *Children and Society* 23(5): 347–63.

Milson, F. (1970) *Youth Work in the 1970s*, London: Routledge and Kegan Paul.

Mitchell, J. and Rose, J. (eds) (1982) *Feminine Sexuality: Jacques Lacan and the école freudienne*, London: Macmillan.

Moore, G. (1994) *Student Placement Report*, Manchester Metropolitan University.

Morgan, S. and Harland, K. (2009) 'The Lens Model: A Practical Tool for Developing and Understanding Gender Conscious Practice', *Youth and Policy* 101: 67–79.

_____ and McCardle, E. (2009) 'Long Walk from the Door: A History of Work with Girls and Young Women in Northern Ireland from 1969 to the Present', in Gilchrist, R. et al. (eds) *Essays in the History of Youth and Community Work – Discovering the Past*, Lyme Regis: Russell House Press.

Morris, J. (2001) 'Social Exclusion and Young Disabled People with High Level Support Needs', *Critical Social Policy* 21(2): 161–83.

Morris, L. (1994) *Dangerous Classes: The Underclass and Social Citizenship*, London: Routledge.

Mullender, A. and Cohen, M.B. (2003) *Gender and Groupwork*, London: Routledge.

Murray, C. (1994) *The Emerging British Underclass*, London: Institute of Economic Affairs Health and Welfare Unit.

Naples, N. (ed)(1998) *Community Activism and Feminist Politics Organising Across Race Class and Gender*, New York: Routledge.

National Youth Agency (NYA)(2000) *Ethical Conduct in Youth Work: A Statement of Values and Principles from the National Youth Agency*, Leicester: The National Youth Agency.

Nava, M. (1992) *Changing Cultures: Feminism, Youth and Consumerism*, London: Sage.

Newman, E. and Ingram, G. (1989) *The Youth Work Curriculum*, London: Further Education Unit.

Nicholls, C. (1994) conversation with the author.

NOWGYW (National Organisation for Work with Girls and Young Women) (no date) *Background and History*, London: Amazon Press.

Ord, J. (2007) *Youth Work Process Product and Practice Creating an Authentic Curriculum in Youth Work*, Lyme Regis: Russell House Press.

_____ (ed) (2011a) *Critical Issues in Youth Work Management*, Abingdon: Routledge.

_____ (2011b) 'John Dewey and Experiential Learning Developing the Theory of Youth Work', *Youth and Policy* 108, Winter.

Osborne, L. and Walmsley, M. (1995) 'The National Organisation for Work with Girls and Young Women (1981–1994)', Manchester Girls' Project, unpublished.

Packham, C. (2008) *Active Citizenship and Community Learning*, Exeter: Learning Matters.

Parkes, J. and Connolly, A. (2011) '"Risky positions" Shifting Representations of Urban Youth in the Talk of Professionals and Young People', *Children's Geographies* 9(3–4): 411–23.

Parmar, P. (1989) 'Black Lesbians', in Phillips, A. and Rakusen, J. (eds) *The New Our Bodies, Ourselves*, Harmondsworth: Penguin.

Pearson, G. (1983) *Hooligan! A History of Respectable Fears*, Basingstoke: Macmillan.

Peerman, P. and Keenan, J. (1993) 'Hag Fold Young Women's Centre Aims and Objectives 1993', Wigan Youth Service, internal document.

Percy-Smith, B. and Thomas, N. (2010) *Handbook of Children and Young People's Participation Perspectives from Theory and Practice*, London: Routledge, 2010.

Phillips, A. and Rakusen, J. (eds) (1989) *The New Our Bodies, Ourselves*, Harmondsworth: Penguin.

Phoenix, A. (1991) *Young Mothers?* Cambridge: Polity.

Plummer, K. (1995) *Telling Sexual Stories: Power, Change and Social Worlds*, London: Routledge.

Podd, W. (2010) 'Participation', in Batsleer, J. and Davies, B. (eds) *What is Youth Work?* Exeter: Learning Matters.

Pring, R. (2009) *Education for All: The Future of Education and Training for 14–19 year olds*, London: Routledge.

QAA (2009) *Subject Benchmark Statement Youth and Community Work*, Gloucester Quality Assurance Agency for Higher Education. www.qaa.com.

Quinn, S. (1993) 'Let's advocate', *Youth Clubs* 73, September.

Reynolds, M. and Vince, R. (eds) (2004) *Organising Reflection*, London: Gower Ashgate.

Rich, A. (1980) 'Compulsory Heterosexuality and Lesbian Existence', in *On Blood, Bread and Poetry*, London: Virago.

Riley, D. (1988) *'Am I that name?' Feminism and the Category of 'Women' in History*, London: Macmillan.

Ringrose, J. (2007) 'Successful Girls? Complicating Post-feminist Neoliberal Discourse of Educational Achievement and Gender Equality', *Gender and Education* 19(4): 471–89.

_____ (2011) 'Are You Sexy, Flirty, or a Slut? Exploring "Sexualization" and how Teen Girls Perform/Negotiate Digital Sexual Identity on Social Networking Sites', in Gill, R. and Scharff, C. (eds) *New Femininities? Postfeminism, Neo-liberalism and Subjectivity*, London: Palgrave Macmillan.

Robb, M. and Thomson, R. (eds) (2010) *Critical Practice with Children and Young People*, London: Sage Open University.

Ronan, A. (1994) Dissertation Proposal, Manchester Metropolitan University.

Rossi, H. (1988) *Great Britain Local Government Acts 1987 and 1988 Annotated by Sir Hugh Rossi*, London: Shaw and Sons.

Russell Commission (2005) *Report: A national framework for Youth Action and Engagement* Russell Commission London HMSO

Sawbridge, M. and Spence, J. (1991) *The Dominance of the Male Agenda in Community and Youth Work*, Durham: University of Durham Press.

Sayce, L. (2000) *From Psychiatric Patient to Citizen. Overcoming Discrimination and Social Exclusion*, London: Palgrave Macmillan.

Schneider, M. (1989) 'Sappho was a Right On Adolescent', *Journal of Homosexuality*, 17(1/2).

Seabrook, J. (1978) *What Went Wrong? Working People and the Ideals of the Labour Movement*, London: Gollancz.

Selman, P. and Glendinning, C. (1994–95) 'Teenage Parenthood and Social Policy', *Youth and Policy* 47, Winter.

Sercombe,H.(2010) 'Youth Workers as Professionals: managing dual relationships and maintaining boundaries.' In Banks, S. (ed) *Ethical Issues in Youth Work* (second edition),London: Routledge.

Shain, F. (2003) *The Schooling and Identity of Asian Girls*, Stoke on Trent: Trentham.

Sharma, U. and Berry, H. (eds) (2008) *Am I Safe Yet? By Women Asylum Seekers Together*, Manchester: Ahmed Iqbal Trust.

Shildrick, T. et al. (2010) *The Low-pay, No-pay Cycle. Understanding Recurrent Poverty*, York: Joseph Rowntree Foundation.

Shukra, K. (2010) 'From Anti-racism to Community Cohesion' in Batsleer, J. and Davies, B. (eds) *What is Youth Work?* Exeter: Learning Matters.

Sivanandan, A. (1990) 'Left, Right and Burnage', in *Communities of Resistance: Writings on Black Struggles for Socialism*. London: Verso.

Skeggs, B. (1997) *Formations of Class and Gender: Becoming Respectable*, London: Routledge.

Smith, M. (1988) *Developing Youth Work: Informal Education, Mutual Aid and Popular Practice*, Milton Keynes: Open University Press.

Social Exclusion Unit (SEU)(1999) *Teenage Pregnancy* Cm 4342 HMSO London.

Solomos, J. (1993) *Race and Racism in Britain*, Basingstoke and London: Macmillan.

Soni, S. (2011) *Working with Diversity in Youth and Community Work*, Exeter: Learning Matters.

Spence, J. (2010) 'Collecting Women's Lives: The Challenge of Feminism in UK Youth Work in the 1970 and 80s', *Women's History Review* 19(1): 159–76.

Spivak, G., with Rooney, E. (1989), 'In a Word. Interview', *Differences* 1(2).

Stanley, M. (1890) *Clubs for Working Girls*, London: Macmillan.

Steinberg, S. (2011) *Kinderculture The Corporate Construction of Childhood*, Boulder, CO and Oxford: Westview.

Szirom, T. and Dyson, S. (1986) *Greater Expectations: A Source Book for Working with Girls and Young Women*, Wisbech: Learning Development Aids.

Taylor, T. (1987) 'Youthworkers as Character-builders: Constructing a Socialist Alternative', in Jeffs, T. and Smith, M. (eds) *Youth Work*, Basingstoke: Macmillan.

Terry, I., Davis, M. and O'Neill, N. (1993) 'In the Neighbourhood', *Youth Clubs* 74, October.

Thomas, P. (2006) 'The Impact of Community Cohesion on Youth Work: A Case Study from Oldham' *Youth and Policy* 93: 41–61.

_____ (2011) *Youth Multiculturalism and Community Cohesion*, Basingstoke: Palgrave Macmillan.

Thompson, D. (1985) 'Anger', in Browne, S.E., Connors, D. and Stern, N. (eds) *With the Power of Each Breath: A Disabled Women's Anthology*, Pittsburgh, PA: Cleis Press.

Thompson, N. (1998) *Promoting Equality. Challenging Discrimination and Oppression in Human Services*, Basingstoke: Palgrave Macmillan.

Thompson, N. (2006) *Anti-Discriminatory Practice*, Basingstoke: Palgrave Macmillan.

_____ (2007) *Power and Empowerment*, Lyme Regis: Russell House.

Thomson, R. and Scott, S. (1991) *Learning about Sex: Young Women and the Social Construction of Sexual Identity*, London: Tufnell Press.

Tiffany, G. (2009) 'Learning from Detached Youth Work Democratic Education', in Pring, R. (ed.) *Education for All: the Future of Education and Training for 14–19 year old,*. London: Routledge.

Trimbell, J. (1990) *Equality of Opportunity Provision for Girls and Young Women in the Full-time Sector of the Northern Ireland Youth Service*, Belfast: Youth Action Northern Ireland, May.

Troiden, R.R. (1989) 'The Formation of Homosexual Identities', *Journal of Homosexuality* 17(1/2).

TUC (1995) *Civil Rights for Disabled People: A TUC statement*, London: TUC.

Walby, S. (2009) 'Gender and the Financial Crisis', paper for the UNESCO Project 'Gender and the Financial Crisis'.

Ward, D. and Mullender, A. (1992) 'Empowerment and Oppression: An Indissoluble Pairing for Contemporary Social Work', *Critical Social Policy* 32, Autumn.

Warner, S. and Reavey, P. (2003) *New Feminist Stories of Child Sexual Abuse: Sexual Scripts and Dangerous Dialogues*, London: Routledge.

Weller, P. (1987) *Sanctuary: The Beginning of a Movement?* London: Runnymede Trust.

Wenger, E. (1998*) Communities of Practice: Learning, Meaning and Identity*, Cambridge: Cambridge University Press.

Williams, F. (2004) *Rethinking Families*, London: Calouste Gulbenkian Foundation.

Williams, R. (1989) 'The Idea of Community', in *Resources of Hope: Culture, Democracy, Socialism*, London: Verso.

Williamson, J. (1986) *Consuming Passions: The Dynamics of Popular Culture*, London: Boyars.

Wilson, A. (2006) *Dreams, Questions, Struggles – South Asian Women in Britain*, London: Pluto.

Wilson, M. (ed.) (1994) *Healthy and Wise: The Essential Health Handbook for Black Women*, London: Virago.

Wright Mills, C. (1959,2000) *The Sociological Imagination* Oxford: Oxford University Press.

Young, I.M. (1994) 'Gender as Seriality: Thinking about Women as a Social Collective', *Signs: Journal of Women in Culture and Society* 19(3).

Young, K. (1992) 'Work with Girls and Young Women: Losing the Purpose?', *Youth Clubs* 67, April.

_____ (2006) *The Art of Youth Work*, Lyme Regis: Russell House Press.

Youth Support Project (1986) *Annual Report*, Manchester: Project Report.

Youth Work Unit (1983) *Looking Beyond Street Level: Detached Youth Work with Young Women*, Leicester: National Youth Bureau.

Zion Community Health and Resource Centre (1993–94) *Amidst the Change*, Manchester: Project Report.

Websites

www.brook.org.uk
www.fawcettsociety.org.uk
www.feministwebs.com
www.geogov.uk
www.lowpayunit.org

www.poverty.org.uk
www.thefword.org.uk
www.gingerbread.com
www.womenagainstfundamentalism.org.uk
www.ukfeminista.org.uk
www.waronwant.org/olympics

Index